LAW

for the

VETERINARIAN

and

LIVESTOCK OWNER

LAW
for the
VETERINARIAN
and
LIVESTOCK OWNER

by

H. W. HANNAH, B.S., LL.B.
Associate Dean of College of Agriculture and
Professor of Agricultural Law
University of Illinois
and
DONALD F. STORM, B.S., J.D.
Attorney at Law

SECOND EDITION

Danville, Illinois

THE INTERSTATE
PRINTERS and PUBLISHERS, INC.

First Edition, 1959

Printed and Published by

THE INTERSTATE PRINTERS & PUBLISHERS, INC.

Danville, Illinois

Library of Congress
Catalog Card Number 64-25222

PRINTED IN U.S.A.

PREFACE

There is only one good excuse for a book about law for the layman: to fulfill his need to know more about law. This book is mainly for two particular kinds of laymen, veterinarians and livestock owners. Chapters and sections reflect the writers' success (or lack of success) in pulling from the whole body of the law those segments which seem pertinent. With some exceptions each section represents a concrete problem as it is likely to arise in the practice of veterinary medicine or in the minds of practitioners and livestock owners.

Books of this kind are to supplement an existing knowledge and judgment. They are not to serve as substitutes for either. Neither are they to serve as substitutes for professional help. Veterinarians know that livestock owners risk the health of their herds when they try to be their own veterinarian; livestock owners know that animals are not finished for market by tacking a table of digestible nutrients on the barn door, and lawyers know that laymen sometimes find themselves in legal hot water because they try to handle their own cases.

For the person with judgment, knowing more about law should have many beneficial effects; it should enhance his judgment, increase his use of the legal profession for preventive as distinguished from remedial purposes, enable him better to organize and handle the details of his business and give him further insight into that most important sphere—human relations.

H. W. HANNAH
DONALD F. STORM

TABLE OF CONTENTS

CHAPTER 1

THE STRUCTURE OF OUR GOVERNMENT

1. **The Objective of American Government.** Free peoples look at the State as a means of achieving their desire for an organized political life, not as a means of establishing a regimen in their lives. Though the form alone does not determine the extent to which a particular government will satisfy a free people, the democracy as we have come to define it seems best suited. Madison, Hamilton, Jefferson and other architects of the Federal Constitution gave a great deal of thought to the structure of the new National government. They wished to give it strength but still make it responsive to the people. This is not easily done. Abraham Lincoln once said, "Is there, in all republics, this inherent and fatal weakness? Must a government, of necessity, be too strong for the liberties of its own people or too weak to maintain its own existence?"

2. **The Functions of American Government.** Our governments, both federal and state, have three main functions—to make law, to administer and enforce the law, and to settle disputes which arise under the law. Accordingly, three divisions of government exist to accomplish these functions: a legislative branch to make the law, an administrative or executive branch to administer and enforce, and a judicial branch to settle disputes and interpret the law. Congress, the President and the federal courts accomplish these functions for the federal government; the General Assembly, the Governor and the state courts for the states.

3. **Checks and Balances.** When the powers of government are divided between three agencies, each independent of the other, the likelihood that government will become too strong and dictatorial for the best interests of the people is greatly reduced. Congress cannot enforce a law or sit as a court and decide that a law made by it is constitutional. But it can make laws, including laws creating enforcing machinery and additional courts,

The administrative branch of government, including the President or Governor and all the agencies spread out below, cannot make a law or decide that a law is unconstitutional. But it can effectuate the law, and in so doing may establish rules and regulations which have the same force as a law passed by the legislative branch, providing the rule or regulation is not unreasonable and that it does not transcend the authority conferred by the law. Also, the President or Governor may create additional administrative machinery by his own order, when such machinery is essential. Courts do not make laws, at least not in the legislative sense, and they do not administer laws. But they do interpret the law and they do enforce their own decisions and judgments. So, as an adjunct of the court's power to adjudicate, it has some law making and some law enforcing power. Many statesmen, lawyers and students of government complained bitterly when the United States Supreme Court, under the leadership of Chief Justice John Marshall, declared that a federal law contravened the Constitution and was therefore void and unenforceable: They argued that the function is to settle controversies, not to pass on the validity of laws involved. But "judicial review"—the right of the court to consider constitutionality—has become a well established principle in our government and is regarded as one of the prime safeguards of our individual freedom and liberty.

During the past few decades the administrative branch of government, particularly that of the federal government, has been greatly expanded. Along with this expansion has developed a greater necessity for rules and regulations, and for resort to the administrative hearing as an initial means of determining controversies that arise under the enforcement of rules and laws. In so far as a democracy may be endangered by changes in its government as distinguished from changes in its citizens and their thinking, this growth of the administrative branch, with its greater power to make rules and adjudicate disputes is a significant development.

4. **Representation.** Citizens cannot participate directly in the lawmaking process. They must do it through representatives. Two principles are regarded as basic in the American scheme of representation; one, that the states shall be equally represented in one house of congress—hence the senate with its 100 members —the other, that all representatives shall be elected by the people and except for senators, apportioned according to population.

This same scheme is followed by each of the states in the establishment of general assemblies or state representative bodies. However, there is no federal constitutional requirement that the representative bodies elected in the states be composed of a senate and house of representatives: Nebraska, for example, has only one "house."

5. **The Citizen's Role.** Though the individual citizen cannot participate directly in lawmaking, there is a great deal he can do indirectly if he is so inclined. Legislators are subject to influence. Regardless of their integrity and wisdom they cannot escape the arguments which are laid on their doorsteps by organizations and individuals. Veterinarians, for example, have legislative interests outside their general interests as a citizen. If a veterinarian believes a particular animal disease law is needed—or not needed—he can make his voice heard in many ways. He can encourage his organizations to take a stand and be represented at committee hearings; he can himself appear at hearings if he feels strongly enough about the matter; he can write to his representatives and encourage others to do likewise; he can think and analyze and prepare statements; he can make his views known to the administrative officials of the federal or state agency which would be or is concerned with the administration of the law. Obviously, these pursuits take time. But, then, democracies thrive only when some essential minimum number of their citizens are willing to engage in such pursuits.

CHAPTER 2

SOURCES OF LAW

6. **What Is Law?** Through the mind of the average American runs the feeling that if he leads a reasonably moral life and pays his debts he will not run afoul of the law! Fortunately, this is true—not completely true—but sufficiently accurate to support the admonition that if one wishes to stay out of legal trouble, he should at least pay his debts and lead a reasonably moral life. Beyond this, living within the law becomes a matter of knowing. And the more complicated and involved one's calling, the more "knowing" he must have. Fortunately or unfortunately, depending on one's point of view, veterinarians and livestock owners need to know a great deal about some laws which have nothing to do with one's instinctive feelings about right and wrong. Law is something more than a moral code. It is a composite of all the ways in which some force superior to ourselves can make us conform or punish us if we do not. It is like fire and water—a great boon to mankind when properly used, and the certain means of his destruction when it gets out of hand. Constitutional provisions, statutes, city ordinances, the regulations of administrative agencies, rulings of a court in a particular case—these are all law because there is a force greater than the individual standing behind each one, ready to make the individual conform if he fails to do so voluntarily. If such a force is not present, then the requirement cannot be a law. It may be a custom or a moral or ethical principle, but it cannot be a law. Sometimes laws are not enforced. Technically, they are still laws; practically, they are not.

7. **How Laws Are Made.** Men make laws. Consequently, many imperfections exist in the laws themselves and in the processes used to establish them. In a democracy the only laws which will be effective over a long period of time are those the people are willing to ratify by usage. Laws generally come into being because somebody wants them. Legislative bodies do not originate very many laws, they act more as a screening device for the

countless bills fostered by pressure groups, government agencies, associations and organizations of all kinds, the chief executive and others. When bills are introduced, they are referred to an appropriate committee. This is generally where they receive the most thorough consideration and is a point at which those interested can get in their licks for or against. Many bills die in committee. Those that do not are brought to the whole legislative body, read, reread, sometimes debated and then voted on and sent to the other legislative chamber. Following final passage, the chief executive has an opportunity to veto or approve. If he approves, then some agency of government becomes responsible for enforcement. The agency is generally named in the law, but if not, the chief executive designates the appropriate one.

All laws are not statutes. Administrative regulations are made and published by the various agencies of federal and state government, in accordance with directives contained in the law. City ordinances are enacted by city councils, county ordinances by county boards of supervisors, and rules or orders of all kinds are adopted and enforced by countless local agencies in carrying out their legal responsibilities.

WHERE LAW ORIGINATES

Sources of law in the United States	Where the law may be found
International treaties and agreements	"Treaties, Conventions, International Acts, Protocols and Agreements," Treaty Series.
Federal constitution	United States Code. Any History or Political Science text.
Congress (federal statutes)	United States Code. Statutes at large. Slip laws.
Federal administrative agencies (rules and regulations)	Federal Register. Code of Federal Regulations.
State constitution	Revised or compiled Statutes. Pamphlet issued by Secretary of State or similar officer.
State legislatures (state statutes)	Revised or compiled statutes. Annotated statutes. Session Laws.
State administrative agencies (rules and regulations)	Separate publications by departments and divisions.
Political subdivisions of the state (ordinances)	Minutes of the governing body.
Municipal corporations (ordinances)	Printed copy of ordinances—book or pamphlet.
Public corporations (rules, regulations, ordinances)	Minutes. Proclamations.
Quasi-public corporations (rules, regulations, rates)	Letters, minutes, published records and schedules.
Courts (common law)	Court records and case reports—digests and encyclopedias.
Contracts (enforceable private rights)	Written or oral agreements.

8. **Constitutions.** Some countries do not have written constitutions. But our federal government and our states do. The purpose of a constitution is to prescribe the basic framework for the governmental structure, grant powers to the government, place limitations on the government in the exercise of certain powers, and guarantee in positive language that certain freedoms and immunities shall inhere in each citizen. As a source of law, constitutions are basic, and statutes, regulations, private contracts, or any other instrument creating legal obligations must be in conformity with the federal constitution and with that of the particular state. The federal constitution is supreme and the powers granted the federal government under it are controlling over state constitutions and statutes. However, the federal constitution is a grant of power, and the federal government has only those powers specified in it or implied from it, whereas state constitutions simply act as limitations on the authority of the state since it is the repository of legislative power.

Veterinarians and livestock owners are affected very little by constitutional provisions applying directly to their calling, but they are affected greatly by those provisions which define the powers of government and place limitations on their exercise. Whether or not the federal government can enforce a particular regulation on the interstate shipment of livestock or whether a state can adopt a particular animal disease statute will depend upon how these laws meet the test of constitutionality. The treaty-making authority of the federal government is contained in the federal constitution: This is important to the livestock industry because it gives the government a means of controlling the import and export of animals and animal products, and hence another means of controlling animal disease. Further applications of constitutional theory to the business of the veterinarian and livestock farmer will appear in appropriate sections throughout this book.

9. **Statutes.** The laws enacted by legislative bodies are more important to the average veterinary practitioner than those derived from any other source. These laws are written, they are definite, and they are put into operation by appropriate agencies of federal and state governments. They are augmented annually

by Congress and the state legislatures, and now provide control or regulation in varying degree over such matters as livestock shipments, food processing and shipment, animal disease eradication, the practice of veterinary medicine, the handling and dispensing of narcotics, serum manufacture and sale, dead animal disposal, community sales, livestock auctions, milk distribution and stockyards operations—to mention only a few.

The constitutional right of the federal government to make laws like some of those listed above depends largely on the interpretation which has been placed on the so-called commerce clause of the federal constitution, the clause giving the federal government authority to control commerce between the states and with foreign countries. The definition of "commerce" long ago ceased to be a literal one, and federal control may now be exercised over movements of goods or services that "affect interstate commerce." Once a federal law meeting the test of constitutionality has been adopted, state laws on the same subject become ineffective in so far as they are in conflict. Actually, many control measures have been worked out cooperatively between the federal government and the states so the laws complement each other—bovine tuberculosis eradication, for example.

Federal statutes currently in effect are all contained in a publication known as *The United States Code,* sold and distributed by the Government Printing Office. There are many special compilations of federal law, some of which contain those pertinent to agriculture and the livestock industry. Those in which veterinarians and livestock owners are interested may be procured from the USDA-Agricultural Research Administration. State laws are generally published as compiled or revised statutes, sometimes by the state, sometimes by private publishers. These works are generally inexpensive, considering their completeness. A veterinarian who wishes to have in his office a complete set of all the laws of his state affecting his profession is virtually compelled to purchase such a set because many states make no separate compilation of animal disease laws, and even when they do, all the laws affecting the profession are not apt to be included.

10. **Rules and Regulations.** Statutes are seldom complete enough in detail to provide for their own administration. As a matter of good legislative policy they should not be that complete. The legislature should prescribe the essential conditions under which the law is to operate and leave the minute or "minis-

terial" details to the enforcing agency. Naturally, laws vary in
their completeness, depending on the nature of the subject matter. A statute prescribing standard weights for a number of
commodities leaves little to an administrative agency, but a
statute providing that grades for agricultural products may be
established by a state department of agriculture, following a publication of proposed grades and hearings, leaves a great deal of
discretion in the hands of a director of agriculture. In the animal
disease and food fields particularly, many rules and regulations
have been adopted by both federal and state administrative agencies. Generally, these rules are promulgated directly by the chief
administrative officer, presumably after a thorough investigation
of the need. Sometimes, however, the law requires that proposed
regulations be presented to an advisory body composed, in part
at least, of persons from the particular industry affected, and
that this body may, within a prescribed time, either require or
suggest that modifications or changes be made.

Federal regulations are all contained in *The Federal Register*, a publication issued daily. The permanent repository for
such regulations is *The Code of Federal Regulations*. Though
not essential, it would be convenient for a veterinarian to receive
The Federal Register. Separate publications containing federal
regulations on animal disease and related subjects may be procured from the USDA-Agricultural Research Administration
and from state livestock sanitary officials. Most states have no
publication corresponding to *The Federal Register*. The best
source, therefore, is the state livestock sanitary agency. Sometimes even this source is not completely reliable because state
administrative agencies have a habit of permitting regulations
to accumulate so that it is not always possible to tell just what
the current regulatory provisions on a particular subject are.
However, many states have codified these regulations and keep
the codification up to date.

11. **Ordinances.** Municipalities, particularly the larger ones,
exert a great deal of control over the practice of veterinary medicine and the sale and distribution of livestock and livestock products within their limits. As separate political entities they have
legislative authority and may adopt laws—referred to as ordinances—for the welfare of their inhabitants and for the accom-
plishment of their various functions. These ordinances are as

binding as statutes on those within the jurisdiction of the municipality. A city, for example, may legally regulate the location of
various types of business and industry, including the location of
an animal hospital or any other establishment that may affect
the public. City milk ordinances are long-standing examples of
the right to control the purity of food products brought inside
city limits for processing and distribution. Though occupations
outside the city may be materially affected by the nature of
particular ordinances, municipalities ordinarily have no right to
enforce their ordinances outside their own limits.

Cities are not the only agencies with ordinance-making authority. Health districts, county boards, township electors, school
boards, sanitary districts, and a large number of public agencies
may adopt ordinances reasonably designed to carry out their
authority.

Copies of ordinances are sometimes difficult to procure. As
a last resort, the best possibility is the clerk or secretary of the
particular agency.

12. **Unwritten Law—The Common Law.** Theoretically,
courts act only to settle controversies—they do not make any
law. Actually, the courts make law in two ways; they interpret
constitutional provisions and statutes, thus adding to, subtract-
ing from, or completely nullifying the written law involved, and
they invoke custom and precedent as aids in reaching decisions,
thus establishing rules which, though not written in the legislative sense, are nevertheless available for future reference and
for any influence they may have on courts and lawyers. The vast
body of precedent thus officially recorded in the reports of cases
settled by our federal and state courts—and by the courts of
other English-speaking countries as well—constitutes what is
known as the unwritten or common law. These common law principles are highly important because, in effect, they are the law
when a statute, regulation or written law of some kind does not
supply the answer. They fill the great void which must always
be left by statutory enactment. There are variations in their
applicability, depending on how completely the written law covers
a particular subject. For example, the statutes are quite complete
on the making of wills, and for the most part any question about
the validity of a will can be answered by reference to an appropriate section in the probate act of the particular state. But

statutory provisions are very sparse on the contractual relation of veterinarian and client. So, questions like, "What is a veterinarian's duty to answer a call? What is his duty to continue attendance on an animal? What constitutes negligence in the handling of animals while being vaccinated?" are all questions that, for the most part, must be answered by reference to common law principles. Actually, there are very few reported higher court cases involving veterinarians, so that much of the precedent used in cases involving veterinarians must come from medical practice and from other related areas.

Needless to say, not all higher court decisions are sound. Because of this, "bad" precedents are sometimes established, and so long as the courts feel bound by the precedent thus established, inequitable results will follow. Hence, the legislators are frequently called upon to pass laws on the subject, thus rendering the common law inoperative. Also, precedents, once sound, may become outmoded. If the courts do not modify or overrule such precedents, the legislature may again be called upon.

13.   **Contracts.** Contracts are sources of law because they create enforceable obligations. If a man contracts to perform a service for another, he can be legally held to his agreement or made to pay damages for not performing. All agreements are not contracts. To constitute a contract, an agreement must be clearly understood by both parties and must involve an exchange of things having value (consideration). When a veterinarian treats a client's animal, a contract arises and certain legal rights and obligations come into being.

14. **Custom and Usage.** Though customs are not legally binding, courts frequently admit evidence of prevailing usage or practice when a specific agreement cannot be proved. If, for example, a farm were rented and no specific agreement made as to the share of the crop reserved for rent, the customary division of the crops in the locality would carry much weight with a court. In malpractice suits involving veterinarians, evidence of what is customary or usual in the practice is highly important. Once a custom or usage has been recognized by a court, it carries greater weight because it then bears the stamp of legal precedent.

CHAPTER 3

COURTS AND LAWYERS

15. **The Enforcement of Legal Rights.** Justice Holmes once said, "Just so far as the aid of the public force is given a man, he has a legal right, and this right is the same whether his claim is founded in righteousness or iniquity." Law is meaningless if it is not enforced. As a matter of fact, it is worse than meaningless because the absence of law would be more certain and less misleading.

The enforcement of statutes is primarily a job for the administrative arm of government, backed by the courts. Quite apart from the enforcement of statutes is the enforcement of individual legal rights. When one is injured by another, whether contractually or in any other way, redress is not automatic: something has to be set in motion. Even criminal acts committed against one's person or property will go without redress as to his personal right to damages unless he sets the law in motion by filing a suit for damages. Prosecution by the public and suit by the owner for damages are separate and distinct actions. But one is not always in the position of the injured party: He may be the one sued for damages or the one indicted for a criminal offense. In either case, he has some very definite and very important legal rights. Here again, however, the extent to which these rights are urged will depend largely upon the defendant himself. If one is criminally accused, the court will see that certain constitutional and statutory rights are preserved, but it is up to the individual to develop and present any defense he may have to offer. In civil cases the court is not so solicitous of defendants, and if one doesn't appear and urge his defense, he may lose by default.

There are two important entities in the enforcement of legal rights: the court, which hears the parties and passes judgment and the lawyer, who assembles all available evidence, studies the law involved, and presents the best possible case for his client.

16. **Our System of Courts.** In this country there are two

11

systems of courts—federal and state. The Constitution of the United States created the Supreme Court and gave Congress power to create inferior federal courts. Pursuant to this authorization, Congress has established more than eighty Federal District Courts. District Courts vary in territorial jurisdiction from a whole state to a small part of a state or a large city, depending on population. They are known as courts of original jurisdiction and suits involving federal law are commenced in them. Between the District Courts and the Supreme Court are the Courts of Appeal. There are eleven of these, and it is their function to accept appeals from the District Courts. These courts are able to dispose of large numbers of cases which otherwise would go to the Supreme Court, thus filling a practical and necessary requirement in the federal judicial system. The Supreme Court is composed of nine judges, appointed for life by the President. It accepts appeals from the federal courts and from State Supreme Courts.

State courts have been established after the fashion of federal courts. Each county ordinarily has an inferior court corresponding to the Federal District Court. They may be called Circuit Courts, County Courts, or by other names. Intermediate between these courts and the Supreme Court of the state are Appellate Courts, fulfilling for the state the same function served by the Courts of Appeal in the federal system. In addition, each county has a Probate Court concerned mainly with estates, inheritance, drainage, guardianship, and other matters of a local administrative nature. In some states Justice of the Peace Courts are still used to settle local suits involving misdeameanors or minor infractions of the law. In a few states Land Courts have been established to deal exclusively with property matters. There has been a trend toward the establishment of special courts to handle frequently recurring violations—Traffic Courts for example—or to handle suits that recur frequently and have important social implications—Divorce, Domestic Relations and Juvenile Courts, for example. By thus specializing, these courts have been able better to understand and protect not only the legal rights of the parties involved, but also their emotional and social well being.

Once a court has rendered a judgment, it has the authority necessary to enforce its decree. It may seize and sell property or fine and jail those who stand in contempt of its orders. The sheriff is the court's agent for the enforcement of its decrees.

17. **Administrative Hearings.** When a person fails to abide by the regulations of an administrative agency of government, feels that he is injured by the action of an administrative agency, has a license of some kind revoked or denied, or for any other reason falls into controversy with such an agency, he is ordinarily accorded a hearing before the administrative head or other proper officer of the agency. In many respects this hearing is like a court trial. Both sides present arguments, counsel may be employed, a record is kept, and a decision is rendered. Much criticism has been leveled at this method of settling controversies, the chief argument being that in reality these hearings are trials at which legal rights are determined without the safeguards and experience afforded by a court, and that in fact such hearings are infringements of the judicial authority by the administrative branch of government. Nevertheless, hearings are an important medium, and generally an expeditious one, for determining certain rights. Many states now have an Administrative Review Law which requires that certain uniform records be kept by officers at such hearings and which clearly establishes and outlines the method of appeal to the courts—a right which has always existed, but which is not always clearly spelled out in the absence of such a uniform provision. Veterinarians are especially interested in the administrative hearing because any refusal of a license to practice or any attempted revocation would be heard initially by the state agency administering the Veterinary Practice Act. Also, the enforcement of animal disease laws gives rise to many circumstances in which both veterinarians and livestock owners may either be defending their actions or claiming some right before the livestock sanitary officials of the state.

18. **Lawyers.** Lawyers are a necessity in our judicial system. Finding the law, interpreting its meaning, handling cases in court, following the directions of a law or regulation and filing necessary documents, searching records, drafting instruments, appraising the legal factors in a given situation—these are highly technical tasks which one without legal education and experience is not qualified to undertake. Lawyers are not, as many people declare, a seemingly necessary evil. In every profession, and among the nonprofessional as well, are those who place their own interests so high that others suffer. Lawyers who do this are not in good repute either among members of the public or the members of

their profession. Too often the advice of a lawyer is sought when all that is left for him to do is invoke the procedural machinery of the law. In such circumstances, a lawyer has to assume control of the situation, and in doing so may create a feeling of awe and helplessness in his client—feelings the client does not enjoy. This leads many people to feel that the last thing they want to do is go to a lawyer, when seeing one earlier might have saved them much grief and expense. When approached about matters which can be discussed free from prejudice and impending action, the lawyer can view the client as a rational human being capable of understanding anything explained in a reasonable manner. Any person whose business brings him into contact with an appreciable number of laws and regulatory measures, or who is confronted with personal situations having legal implications, can well afford to bring his problems to a lawyer and consult him frequently. The cost of such service is small compared to litigation.

Once a lawyer accepts a case, it becomes his duty to ascertain all pertinent facts, contact all persons who might be valuable witnesses, make appearances and pleadings before the court, file necessary documents and do everything legitimately within his power to make the wheels of justice turn smoothly in favor of his client. The cost of legal service depends on many factors—the length of time counsel is employed, the amount of time spent in court, travel and time away from the office, the kind of legal work involved. Local bar associations generally adopt a schedule of charges which the members feel morally bound to follow.

19. **Evidence.** Rules of law can be applied only to factual situations. To determine what the facts are in a particular situation, all kinds of evidence are necessary. Evidence is simply the means by which allegations are proved—or disproved. It comes in many forms. Letters, written instruments, the accounts of eyewitnesses, the condition of a person or an animal or an item of property, records, reports, instruments or properties used, the testimony of experts—these and many other things may all be evidence if they are relevant to the situation about which facts are being established. Some evidence is direct. Suppose a veterinarian becomes unduly irritated by a calf he is trying to treat. He seizes a baseball bat left conveniently in the manger by the client's young son and gives the calf a blow across the head. It dies. There is a suit for damages. Suppose the client's hired man

was helping the veterinarian and saw the whole incident. His testimony will constitute direct evidence—he saw the act alleged. But suppose no one was with the veterinarian. The young son is called and testifies that he left his baseball bat in the manger the day before, that he went to the manger to get it the evening after the calf died and found it lying on the floor of the stall with the handle cracked and what appeared to be a patch of hair and blood on the business end. This would be indirect or circumstantial evidence. Standing alone it proves nothing; coupled with other evidence it may establish the factual situation as well as direct testimony. Veterinarians may be asked many times by their clients to help establish certain facts—that an animal was vaccinated, that it was examined as required by law, that it died of a particular disease. On many such questions the veterinarian will be in a position to give direct testimony because he was there, he made the diagnosis, he administered the vaccine. Obviously, the value of such testimony will be greatly enhanced if records or memoranda of some kind are available. A veterinarian who is careful about making records and who makes it a practice to retain copies of all certifications made by him will not only be able to help his client more when a controversy arises, but will also be better able to protect himself not only from charges that he is not telling the truth, but also from accusations that he did not comply with the law. From the standpoint of evidence alone, good record keeping pays off.

Apparently veterinarians are not included in statutes or common law precedent giving physicians and lawyers the right to refuse to testify on matters which are considered privileged communications with their clients. In an Iowa case[1] it was held that the testimony of a veterinary surgeon should not have been excluded under a statute relating to privileged communications of a physician or surgeon; and in a South Dakota case[2] it was considered proper at the trial to ask witnesses what the defendant veterinarian said to the plaintiff about the responsibility or blame for the loss of the sheep involved in the suit.

20. **The Veterinarian as an Expert Witness.** Persons possessing special knowledge or skill about a subject are sometimes asked to give opinions in law suits on questions involving their special

---

[1]Each case cited in this book is numbered and listed in the TABLE OF CASES on pages 181 to 191 for your ready reference.

learning and skill. They may be called by either party to a suit. Such testimony is based entirely on their expert appraisal of the situation in controversy and not on direct or indirect knowledge of the facts. The trial court may always determine if an "expert" is qualified. Merely having a license is not a sufficient qualification. It may be shown that one called as an expert has not practiced his profession, or that he is not an expert on the particular question involved. For example, it has been held that no amount of experience as a veterinarian will qualify one to testify on a question involving a technical knowledge of bacteriology. Among the things on which our American courts have said a veterinarian is qualified as an expert are the effect of medicines, drugs and surgery on animals; gestation and lactation periods; heat periods; sterility and impotency; the physical structure of animals; diseases of animals and cause of death; physical and chemical changes in animals, and temperament. Unless there is a statute like the one in Wisconsin, which provides that no person shall be competent to testify on matters pertaining to animal disease unless he is a licensed veterinarian, any person with special knowledge and experience may qualify to give expert testimony. In the Illinois case of Pearson v. Zehr[3] the court said, "We are not prepared to hold that no one but a veterinary surgeon can properly testify in respect to the appearance and symptoms of diseased horses, and give an opinion upon the existence or non-existence of a particular disease or malady in such horses. It would seem that farmers and other persons who for many years have had the personal care and management of horses, both sick and well, and have had an extensive practical experience with such animals, and with some particular disease to which they are subject, and ample opportunity to observe and know the characteristics and symptoms of such disease, are qualified to state whether in a particular case such characteristics and symptoms do or do not exist." There is a Kansas case, however, which seems to set a more strict test as to the competence of one not a veterinarian. In Rouse v. Youard[4] the court held that a witness who is not educated in any particular profession or trade is not competent to give an opinion in any matter that requires science or skill to determine, although he may have frequently seen the treatment of diseases by physicians, or operations made by surgeons, and have assisted veterinarians in the treatment of stock for diseases, and have read extensively from books and papers treating on diseases of stock.

In the United States Supreme Court case of Grayson v. Lynch,[5] it was held that professors of veterinary medicine, employed for many years by the Department of Agriculture in the investigation of the diseases of animals are competent to testify as to the nature and symptoms of Texas cattle fever. This seems like a reasonable decision and no doubt would apply to professors of veterinary medicine generally under state as well as federal precedent.

Witnesses are entitled to compensation. State law ordinarily prescribes the fee to be paid witnesses of fact, but is generally silent on the fees of expert witnesses. Some states, however, do prescribe fees for expert witnesses. Generally it is best if the expert witness agrees beforehand with those who ask for his services. This is usually possible since expert witnesses cannot be subpoenaed as witnesses of fact can be. However, if an expert witness performs an autopsy or makes investigations that put him in possession of facts regarding the case, then he may be required to give testimony as a witness of fact. The fact that a veterinarian is in the service of the State does not disqualify him from being an expert witness and receiving fees for his services.[6]

To be a good expert witness one needs more than a knowledge of his specialty—he needs to have a cooperative attitude and an understanding of what the attorneys in the case are trying to do. Trials involve more than a recital of legal principles and their application to a set of facts—they involve people. Here are some pointers on how to make the best impression on the people who will decide the final outcome—the judge and the jury:

Do not make positive, vehement or dogmatic statements— employ the phrase "in my opinion."

Be impartial.

Be truthful.

Avoid technical language—try to make clear explanations.

Know the particular subject involved—refresh your knowledge by study if necessary—do not read from a treatise while you are on the stand.

Be ready with your answers without being hasty.

Try not to act embarrassed by anything you are asked—remember it is customary for the party calling an expert witness to pay him.

Be patient.

Give evidence of having a sense of humor without trying to be funny.

Be able to say "I do not know"—it sounds better than "I am not certain."

CHAPTER 4

THE POLICE POWER

21. **Definition of Police Power.** Governments are expected to protect citizens from each other. If the citizens of a country were all moral perfectionists, no such protection would be needed. In a sense, the "police power"—which has nothing directly to do with the police—is the inherent power which reposes in all governments to regulate, restrain, direct, prohibit, control, or take any action deemed necessary to protect its citizens from practices, activities or devices which would otherwise result in harm to the public. City milk ordinances prevent one citizen from selling impure milk to another; the Federal Food, Drug and Cosmetic Act restrains those citizens in the food processing and distributing business from handling impure, adulterated or misbranded products; veterinary practice acts prevent unlicensed persons from injuring livestock owners with their lack of skill and understanding. These are examples of the police power. Theoretically, there is no limit to the police power, except what seems to be best for the most people. The number of things regulated and controlled increases as population increases and as people have increased means of communication. Controls regarded as unnecessary in an earlier day are provided today—controls we would not sanction today will become the law tomorrow. Abuse of the police power can easily lead to despotism and the loss of freedoms guaranteed. Our protection from abuse lies mainly in the courts and in the good sense of our legislators.

22. **Federal, State and Local Use of the Police Power.** The tenth amendment to the Federal Constitution provides that the powers not delegated to the United States by the Constitution nor prohibited by it to the states, shall be reserved to the states. Because of this amendment and because all the powers of government resided in the states prior to the adoption of the Federal Constitution, it is frequently stated that only the states can exercise the police power. As a matter of political theory this may be correct, but as a matter of fact it would be misleading, since

the federal government does in so many ways exert a tremendous influence and control over the very things the states control through use of the police power. For example, the states may adopt meat inspection laws and condemn meat unfit for human consumption: This is an exercise of the police power. But the federal government, under its authority to regulate commerce between the states—or anything that affects interstate commerce—may adopt federal meat inspection laws and do the same thing with respect to any meat which enters into or affects interstate commerce. Hence, the federal government adopts many of its regulatory laws for the same reason the states exercise the police power. The main difference lies in the fact that the need for the law is justification enough in the case of the state, whereas in the case of the federal government, there must be a need plus some grant of authority in the Constitution—either express, implied, or resulting from judicial interpretation. Lack of uniformity in state laws and inability of the federal government to legislate unless there is constitutional authority has led to the use of federal legislative devices such as the grant-in-aid or other assistance programs, in which matching funds and other types of aid will be provided if the state will adopt and carry out a type of program advocated by the federal government. Bovine tuberculosis eradication is an example. But the effect of federal activity extends much beyond anything that can be inferred from a summary of statutes and regulations. The United States Department of Agriculture, for example, must employ large numbers of veterinarians in its animal disease and meat inspection programs. In hiring these veterinarians it may establish its own standards. But the training and licensing of veterinarians is a function of the states. No state would wish its veterinarians to be unable to qualify for federal employment. Hence, indirectly, but very forcefully, the federal government influences the use by the state of its police power in licensing and regulating the practice of veterinary medicine and surgery. Under different circumstances and in different degree this example can be duplicated many times over.

Municipalities partake of the police power inherent in the state. A city may pass ordinances to protect the health, welfare or convenience of its residents. Milk ordinances, zoning laws restricting buildings of certain kinds, restaurant inspection,

scale and weight standards, dog licensing and quarantine are
typical regulations. Other local political agencies such as the
county, township or public health district may also have a slice
of the police power and may wield it potently within the scope
of their authority.

   23.   **Due Process of Law and Limitations on the Police Power.**
No government in history ever admitted that any of its laws
were unreasonable. But all governments adopt some unreasonable laws. The number of such laws a government can get by
with and how unreasonable they can be depends on the nature
and extent of the curbs which have been provided. In a democracy there are several. Some of them were explained in Chapter
1. There are two curbs of great importance to individuals subjected to any exercise of the police power. One of these provides
that no person shall be deprived of his life, liberty or property
without due process of law. The other is a general prohibition
against unreasonable or arbitrary authority. The due process
provision is in the fifth amendment to the Federal Constitution
and is also contained in one form or another in the constitutions
of the states. It prevents persons who have violated or failed
to abide by a law or regulation from being summarily punished.
They are entitled to "due process of law," which gives them an
opportunity to prove that they are innocent, that the penalty
is too severe, or that the law or regulation is invalid. In a Massachusetts case,[7] the owner of a horse destroyed by the State
Board of Health because it had glanders recovered the value of
the horse by refuting the Board's evidence that the horse had
that disease: It was not "due process" to seize an animal except
in strict accord with the statute conferring the authority.

   Statutes or regulations that are unreasonable or arbitrary
present a peculiar problem. Theoretically, the legislature determines what laws are needed. The courts are not to interfere with
this authority. But suppose the court has to decide a suit in
which a cattle owner is being prosecuted because he has a white
cow, there having been passed by his state legislature a law
prohibiting the raising or keeping of any but red cattle. Will
the court say: "The defendant is guilty. We do not think this is a
reasonable law, but it is in the province of the legislature to
make the laws. If this is objectionable, then the legislature
should be induced to change it"? Probably not. But courts do

say this sort of thing about laws. A Kentucky court used just about this language in upholding a Kentucky statute which declared as a matter of law that milk from a cow fed distillery waste is impure, though the testimony showed that such feed had no effect on the purity of the milk.[8] Actually, courts do consider reasonableness, whether or not they say so in express words.

There are some other safeguards in the exercise of the police power besides due process and the test of reasonableness. One of these has to do with the delegation of authority. If a state legislature were to pass a law which said "the commissioner of agriculture shall examine all the animals in this state and order the immediate destruction of those he deems to be a menace to the public," it would beyond a doubt be held invalid. The courts would say that such a law places too much authority and discretion with an administrative officer and gives him the power to make decisions which the legislature should have made. No state law on animal disease is quite this broad. Such legislation commonly specifies not only the disease which will permit state officials to destroy an animal, but outlines the circumstances under which the authority may be exercised, the rights of the livestock owner, and how the indemnity, if any, shall be determined. Obviously, some discretionary power must be created in administrative officers—the legislature cannot examine cattle to see if they have brucellosis, or a dairy farm to see if proper sanitary standards are maintained. But when the legislature places this discretionary authority with a particular officer or board or commission, these agencies cannot delegate to someone else the power to make the decisions required of them by law, but they may—and as a matter of fact normally must— base their decisions on the information and facts supplied by their inspectors, field men or other ministerial officers. Still another safeguard exists in the form of technical requirements in the drafting and wording of statutes. If a law is repugnant to another law or cannot be construed so they both make sense, if it contains conflicting provisions, if it violates a constitutional or statutory directive that the title of the act shall be a fair indication of its contents and that not more than one subject shall be embraced under one title, it may be void or partly unenforceable.

One of the most effective limitations on the exercise of the police power is an informed and articulate public. If the individ-

uals and organizations most affected by proposed regulatory
laws will study the proposals and make their opinions felt in
the legislature, particularly in committee hearings and by dis-
cussions with the proponents of the laws, the chance that an unreasonable or unnecessary law will be passed is greatly reduced.
Some proposed laws, of course, are quite controversial in nature,
and the individuals and agencies concerned need no prodding—
a state law permitting the scientific use of dogs and cats from
public pounds, for example. But many laws are not so exciting.
The writer remembers a midwestern legislature's agriculture
committee hearing on a proposal to declare bull thistles a noxious
weed. The proponents had been impressed with the complaints
of some of their farmer constituents whose neighbors did not
control bull thistles. They argued that these thistles were as real
a nuisance as Canada thistles, which were noxious weeds under
the laws of this state. The proposal failed, largely because the
committee members themselves felt it to be unnecessary and im-
practical. But for this it might have received a favorable report
from the committee because there were no persons there to
testify against its inclusion. Many laws "get by" through default. The more thoroughly they are aired and the more interest
people take in them, the less probable will be their enactment
if they are not needed and the more probable will be their enactment if they are.

24. **The Law of Nuisance.** In a sense the law of nuisance
takes up where the exercise of the police power leaves off. When
a danger is widespread, or something needs to be regulated to
protect large segments of the population, a state law or a city
ordinance is the best answer. But when there is no law or ordinance, and particular individuals or groups are injured by the
actions of others in the use of their property, then recourse
must be had to some other kind of protection. This is where the
law of nuisance fits in. It is a qualification of the principle that a
man may use his property as he sees fit, and results in another
principle—that a man shall not use his property so as to injure
another. The extent to which the principle applies depends on
circumstances. If one owns property in a crowded city residential
area, he might be enjoined, under the nuisance theory, from
keeping chickens or goats, piling manure in his back yard, operating a small animal hospital in his home, or doing any of a num-

ber of things that would inconvenience his neighbors and reduce the enjoyment by them of their property. These same acts would not amount to nuisances in the country because no one else would be injured. However, there are some things that are a nuisance regardless of circumstances: A rabid dog is a potential danger to all members of the public and may be abated without instituting a suit to determine if he should be permitted to run at large. Dumping dead animals in a stream is another example of something that is a nuisance "on its face." They are referred to as nuisances *per se*. Generally, however, the determination of whether a thing is a nuisance is a question of fact. Furthermore, the determination of whether a nuisance is private or public is a question of fact: It is a public nuisance if the public generally is injured, a private nuisance if an individual or a small group of individuals are injured. A rabid dog or an animal with an infectious disease would normally be classed a public nuisance —an outdoor toilet next to someone else's house, or chickens that take up residence in a neighbor's garden are private nuisances. Some things may amount to a public and private nuisance at the same time. A Colorado court so held with respect to the maintenance near town of a hog ranch where garbage was fed.[9] The discoveries of science have much to do with the determination of nuisances and with the eventual exercise of the police power. Knowledge of where flies breed and of how far they travel, where mosquitoes breed, the habits of rats, how disease organisms are propagated and spread, can easily result in a change of opinion as to whether a garbage dump, a stagnant pool of water, waste piled in the alley, or a sick animal is a nuisance.

Many things may constitute nuisances. An interference with free movement (obstructing a private way), offending the sense of smell (a privy too near another's property), offending the senses of hearing or sight (loud and continuous screaming and indecent exposure), causing bodily discomfort (cinders piled so they blow across another's porch), creating mental disturbance (a funeral parlor in a residential block), and the more familiar one of endangering health, are common causes of nuisance suits.

25. **Legal Remedies for Nuisances.** A nuisance, whether public or private, may be abated, prohibited, or modified. When a nuisance is abated, it is terminated. Killing a rabid dog, filling a dangerous hole, destroying an illegal dam are examples. Sum-

mary abatement (taking action without court or other authority) is justified only when life or health are seriously endangered
and immediate action is required. Even then the one acting does
so at his peril: The danger may not have been as imminent as
he thought, the dog may not have had rabies, the peril may not
have seemed great to the average man. One is not privileged to
destroy a building, though it contains a stable which may be a
nuisance.[10] The abatement of nuisances, except for authority
conveyed by statute to administrative officers to seize, destroy
or otherwise exercise control over property, is accomplished under
an order of the court, issued in a suit which determined that the
thing complained of was a nuisance and that abatement was a
proper remedy. Officers of the court are responsible to see that
the order of the court is carried out.

The prohibition of a nuisance comes about by injunction. In
a civil suit to secure damages caused by a nuisance, the court
may issue an order forbidding a repetition of the nuisance. Violation of such an order subjects the offender to a penalty and
makes him liable to a further recovery of damages by the injured
party.

Sometimes in a suit to enjoin an activity it is apparent that
with some modification of the activity it would no longer constitute a nuisance. Fumes from a copper smelter may destroy
vegetable crops, thus giving the vegetable growers a right to file
a suit and seek damages and a restraining order. But if the court
has evidence that fumes may be removed from the smoke and
that the defendant may be able to render it harmless, injunction
may be withheld for some reasonable period of time to give the
defendant an opportunity to make the correction.

When one is injured by a nuisance, there are a few steps
which should be taken. First, one must decide if the injury is
great enough to complain about. If it is, the next line of approach
would be a talk with the offending party. If no settlement or
compromise can be reached after a bona fide effort, then one must
decide if the matter is important enough to take "to the law."
At this point an attorney should be consulted. It may be that the
act complained of is a violation of some statute, ordinance, or
regulation, in which case you can enlist the aid of the public.
Also, it should be determined whether a public nuisance is being
created and if there are others who will join in an action to abate

or correct it in some other way. Following this a case must be made. This means that facts must be assembled to show the nature and extent of your injury, the steps you have taken to alleviate it, the period of time the injury has continued, the intent of the offender, and the necessity of his continuing the damage to you: In short, your legal counsel must take every precaution to see that nothing is left to conjecture and that your case receives a strong presentation. The burden of showing that your neighbor, or whoever the offender may be, is not making a lawful use of his property rests with you, and the courts are not inclined to interfere unless the facts clearly indicate that a nuisance does exist.

CHAPTER 5

REGULATION OF THE PROFESSION

26. **The Purpose of State Veterinary Practice Acts.** Were it not for the veterinary practice acts, anyone could practice veterinary medicine, whether qualified or not. Under such circumstances, the only protection the public would have against ignorant or careless practitioners would be that afforded by civil actions for damages. This is not always a satisfactory remedy, because at the time such a suit is instituted, the damage has already been done. Also, many cases of incompetence—malpractice —would not be recognizable to the owner. Perhaps the practitioner employed was the only one available, and there was no one from whom the owner could learn that the treatment used was grossly wrong. The owner would not consider himself as well acquainted with animal diseases as one who professed such an acquaintance and knowledge—though often he might be—and would rely absolutely upon the diagnosis and treatment prescribed by the practitioner, never questioning the correctness of the diagnosis or treatment. To afford adequate protection to the public from the ignorant, the unscrupulous, and the charlatans, there must be some means for preventing them from ever starting to practice. Today, except for Alaska, every state of the United States has a veterinary practice act which requires all practitioners to be licensed by the state. Under these practice acts, the would-be practitioner must prove to a board of competent veterinarians that he is qualified to practice. He must prove that he has met the educational requirements for practice, and also that he possesses the necessary moral qualifications. In a very real sense, a license issued today is a certification that the holder is qualified to practice veterinary medicine.

Clearly, the main purpose of these statutes is to provide a scheme whereby the state can regulate the practice of veterinary medicine. The enactment of these statutes shows that the states have recognized the important part that veterinarians play in

27

our national and community life, and are trying to protect the public by prescribing certain standards which a person must meet if he intends to practice veterinary medicine. Further, the state is assisting the qualified veterinarian by excluding from practice those persons not properly qualified.

It is natural, when a state so regulates a profession, for someone to contest such legislation on constitutional grounds. The usual arguments are that such regulation is arbitrary or a deprivation of due process of law. The veterinary practice acts have been so tested and held valid.[11] In Barnes v. State,[12] the court said:

> For one who has had no training of the kind to assume a title which indicates that he is a graduate of a veterinary college, is a species of deceit, which, if practiced with a view of thereby obtaining business, amounts to an attempt to obtain money by false pretenses, which is not only reprehensible, but unlawful.

27. **Scope and General Content of the Practice Acts.** The veterinary practice acts apply to all persons acting in a veterinary capacity, and to all acts of a veterinary nature. These statutes define "veterinary practice," provide for administration of the act by creating a Board of Examiners, enumerate certain prerequisites for practice, set forth grounds for refusal or revocation of licenses, and in many cases enumerate the subjects to be covered on an examination of applicants. In addition to defining "veterinary practice," the acts set forth exceptions to the definition—both as to persons exempted and acts excepted. Reciprocity provisions, if any, are in the practice act.

Analysis of a typical state law reveals that it does the following important things:

Prohibits the practice of veterinary medicine and surgery except by those with a valid and existing license.

Defines the practice of veterinary medicine and surgery and lists exceptions and exemptions.

Gives an agency of state government the responsibility of approving schools and courses of study, determining qualifications of applicants for a license, administering examinations and issuing licenses.

Defines an accredited school of veterinary medicine and surgery.

Specifies the qualifications, in addition to educational qualifications, for receiving a license and the fees to be charged.

States the grounds for refusing to issue, suspending or revoking a license, and sets forth the procedure to be followed.

Provides that all administrative decisions under the practice act shall be subject to judicial review, and that final orders or judgments of a lower court may be appealed directly to the State Supreme Court.

Provides reciprocity with other states having equal standards.

Requires that the license be recorded in the county in which the veterinarian resides, and that it be endorsed and again recorded if he moves to another county.

Provides penalties for forging a diploma or otherwise violating the law and makes it the duty of the state's attorney in his county to prosecute.

Specifies fines and penalties.

28. **Administration of the Practice Acts.** The administering agency is the "Board of Examiners," and its composition is prescribed by the practice act. Usually, the statute requires that the governor of the state appoint from three to five graduate veterinarians to receive applications, examine the applicants, and otherwise to administer the act. The term of office for a member of the Board varies from two to six years, and it is common for the statute to provide that one office shall be vacated each year. Some sixteen states list, within their practice acts, the subjects which are to be included in the examination. Such a statute ordinarily provides that the examination shall include such subjects as: physiology; anatomy; obstetrics; pathology; surgery; materia medica; chemistry; therapeutics; and very possibly, sanitation and veterinary practice. The rest of the states either leave the subjects to be covered to the discretion of the Board or state the requirements in very general terms.

Provisions on licensing are to be strictly construed and examing boards have no discretion but to apply the law, administer examinations, and issue licenses to all who qualify. It cannot permit someone to qualify contrary to statutory provisions. For example, at one time the Michigan law required graduation from "a veterinary college with a curriculum of three sessions of six months." An applicant had attended a veterinary college when it was offering only a two year course, but at the time he received his diploma, it had been changed to a three year school. The court held that this technicality did not qualify him to take the examination since the meaning of the law was that he should have himself completed the three year course.[13] Also, it has been held that it is no defense to a criminal prosecution for illegal practice of veterinary medicine that the Board consisted of only five members, instead of the seven called for by the statute, nor because three of the members were graduates of the same school, whereas the statute provided that no more than two shall be graduates of the same school. "This court cannot assume and will not presume that the Governor, a coordinate branch of the government, has violated his sworn duty."[14]

29. **Definition of Veterinary Practice.** The tests ordinarily prescribed by the practice acts to determine whether a person is practicing veterinary medicine are: (1) Is he appending to his name words or initials indicating that he is a qualified veterinarian? (2) Is he publicly professing to act as a veterinarian? (3) Is he treating or prescribing for animals? It could be well argued that #2 is broad enough to include any act which would come within #1. An ordinary qualification upon the test of prescribing or treating animals is that the prescription or treatment be for domestic animals, and that it be given for compensation. Nine practice acts give no definition of veterinary practice. The common statutory exceptions to the practice acts are: (1) Veterinarians from other states; (2) Owners and their employees (however, when an owner is treating his own animal, his services are gratuitous and, therefore, would come under that exception, or a similar one which states that treating or prescribing for animals constitutes veterinary practice only when done for compensation); (3) Students; (4) Veterinarians of the U. S. Army or U.S.D.A.; (5) The administration of serums; (6) Castrating, spaying, and dehorning; (7) Gratuitous services. Several states do not expressly except gratuitous services, but say that treating or prescribing for animals constitutes practicing veterinary medicine *when done for compensation.* Five states do not exempt owners, nor do they except gratuitous services; but of these, one (Rhode Island) does not define veterinary practice, one (Massachusetts) does so in very general terms, and three (Georgia, New Hampshire, and Vermont) define it merely as representing one's self to be a veterinarian. Thus, it appears that in no

state is an owner precluded from treating his own animals. It further appears from this analysis, that anywhere in the United States (with the possible exception of Delaware), any person may treat or prescribe for an animal if he does so gratuitously and without representing that he is a qualified veterinarian.

Although the question of what constitutes an unlawful representation as a veterinarian has been raised in this country, the English courts have considered the question several times and show a clear definition of what constitutes a representation that one is a veterinarian. A defendant who displayed on his premises a sign: "J. Robinson, veterinary forge" was held liable for the statutory fine exacted upon violation of the statute prohibiting anyone not registered from taking or using "any name, title, addition, or description stating that he is a veterinary surgeon or a practitioner of veterinary surgery, or of any branch thereof, or is specially qualified to practice the same. . ."[15] A chemist published a book dealing with the diseases of horses, recommending medicines which he kept, and advising people in some cases to consult a veterinary surgeon. He described himself in the book as a "pharmaceutical and veterinary chemist." The court held that this was not unlawfully using a description that he was a veterinary surgeon.[16] A limited company caused the following notice to be displayed above its premises: "Churchill's Veterinary Sanitarium, (Ltd.). Dogs and Cats boarded here." James Churchill, the managing director of this company, was not a duly qualified veterinary surgeon within the meaning of the statute then in effect. The court held that the notice amounted to a false representation that Churchill was a duly qualified veterinary surgeon, and, therefore, was in violation of the statute. It was further held that, although no penal action could be taken against a limited company, an injunction could be granted against it and against Churchill personally to restrain both from continuing to make this representation.[17] It has been held, in the absence of a statutory definition of "veterinary," that a defendant who put up "M. Collinson, Canine Specialist, Dogs and Cats treated for all diseases," was violating the Veterinary Surgeons Act of 1881,[18] which prohibited unqualified persons' representing that they were competent veterinarians.[19] However, in Royal College of Veterinary Surgeons v. Kennard,[20] the court decided that the statute prohibits a description of the *person,* as distinguished from a description of the place. Hence, it was no offense for the defendant to append to his name the words: "Canine Surgery." One of the judges, concurring specially in the decision, said: "I will only say that it appears to me that the net result arrived at from a consideration of the cases is that it is probably an offense to say 'I am a canine surgeon,' but that it is no offense to say 'I have a canine surgery.' "

It has been held in this country that holding one's self out as a "Horse dentist," advertising one's self as "doctor" at a place where horses are kept, and primitive treatment of horses' teeth rendered the defendant subject to conviction of the crime of practicing veterinary medicine without a license.[21] By way of dictum, another court has said that the use of instruments upon the teeth and mouths of horses for remedial purposes constitutes the practice of veterinary surgery.[22] The Supreme Court of Pennsylvania has said that veterinary dentistry is a branch of veterinary medicine or surgery within the meaning of the practice act, and the title "doctor" used in connection with the initials "V.D." is an analogous title to "Veterinary Surgeon" within the prohibition of such act.[23] Thus, it is evident that a court will not hold that, merely because a certain title is not expressly condemned by statute, it is permissible for an unqualified person to attach it to his name.

30. **Prerequisites for Practice.** The most common prerequisites for practice enumerated by the statutes are: 1. possession of a license or permit to practice; 2. payment of certain fees; 3. passing an examination; 4. graduation from a veterinary college; and 5. furnishing evidence of good moral character.

When a statute sets forth conditions which must be performed before one is entitled to a license, or to practice, substantial performance of those conditions is not enough; there must be *literal* compliance with the statutory conditions. A South Carolina statute provided for the licensing of nongraduate veterinarians who had engaged in the practice of veterinary medicine as a vocation for five years immediately prior to the enactment of the statute, upon their application, accompanied with affidavits to that effect by five disinterested freeholders, such application and affidavits to be submitted within six months from the date of the passage of the act. The Board retained, without protest, a petitioner's application and affidavits for three months, and then, after the six month period had elapsed, informed the petitioner that his application was denied because two of the affiants were not freeholders. The applicant immediately forwarded five additional affidavits, all of freeholders, and the Board refused to issue a license because the six month period had elapsed. The applicant sought a writ of mandamus to compel the Board to issue a license, but the Supreme Court denied his petition, saying that the clear requirements of the statute were five freeholders within six months; he had not complied with the statute, and therefore was not entitled to a license.[24]

31. Who May Practice. Upon performance of all conditions enumerated by the statute, a man may practice veterinary medicine. But it is not enough that a person have all the educational prerequisites, nor is it enough that he has fulfilled all the other statutory requirements; he cannot practice *until a license has been issued to him.* The Texas Court of Criminal Appeals affirmed the conviction of a man who was otherwise qualified to practice, but who had never applied for a license, taken the examination, or been issued a license.[25] In an Iowa case,[26] the plaintiff sued to recover the value of services rendered in the care of the defendant's hogs. The plaintiff had taken the examination before the Board of Examiners; he had been orally informed by members of the Board that he had passed; but he received his license some six weeks after he had treated the defendant's hogs. The plaintiff, in treating the hogs, diagnosed their ailment as cholera, and administered virus and serum. The court held that the plaintiff could not recover, saying that he had not complied with the statutory prerequisite; that good faith would not substitute for such compliance; that he was engaged in a criminal act (a misdemeanor); and that he could not require compensation. As to the plaintiff's contention that a person did not have to be a veterinarian to administer anti-hog-cholera serum and virus, and that he had complied with the statutory prerequisites for such administration, the court said that the administration of the serum and virus was not severable from his holding himself out as a veterinarian and diagnosing animal disease.

The original practice acts commonly contained provisions permitting existing practitioners to continue to practice, upon the performance of certain conditions, such as registration and payment of fees. In a Michigan case,[27] the petitioner sought a writ of mandamus to require the Board to issue him a license to practice. The practice act, adopted on June 27, 1907, provided that applications by practitioners who had engaged in the practice for five years prior to the passage of the act would be granted if such applications were filed before January 1, 1908. The petitioner applied on May 26, 1908, and his application was rejected by the Board. He then filed his mandamus proceeding. The Michigan Court ruled that, under the statute, an existing practitioner would have to apply within a reasonable time; that the legislature determined what would constitute a reasonable time when it specified that applications should be filed before January 1, 1908. Therefore, the petition was refused. However, it was held proper for the Board to issue a license where the applicant had submitted his application before January 1, 1908, failed to state therein that he had practiced for five years, but subsequently corrected this defect.[28] It would appear that when an application is defective, it is discretionary with the Board whether or not it will permit the applicant to remedy the defect and qualify for a license. This conclusion is strengthened by the result in Dusaw v. State Veterinary Board.[29] In this case, the statute involved provided that

> Any person who has practiced veterinary medicine or surgery in their various branches in this State for five years prior to . . . this act shall be eligible to become registered as an existing practitioner, and receive a certificate of registration. . . . *Provided*, that . . . (he) shall, . . ., file with the Secretary of the veterinary board, an affidavit, showing that he has been continuously so engaged, and shall also present letters of recommendation from ten reputable stock raisers of this State, who shall have employed him, showing him to practice veterinary medicine or surgery as above set forth.

The court held: 1. That in the omission of the words "in their various branches," the affidavit fell short of the statutory requirement; 2. The letters submitted did not fulfill the statutory requirements because they spoke in terms of generalities and conclusions, and did not show that the time of employment covered the statutory period; 3. The Board was correct in refusing to issue the certificate.

It must be noted that not all practice acts have been interpreted to prohibit practice by one not licensed under them. The Iowa court has held that nothing in the act precluded a man of good moral character, who had practiced as a veterinarian for more than five years prior to the passage of the act, from continuing such practice although he had never applied for a certificate of qualifications under the practice act. In Pennsylvania, a district court has held that the continuance of practice by one practicing veterinary medicine for two years prior to the enactment of the practice act did not place the defendant within the statutory prohibition.[30]

32. **Legislative Grants of Licenses.** With the advent of the practice acts, occasions arose when state legislatures felt that a legislative grant of a license to a previous practitioner was justified. Where a veterinarian had been given such legal status by an act of the legislature and had been permitted to continue his practice of veterinary medicine and surgery without taking an examination, the Ohio court held that he was a "license holder" within the statute requiring a license of everyone engaged in the practice of veterinary surgery and, therefore, within the exception providing that the statute does not apply to one duly licensed under the laws of the state at the time the statute was enacted.[31] In 1946, the Kentucky General Assembly, by a special law, granted to a certain person the right to practice veterinary medicine because he had "professional training in the practice of veterinary medicine, surgery and dentistry. . ." for more than one year prior to July 1, 1916 (effective date of the Kentucky Practice Act). The Kentucky Supreme Court held this act invalid as violative of the Kentucky Constitutional prohibition of special laws or exclusive grants. Further, the court said that the practice of veterinary medicine is not a "public service" within the constitutional exception to the prohibition.[32] A year later, however, the legislature achieved the desired result by enacting a statute providing that any person who had practiced veterinary medicine for one year prior to March 24, 1916, could obtain a license to practice, if he applied to the Board and paid a $25 fee. It further provided that no license should be so issued after June 30, 1948. The court held this statute valid, as general legislation, regulating the practice of a profession.[33]

33. **Reciprocity.** The federal constitution requires that each of the states give "full faith and credit" to the laws of the others. But this has not been interpreted to mean that a professional man licensed in one state shall be legally entitled to practice his profession in another state. The courts have said that despite the full faith and credit clause, a state may still determine what

standards are deemed necessary for the adequate protection of its citizens. Hence, a veterinarian licensed to practice in one state may not practice in another unless he in some way meets its requirements. If the states involved have a mutual understanding—a "reciprocity" agreement—it is possible for a veterinarian licensed in one of these states to secure a license in the other without examination. Usual requirements for the issuance of a license by reciprocity are educational standards as high as the reciprocating state, a stated number of years of experience, and a declaration of intention to become a resident of the reciprocating state. As an example, there is reproduced below the rules on reciprocity adopted by the Illinois Department of Registration and Education:

RULES RELATING TO LICENSING OF VETERINARIANS BY RECIPROCITY

1. The Department shall issue licenses to veterinarians licensed in foreign states upon a basis of equal educational standard and mutual recognition, which educational standard shall not be lower than the requirements of the Illinois Veterinary Medicine and Surgery Act.

2. The application for license by reciprocity shall be upon forms prescribed and furnished by the Department.

3. The application must be signed by the applicant and sworn to before a notary public or some other person duly authorized by law to take acknowledgements.

4. Applicants for license on the basis of reciprocity shall make a declaration of intention to become a citizen of this State for the purpose of practicing veterinary medicine.

5. The license of an applicant who seeks a license to practice in this State by reciprocity must have been issued upon passing a written or written and oral examination.

6. The applicant for a license by reciprocity shall appear in person before the Veterinary Examining Committee for an oral interview and shall exhibit the license he received from the foreign state, issued upon the basis of an examination.

7. The applicant shall furnish proof of good moral character and temperate habits.

8. A recent personal photograph must accompany the application.

9. The fee required is $50.00, but should not be forwarded until the applicant is notified that application is in complete form.

One interested in the reciprocity provisions of his own state or of one or more other states where he may contemplate moving to practice, should obtain detailed information by writing to the examining boards of the states involved.

The cases arising under the reciprocity provisions of the practice acts illustrate the same "literal meaning" interpretation of the statutes noted in connection with other provisions of the practice acts. In an action by a veterinarian, holding an Indiana license, to obtain a license to practice in New Jersey, the court held that since the applicant relied on the provisions of the statute, and the section of the statute on which he relied clearly comprehended that he should have been examined in the state whose license the Board is asked to honor, and he had not been so examined; and since the statute required that the preliminary educational requirement be substantially the same, and it was not, the applicant was not entitled to a license. Here the applicant had been excused from taking the Indiana examination because he had been in practice eight years prior to the date of the Indiana Practice Act, and it was not apparent in the case that the requirements were the same in Indiana when he obtained his license as they were in New Jersey when he filed suit.[34]

A Board may not discriminate against graduates of out-of-state veterinary schools. In Robertson v. Schein,[35] a Kentucky case, the plaintiff had graduated from a Massachusetts veterinary college, passed the examination required by statute in Kentucky, and was issued a license as a nongraduate veterinarian. He filed an action for a mandamus order directing the Board to issue to him an unrestricted license to practice veterinary medicine, surgery and dentistry as defined by the Kentucky statute. The court held for the veterinarian. It said that the Kentucky statute nowhere expressly conferred upon the Board the authority to issue two classes of licenses or certificates,

one based upon graduation from the recognized veterinary college and one based upon successful examination by one from a veterinary college not recognized. That the statutes require the State and Deputy State Veterinarians to be residents of the State and graduate veterinarians is not an implied authorization for the Board to distinguish between graduate and nongraduate veterinarians in issuing the private licenses.

This decision leaves open the question whether or not the legislature could, by express declaration, create this distinction. Might such legislation be a deprivation of due process? Probably not, for the legislature concededly has the power to prescribe reasonable regulations for the profession, and this classification does not appear unreasonable when exercised by the legislature, at least if such regulation does not operate retroactively. In Wise v. State Veterinary Board,[36] a Michigan case, it was held that the State Veterinary Board has no power to define "regular veterinary college or school" as used in the statute; that this phrase simply gives the Board authority to determine if an institution is a *properly incorporated veterinary college or school.*

34. **Violation of the Practice Acts — Practice Without a License.** It has been pointed out that lack of a license may be interposed as a defense to a suit for compensation for services rendered as a veterinarian.[37] Also, it has been intimated that the practice of veterinary medicine without a license is a crime, for which the offender may be prosecuted by the state's attorney. These are the ways in which the matter is likely to be brought before a court. Another is when the owner of an animal sues a veterinarian for injuries caused to an animal by his mistreatment of it, and lack of a license is brought in to prove lack of ability to treat the animal.

It appears that no private citizen may maintain an action to restrain a man from practicing, unless such citizen has a substantial interest in the litigation. It was held by the Virginia Supreme Court that four legally licensed and practicing veterinarians could not maintain an action to enjoin another's practice of veterinary medicine because he had illegally obtained his license. (The board had not required him to take an examination.) The court said that this practice by the defendant was no invasion of either the property or civil rights of the complainants, and that, "Equity will not assume jurisdiction at the instance of a private individual, who shows no special damages, for the sole purpose of declaring an act of a quasi judicial board illegal."[38]

If the practitioner is suing for compensation, it has been held that he must be licensed to recover. It is not enough that he has the educational requirements, has taken the examination, and has been informed orally that he has passed and that a license was subsequently issued to him.[39]

As to the question of who has the burden of proof (convincing the jury) of the veterinarian's qualifications—or lack of qualifications—the Michigan court has said that the burden of proof of qualification to act as a veterinarian is upon the alleged veterinarian in an action by him to recover for his services.[40]

In affirming a conviction for practicing without a license, the Oklahoma Criminal Court of Appeals said that

> . . . in order for a person to be held for a violation of said part of the statute, it is necessary for him to be charged with: 1. not having a license, 2. acting for commercial purposes, and 3. (a) prescribing any drug or medicine for any livestock, or (b) applying any drug or medicine to any livestock, or (c) administering preventive treatment to any livestock, or (d) performing any operation for the treatment, relief, or cure of any sick, diseased, or injured animal.[41]

The North Dakota court has held that it is proper, in a prosecution for practicing without a license, to prove that the defendant received compensation for treating the horses, since such proof tended to refute the claim that his treatment came within the statutory exemption of gratuitous and friendly assistance by a neighbor; that it was competent to show by the secretary of the state board of veterinarians, that the records of his office did not show the issuance of any license to the defendant; and that it was competent for the said secretary to testify that defendant had not paid the statutory license fee. In this case, the court held that performance of one or more isolated or occasional acts of dentistry on teeth of animals may constitute the practice of veterinary dentistry, but proof only that on one occasion the defendant filed some sharp corners from the teeth of some horses was not proof of the practice of veterinary dentistry.[42]

Practice without a license is not a public nuisance. Unless a person is directly injured by such practice, he cannot go into court and enjoin the practitioner. In a Missouri case, the Appellate Court held that even the Missouri Veterinary Medical Association was not a proper party to maintain such a suit.[43] The fact that unlicensed practice is punishable under state law does not give a private individual or association the right to enjoin, unless they can show *special* injury.

In all revocation cases, the rights of the accused practitioner are well safeguarded. The practice acts not only specify the causes for revocation, but they spell out the procedure as well.

In addition, any general laws or common law rules on judicial review and appeal could be urged on behalf of the accused. In an Oregon case, for example, it appeared that a letter was written to the veterinarian in reference to revocation of his license to practice. It did not appear that a legal notice was given the veterinarian or that he received a copy of any charge against him. The Supreme Court held that the board had no jurisdiction of the subject matter or of the person of the veterinarian, and that its revocation of his license was void.[44]

35. **Malpractice.** Literally, "malpractice" means bad practice. If a veterinarian fails to measure up to some reasonable standard of performance, is particularly inept or careless or in some negligent manner damages a client, he may lose his fee, be subject to a claim for damages and in some states be liable to lose his license. The practice acts in ten states make "malpractice" a ground for revocation. Regardless of whether the law specifically names malpractice as a cause for revocation, it may constitute a cause for revocation if the charges against a veterinarian are many and serious: After all, one of the purposes of such acts is to protect the public. In any event, the proof of malpractice is a question of fact. Each situation must be judged on its own merits and no veterinarian is likely to be found guilty unless the facts are clear and well substantiated. Further discussion of malpractice and a review of the court cases which help determine what it is appear in Chapter 7.

Terminology used in the various states' acts to define malpractice is interesting. Following is a representative sample taken from the laws of several states:

> gross negligence, ignorance, incompetence, unprofessional conduct, dishonorable conduct, fraud, willful violation, dishonesty, gross inefficiency, dilatory methods, willful neglect, misrepresentation, negligent handling, breach of duty, conduct likely to deceive or defraud, unlawful invasion of other professional fields, gross immorality, manifest incapacity, intemperate habits.

36. **Reporting Communicable Diseases.** Some states require that practicing veterinarians report communicable diseases to the State Sanitary Board, the State Veterinarian, or some similar agency or official. Pennsylvania had such a statute, requiring veterinarians to report the occurrence of tuberculosis to the State Livestock Sanitary Board immediately upon gaining informa-

tion of such occurrence. One veterinary procured the tubercular organs of a cow from a glue factory and exhibited them in his window. He was prosecuted for failing to report the occurrence of tuberculosis. The court held that he was not criminally liable for his failure to report the tuberculosis, and said that the statute referred merely to the attending veterinarian.[45] This seems like a reasonable view and is probably the one which would be followed in those states with similar statutes. Otherwise, it would be difficult to determine when the duty arose.

CHAPTER 6

THE CONTRACTUAL RELATIONS
OF VETERINARIAN AND CLIENT

37. **When Does a Contract Arise?** Two things are necessary to make a contract—an understandable agreement and an exchange of something of value by both parties to the agreement. If Jones agrees to meet Smith on the corner of Dogwood and Vine at four o'clock, and fails to appear, Smith has no cause of action against Jones because there was no consideration or exchange of something of value. But if Jones agrees to meet Smith's mother-in-law at the same corner, at the request of Smith and for a consideration of three dollars, there is a contract. If Jones does not perform, Smith is not obliged to pay the three dollars. Furthermore, Jones may be held liable in damages for the inconvenience caused by his failure to perform. In the case of a veterinarian, a contract arises when he agrees to expend his skill on an animal. An exchange of promises, each containing something of value, is sufficient to establish a contract. A request from a client that his animals be treated and a promise from the veterinarian that he will call and treat them amounts to a contract, because the law will imply consideration—a rendering of skilled service by one party and the payment of a reasonable fee by the other. While it is not necessary that the veterinarian actually make a call or treat an animal to give rise to a contract, it is necessary that a clear and unconditional exchange of promises be made. If, for example, a farmer saw a veterinarian on the street and said, "I have a thin cow that seems to have something wrong with her. Do you suppose you could look at her some day?" and the veterinarian said, "Well, I'm pretty busy right now, but I'll try to stop by in a week or two," there would be no contract, because the exchange of promises is too indefinite. Also, the expression of an opinion by a veterinarian, or even a suggested treatment, does not amount to a contract. In a Georgia case, the State Supreme Court held that there was no contract and no physician-patient relation

established by a physician's suggestion that with the use of a support a certain condition might correct itself.[46]

Once a contract is established and the veterinary-client relation created, certain rights and duties evolve. The veterinarian represents that he is duly licensed, that his training and experience make him competent, that he will employ approved practices with reasonable care and diligence, and that he will continue to handle the case until the contract is terminated. He does not guarantee a cure, and any express promise to do so is regarded as unethical. The owner of the animal is legally obliged to pay a reasonable fee for the veterinarian's services, to render such assistance as is necessary in confining and treating animals, to follow directions, and to assure the safety of the veterinarian by eliminating hazards or dangerous conditions in the premises where the veterinarian must work.

38. **Obligation to Answer Calls.** Regardless of any moral or humane principles that may be involved, there is no duty on the part of a veterinarian to accept a case and enter into a contract. This rule has become well established in the field of medicine, where presumably moral and humane considerations would be even higher. One authority on medical jurisprudence says that "No doctor is bound by law to undertake the treatment of anyone, however great his need (except of a panel patient for whom he has assumed responsibility under a special contract with the state). A doctor who saw a gravely injured man lying in the roadway and chose, like the priest and Levite, to ignore him and proceed on his way, would offend against decency and ethics but not against the law."[47] The current legal view is well stated in an Indiana case where the court said, "It has been occasionally urged that, since the State undertakes the regulation of the practice of medicine, thus affording its protection to physicians, their calling is quasi-public in nature, and that they therefore owe a duty to the public which requires them to respond to all calls and to render assistance whenever their services are required. This theory has not, however, received judicial support, and the courts have uniformly held that, whatever the ethical aspects of the question may be, a physician may capriciously determine what cases he will accept and what he will reject, or whether he will accept any at all."[48] This view is confirmed by decisions from many states. An Iowa case holds that when a physician has ter-

minated his employment, he may arbitrarily refuse to be employed further.[49] An Ohio case holds that a physician or surgeon is not obliged to respond to any and every call made upon him, but he has a right to select his patients and is not liable under any circumstances unless he has entered into a contract to render such services.[50] Since there appears to be no legal duty on the part of a veterinarian to accept cases unless he chooses, his reasons for not accepting are legally unimportant. In a North Carolina case, the court said, ". . . all the evidence tends to show that when the injured man was brought into the hospital, the defendant looked him over, and upon discovering that the patient had been drinking, declined to accept him as a patient or to undertake the necessary treatment. Conceding that the defendant was not justified in assuming that Conie Childers was drunk, still the law did not compel him to accept the injured man as a patient."[51]

The only exceptions to the rule that a veterinarian is under no legal duty to respond to a call are when he is under contract with a client or when his official position with the federal, state, or local government requires.

39. Duty to Attend an Animal. Once a veterinarian has accepted a call, a contract arises, and he is then under obligation to give the animal reasonable attention, the amount and kind of attention resting largely with the judgment of the veterinarian. In a New York case, a veterinarian was denied compensation for his treatment of a client's horse. In affirming the judgment, the higher court said, "The evidence produced by defendant, which the trial judge had the right to believe, showed that plaintiff, being called to treat the animal, and having undertaken its cure, on the day of his last visit—the horse at that time being very ill—agreed to call the next morning early, but neglected to ever call again. I think the action of the plaintiff in leaving the animal he had assumed to take charge of in such a dangerous condition, and failing again to call according to his promise, was such clear negligence as justified the judgment rendered by the trial court."[52] In an action against a veterinarian for negligence in gelding a colt, the Supreme Court of Maine held that, in the absence of special agreement or reasonable notice to the contrary, it was the duty of the defendant to give the colt such continued further attention, after the operation, as the necessity of the case required.[53] The prevailing rule is well stated in the *Cyclo-*

pedia of Law and Procedure: "A physician, responding to the call of a patient, thereby becomes engaged, in the absence of a special agreement, to attend to the case, so long as it requires attention, . . . and he is bound to use ordinary care and skill . . . in determining when it may be safely and properly discontinued."[54] But if a patient is treated at the office of the practitioner and fails to return for further treatments, he cannot hold the practitioner liable for the consequences.[55] Likewise, if a veterinarian were to treat an animal and prescribe certain things for the owner to do, the veterinarian could not be held liable for any damage resulting from a failure of the owner to follow instructions. On the other hand, a veterinarian may be held responsible, even when animals are brought to him for treatment, if their condition clearly indicates further care and treatment and he fails to instruct the client to leave the animal, return with the animal, or does not himself call at the client's premises.

40. **Duties Owed by the Client to the Veterinarian.** When a veterinarian accepts a case, he has a right to expect certain things from the client. Though compensation is the principal expectation, (it is dealt with more thoroughly in section 44), certain duties devolve on the livestock owner. One of these is to make certain that the premises on which the veterinarian must work are reasonably safe. Rotten flooring, lumber or hay insecurely held above a stall, sharp knives or blades on farm machinery concealed by straw or debris—are examples of things that may cause injury to a veterinarian and which may in turn result in liability on the part of the owner. Ordinary hazards are assumed by the veterinarian. Failure to warn may also result in liability. If an animal is particularly adept at kicking, biting, crowding, striking, or otherwise inflicting injury on its human attendants, the veterinarian has a right to know about its vicious habits before he exposes himself. The owner or his agents are expected to render such assistance as the veterinarian needs in treating an animal. This includes rounding up and confining the animals to be treated, helping catch and hold animals, and providing a means for keeping animals separated or sorted in whatever way the treatment may require. If animals are brought to the premises of the veterinarian, there is an implication that they will not be permitted to roam around the premises, exciting other animals and possibly spreading contagious disease. If the owner is asked to give medication between calls or to feed or confine the animal in some

particular way, it is his duty to do so—providing he wishes to hold the veterinarian to his contractual obligations. In rendering assistance to a veterinarian, there is an obligation to do so with ordinary care and not in such a way as may result in personal injury to the veterinarian.

41. **Terminating the Veterinary-Client Relation.** Contracts are fulfilled when each party has done what he agreed to do. But contracts may be legally terminated in many ways. The contract between a veterinarian and his client may be terminated by fulfillment (the cure of the animal), by the death of the animal or animals being treated, by mutual agreement, by inability of the veterinarian to perform because of illness or some other condition making it impossible, by notice to the client that the veterinarian intends to discontinue treatment and that the client should find another veterinarian (this implies a reasonable notice period), by notice to the veterinarian that his services are no longer desired or by the client making it impossible for the relation to continue, removal of the animal from the premises, failure to follow instructions, or other acts of non-cooperation. Regardless of when the contract is terminated, a veterinarian is entitled to compensation for services rendered up to the time of termination, provided he is not guilty of negligence or malpractice. Once the contract is at an end, the veterinarian owes no further duty to the client, and the relationship of veterinary-client will not apply unless a new agreement is entered. This new agreement may concern the same or different animals, or it may concern the same or a new ailment—legally it makes no difference.

42. **Right to Kill an Animal.** Veterinarians have no special right or privilege to kill the animals of a client, even though they honestly believe that killing is the best thing. As an agent of the state or federal government, a veterinarian may be given authority to destroy animals, but this authority is derived from the police power of the state or the constitutional authority of the federal government and not from the fact that he is a veterinarian. Under certain circumstances anyone may be justified in killing animals belonging to another. Killing an animal in self defense (when the person himself is not guilty of inciting the animal), killing an animal to prevent bodily harm to another, and killing a rabid dog[56] are examples. Animals with contagious disease may amount to a public nuisance, and they may be abated by

proper legal action.[57] But here again no special right is given veterinarians: The authority to abate a nuisance must come from a court, and the officers of the court must see that the judgment is carried out. Furthermore, when a veterinarian acts as an agent of the state in determining that animals should be destroyed in accordance with a law providing for such destruction, he acts at his peril—to some extent, at any rate. In a Massachusetts case the court held an agent of the Board of Livestock Commissioners liable for the destruction of a horse under a law permitting the destruction of horses with glanders, where the horse did not actually have glanders. The court said that the commissioners had no power to kill an animal which was not actually infected.[58] Unless laws providing for the destruction of animals are grounded in a public need and clearly worded so that no animal may be destroyed without a determination of disease, they are apt to be declared unconstitutional on the ground that they deprive the owners of property without due process of law.[59] The state has extensive power to legislate against animal disease and to require the destruction of animals, either with or without compensation, but in so doing it must stay within the constitutional safeguards both to property and personal rights.

Sometimes it is urged that one should have a right to kill an animal when such would be justified as a humane act. But no right of this kind is recognized—except in the owner, and even then he must do so under circumstances which will not create a nuisance, "shock the sensibilities" of children or other persons, or violate statutes or ordinances on cruelty to animals. In an Illinois case involving the destruction of certain horses by a humane society, it was held to be no defense against a suit by the owner of the horses that they were killed for humane reasons.[60]

Unless he is acting as an agent of the government or of a municipality, under a law or ordinance which permits the destruction of animals, a veterinarian should not kill an animal without first securing the consent of the owner or the consent of an authorized agent of the owner. It is dangerous to deal with members of the family without ascertaining who the owner of an animal actually is: Instances have been reported in which members of the family, contrary to the desires and without the knowledge of the actual owner, have taken animals to a veterinarian and had them dispatched. Without appearing unduly skeptical, a veterinarian should determine ownership to his own satisfaction, and before destroying an animal secure the signature of the owner or his agent on a consent form which can then be filed. A similar situation may arise under a livestock lease where the tenant and landlord are co-owners of the animals, or in instances where bulls or other breeding animals are owned by several persons.

43. **Gratuitous Service.** Rendering veterinary service for no fee or compensation of any kind does not excuse the veterinarian from the exercise of care and skill. The legal authorities seem to be divided on just how much care and skill is required when no charge is made—whether it is the same as when a charge is made or whether it is somewhat less. In a New York case the court said, "Whether the patient be a pauper or a millionaire, whether he be treated gratuitously or for reward, the physician owes him precisely the same duty and the same degree of skill and care."[61] Certainly, there should be no variation in the skill and care required because of differences in financial position and ability to pay. All authorities seem agreed on this. But some courts hold that if the service is gratuitous, the practitioner is liable only for gross negligence.[62] Even though some jurisdictions adopt this latter view, and even though a good argument may be made for a lesser degree of skill and care in the case of gratuitous service, the wiser course and the more ethical course would be to assume that any and every case is entitled to the utmost skill and care that the practitioner is capable of giving. At any rate, this particular legal question could never be urged if that course were adopted.

In an Iowa case the court stated the law to be that where a veterinarian holds himself out to the public or to the plaintiff as a competent veterinary surgeon, and as such undertakes to treat a horse, he is bound to bring to the service the learning, skill and care which characterize the profession generally in that neighborhood or vicinity, whether he receives compensation for the service or not. But the court held that where the defendant, at the time he treated plaintiff's horse, did not hold himself out as a competent veterinarian, and stated that he was an undergraduate, undertaking the treatment without compensation only on plaintiff's urgent request, he was bound only to perform the service honestly and to the best of his ability, and was not liable for damages for malpractice, even though the service, if performed by one claiming to be a competent surgeon might justly be characterized as negligent and unskillful in a high degree.[63]

In a Canadian case the court held that where a veterinary surgeon gave advice in good faith, gratuitously, and in the honest belief that the best thing to do with horses afflicted with nasal gleet was to shoot them, he was not liable in damages for their destruction.[64]

Actually, these cases do not contravene the rule that a high degree of skill and care are required in gratuitous cases, though they are sometimes cited as being in opposition to such a rule. They both involve points other than gratuitous service. The authorities are well agreed that gratuitous service does not entitle the practitioner to experiment on the patient.

Questions are sometimes raised as to the duty of a veterinarian rendering free service to continue in the care of an animal. There is no such duty, since the rendering of free service does not give rise to a contract. However, if after giving his service once, a veterinarian promises to continue treatment or leads the owner to believe he will continue treatment for remuneration, a contract will arise.

44. **Collecting Fees.** The most ancient legal code known, that established by King Hammurabi of Babylonia about 2100 B.C., contained provisions on fees for the treatment of animals; and the Ecloga, or Greek Farmers Law, dating from about 700 B.C., contained a section which provided, in effect, that if a cow or ass doctor cured an animal, he should be paid its value, but that if it died, he should pay the owner double its value. Since then there have been some changes in the law. Veterinarians are entitled to compensation for their services, whether or not an agreement as to amount is reached before the services are rendered. If no agreement was made—and this is the usual situation—a veterinarian is entitled to recover the reasonable value of his services. A California case states that he is entitled to recover the charges ordinarily made for similar services by members of the same profession of similar standing.[65] The testimony of other veterinarians, or any acceptable evidence which would help establish usual charges—a schedule of rates adopted by a veterinary association for example —would be admissible in determining the amount to be recovered. The veterinarian's own records and testimony and the testimony of others with personal knowledge of the service rendered

are admissible to prove what service was rendered. In the case of a surgeon—and there is no reason to believe the law affecting a veterinarian would be different—it has been held that his services are not to be estimated by the time required for their performance, the measure of their success, or the pecuniary circumstances of the party to be charged.[66] Since the value of a physician's service is not dependent on the saving of a patient's life,[67] it may be safely assumed that the value of a veterinarian's service is likewise not subject to this contingency. Likewise, it has been held that a physician's right to recover for his services depends upon whether he exercises reasonable care and skill, rather than whether he effects a cure;[68] that dissatisfaction with the outcome of an operation will not defeat recovery by the physician,[69] and that the mailing of a check to a veterinarian marked "for mistreatment of dogs in full to date" does not satisfy the veterinarian's claim where the check is not sufficient to cover the charges and where no positive evidence of negligence or mistreatment was submitted.[70] A veterinarian's bill may properly include the cost of service of an assistant,[71] but may not properly include costs which are not professional in nature—an item for effecting a compromise between the client and a third party, for example.[72]

There are about five defenses available to clients when they are sued by veterinarians for compensation. They are lack of license, malpractice, overcharging, that all the service charged for was not rendered, and that non-professional charges are included. Proof that a veterinarian is not licensed is fatal. But the burden of such proof ordinarily rests with the client. The fact normally is not difficult to determine, and if it turns out that the veterinarian is not licensed, he cannot recover his fees.[73] Malpractice may or may not constitute a complete defense, depending on the connotation placed on the term in the particular state. If the practice act lists it as a cause for revocation of a license and malpractice within the meaning of the practice act can be proved, then no recovery could be had. But if it is used to refer simply to negligence and want of care and skill, then it may constitute no defense, a partial defense, or a complete defense, depending upon the facts in the particular case. Failure to comply with other provisions in a practice act, or to comply with general animal disease laws might constitute a defense or a partial defense if the failure affected the client. A client could not refuse to pay an

otherwise valid claim on the ground that the veterinarian did not
comply with a state law requiring the reporting of communicable
disease, but he might very well defend on the ground that the
veterinarian used a vaccine under conditions contrary to state law
and that he suffered some loss because of that fact. Proof that
a client has knowledge of and accepts irregularities in the practice of a veterinarian may prevent or "estop" him from using
such as a defense to payment of the fee. For example, a client
who continued to use the services of a veterinarian, knowing he
was constantly intoxicated, cannot use this as a defense to recovery of the fee.[74] The other defenses—that fees are unreasonable,
that all the service claimed was not rendered, and that non-
professional charges are included—are questions of fact which
must be proved under the usual rules of evidence.

There is another important defense to a veterinarian's claim
for services, but it is not available to a client because the gist of
the defense is that the defendant is not a client—or at least that
there is no contractual relation with the veterinarian and hence
no obligation to pay. When the owner of animals requests the
service, this question cannot arise. But when persons other than
the owner request the service, there must be proof that they have
authority to bind the owner. In most instances it can be assumed
that if a member of the family calls the veterinarian and he
responds, the owner will be contractually bound. Also, an agent
or employee of an owner certainly has the authority to bind the
owner. A livestock share tenant would have similar authority. A
custodian or bailee of animals would have authority to bind the
owner with respect to emergencies, but would probably be without
such authority in other instances: An agister (one who pastures
animals for another for hire) could bind the owner if he called a
veterinarian to treat bloat, but a call to have animals castrated
without the express consent of the owner would be outside the
scope of his authority as an agister and would not be binding on
the owner. In such an instance, the veterinarian would have to
look to the agister for payment. Calls made from the scene of an
accident in which animals are involved would not bind the owner
of the animal unless he accepted the service or continued to have
the veterinarian care for the animal. If the party injuring the
animal calls a veterinarian, there is an implication that he intends
to pay the bill, and a valid claim would exist against him unless
he is not legally responsible for the injury. In that case, the

veterinarian might recover from the owner. Third parties who call a veterinarian are regarded as doing so for humane reasons and cannot themselves be held for the fee. A policeman who calls a veterinarian to treat an animal does not bind the city to pay for the service unless an ordinance so provides. Of course, if a third party agrees to pay the bill, he can be held to his promise.

Complete records and accounts and carefully prepared statements mailed promptly to clients will not only induce payment but will supply the kind of evidence needed if it becomes necessary to sue for a fee.

45.　**Liens for Veterinary Service.** Hotels have claims against a guest's baggage for the payment of his bill, horseshoers have a claim against the horse for the shoeing, agisters have a claim against the animals in their custody for their care and feed, shellers and threshermen have liens, and hospitals have claims against a cause of action existing on behalf of a patient treated for injuries received in the accident giving rise to the cause of action. But veterinarians do not have a prior claim or lien against animals treated for their services unless they retain possession of the animal and the common law of their state gives them a lien. Veterinarians who accept the custody of animals may qualify under the agisters, stablekeepers or a similar lien intended to give these persons a prior claim for feed, care and housing, or they may qualify for a "common law" lien. Certainly, in the absence of specific statutory provisions, a veterinarian acquires no lien by virtue of calls made on the premises of clients. The veterinarian's status with respect to these liens will be discussed in Chapter 18, Animal Hospitals.

In some states a statutory lien is provided for veterinarians. This would seem to be only fair in view of statuory liens provided for other classes of creditors. It should be remembered that a lien is only an additional remedy. The debt remains whether or not the veterinarian has a lien, and he may pursue any other appropriate legal remedy for his fee or for the boarding and care of animals in his custody. Also, some practice acts give the veterinarian the right to dispose of an animal if the owner refuses after notice to come and claim it. By following the provisions of such a law on advertising and disposal, the veterinarian acquires the right to sell the animal. It is not likely, however, that in most such instances the animal would have any value, therefore the main benefit of the law to the veterinarian is his legal right to dispose of the animal.

CHAPTER 7

IMPLIED RIGHTS AND DUTIES —
NEGLIGENCE AND MALPRACTICE

46. **Negligence and Contributory Negligence.** Everything a man does is subject to some standard of performance or conduct. Most things that people do are never measured against such standards because they have no legal effect on other persons. But the moment one's actions affect another to the latter's harm, his manner of acting becomes a question of prime importance. Was he acting like a reasonably prudent man? This is the time-honored standard against which his actions must be judged. If a jury decides that he acted like a reasonably prudent man, then he is free from fault in the legal sense. If a jury decides otherwise, then he is not free from legal fault and his actions are characterized as negligent. Negligence may be defined as the lack of care demanded by the circumstances, the degree of care required being that which a reasonably prudent man would have exercised under identical circumstances. But it frequently so happens that one complaining about the actions of another is himself an actor in the same episode. Therefore, if either party chooses to make a legal issue out of the event, and the other party appears in court and defends himself, the actions of both parties will be measured against the prudent man. And if it appears that the one instituting the action doesn't measure up, he likewise is not free from fault, and is therefore negligent. But the technical name for his negligence, since he instituted the action and expects to prove negligence in the defendant, is contributory negligence.

47. **Liability and the Burden of Proof.** One is not liable simply because his actions injure another or because someone is hurt on his premises. Before there is liability there must be a proof of legal fault. The burden of proving such fault rests with the one claiming injury. Until this has been done, the law will presume that the defendant acted properly. In the case of a veterinarian, the law will presume that he is licensed, that he is

practicing his profession in accordance with all laws, rules, regulations and orders affecting it, that he exercises due care in handling his patients, and that he is possessed of the skill required to meet the standards of his profession. But presumptions do not always win lawsuits. Once a plaintiff in a malpractice suit, or the defendant in a suit by the veterinarian for his fees, has introduced convincing evidence which rebuts any of these presumptions, it then becomes necessary for the opposite party to introduce evidence that he was not negligent or careless as charged. The burden of finding and introducing convincing evidence has been shifted to the veterinarian, though the burden of proving that the veterinarian was guilty as charged still rests with the party claiming injury. By way of defense, a veterinarian may urge the fault of the claimant (contributory negligence) as well as his own freedom from fault. For example, a client who failed to follow directions or who neglected to feed, water or confine a sick animal properly might be barred from recovery, even though the veterinarian was also at fault.

48. **Malpractice and the Law of Torts.** A tort may be defined as a civil wrong for which there is legal redress. One may commit a crime and a tort by the same act. In such cases prosecution by the State for the commission of a crime and suit by an injured party for damages are separate and distinct actions. Malpractice or lack of care, foresight and skill in the treatment of patients is a tort, for which suit may be instituted by the injured party. Whether or not action may be instituted by the State for malpractice depends upon the practice act and upon the nature and seriousness of the practitioner's alleged shortcomings in the particular case. Sometimes the law of torts may be set in motion on behalf of a veterinarian. He may be slandered or libelled, his business injured by loss of good will, his person or property damaged. For these wrongs, if adequate evidence is available, he may recover damages. The profession is concerned about malpractice suits, not only because they are costly in time and money and peace of mind to the parties involved, but because they affect the confidence of the public in the profession. However, they are a reality which must be faced until such time as every case handled by every veterinarian is brought to a conclusion which in the judgment of the client (and of the client's family) is perfect!

49. Care and Skill Required in Diagnosis and Treatment.
Someone once said of a veterinarian, "his manner of treatment
was well considered and he generally avoided heroic means." This
is one way of stating the care and skill required in the treatment
of animals. However, the courts have established some more
definite, if less poetic, guides. One work of law states that "a
veterinary surgeon is bound to use, in performing the duties of
his employment, such reasonable skill, diligence, and attention as
may ordinarily be expected of careful, skillful and trustworthy
persons in his profession, and if he does not possess and exercise
these qualities, he is answerable for the result of his want of
skill or care."[75] He is not required to exercise an extraordinary
amount of care or to have an extraordinary amount of knowledge
and skill. The standard imposed is that of practitioners in his
locality, and is judged according to current practices and methods.
The Supreme Court of New Hampshire stated the rule very well
more than a century ago:

> In the second place, the professional man contracts, that
> he will use reasonable and ordinary care and diligence in the
> exertion of his skill and the application of his knowledge, to
> accomplish the purpose for which he is employed. He does not
> undertake for extraordinary care and extraordinary diligence,
> any more than he does for uncommon skill. The general rule is
> well settled, as in other cases of contracts supposed to be mu-
> tually beneficial to the parties, that the contractor for services
> to be performed for another, agrees to exert such care and dili-
> gence in his employment as men of common care and common
> prudence usually exert in their own business of a similar kind.
> He agrees to be responsible for the want of such care and atten-
> tion, and he stipulates in no event, without an express contract
> for that purpose, for any greater liability.[76]

In a case almost as venerable, the Supreme Court of
Tennessee said:

> A man who enters upon the legal profession and solicits
> business, is required to have such an amount of legal learning
> as will enable him to discharge with reasonable skill and abili-
> ties the duties incumbent upon him in his profession. If, from the
> want of such knowledge and skill, or a proper degree of industry,
> diligence, and attention to the business intrusted to him, his
> client sustains injury, he is responsible in damages. The same
> rule applies to a physician. He impliedly contracts with those
> who employ him that he has such skill, science, and information
> as will enable him properly and judiciously to perform the duties
> of his calling. If he should be deficient in these respects, he has
> violated his contract, and must account, in damages, for any
> malpractice by which those who employ him sustain injury. This

is the general rule applicable to all professions and avocations in which men are employed to act for others in any particular department of business requiring skill, art, or science. The law does not, however, require the *highest degree* of skill and science, but only such reasonable degree as will enable the person safely and discreetly to discharge the duties assumed.[77]

In an action against the United States for alleged erroneous certification of tick infested cattle for interstate shipment, the court said:

> A liability for alleged neglect and wrongdoing of the officials and inspectors of the Bureau in dipping of the cattle, and for their negligence and erroneous certification is to be investigated, and determined on the "same principles and under the same measure of liability as in like cases between private parties."
> . . . The nearest analogy that occurs to us is the duty of one who undertakes a matter requiring expertness to bring reasonable skill and knowledge to his task according to the then state of the art, and to execute it with ordinary care, but involves no guaranty of the results. Such is the duty of a medical practitioner on man or beast.[78]

The diagnosis of animal disease is subject to the same rules as treatment. A veterinarian is not held to a standard of perfection in diagnosing, but may be permitted those errors of judgment made by other members of the profession. In an Iowa case[79] a veterinarian was sued for the loss of 93 hogs out of a total of 137 treated by him. He diagnosed their disease as cholera and vaccinated them. Among other complaints, the plaintiff charged erroneous diagnosis. The court denied recovery, holding that the alleged improper diagnosis should be ignored because "it was, at most, an error of judgment at a point where there was no guide." It held further that for the plaintiff to recover, he must establish a causal relation between the defendant's act and the death of the hogs. This he failed to do. But in a Minnesota case,[80] a veterinarian was held liable in damages for failure to diagnose hog cholera, the court stating that it was no defense that the defendant had been told by the livestock sanitary board that he was not permitted to use serum. Inability to administer a particular kind of treatment was no excuse for an inaccurate diagnosis. In this case, the veterinarian examined the hogs and approved the owner's suggestion that they be given Epsom salts in buttermilk.

In a South Dakota case,[81] the court held it proper for the jury to find that the defendant veterinarian was negligent in the administration of a worm remedy where there was evidence that, if improperly administered, the fluid passes into the animals' lungs and causes strangulation, that almost certain death follows, and that out of 90 sheep treated for the plaintiff, 42 died during the afternoon and night following treatment and another 19 during the next few days. While a veterinarian is not liable for an injury to an animal resulting from an accident while treating it,[82] he may be liable if his negligence causes injury. Where a veterinarian, preparatory to cauterizing a spavin, so negligently threw the horse as to rupture its diaphragm, from which it shortly died, the throwing of the animal constituted part of the treatment and the owner was able to recover damages for negligent and unskillful treatment.[83] In another case the veterinarian was engaged to vaccinate 59 head of cattle. They were all placed in one pen in the barn, and during the process became frightened and crowded and piled upon each other, injuring six head. It was held that the veterinarian was negligent in continuing vaccination under the procedure he had adopted after seeing the effect it was producing on the cattle.[84] According to a New York case, payment of the veterinarian's fee is no bar to a subsequent action against him for malpractice.[85] This seems like a reasonable rule. In the absence of malice or gross negligence on the part of a veterinarian, in which case punitive damages may be awarded, the measure of recovery against him would be the reasonable market value of animals lost, or the depreciation from market value of animals permanently injured or impaired. In a Minnesota case,[86] the court held that hogs which could not be legally sold because they had a contagious disease had no market value. Hence, the measure of damages recoverable from a veterinarian for negligent treatment was the difference between the value of the pigs on the day of the call, assuming proper treatment, and the value of those which survived the defendant's treatment.

A study of the cases on veterinary malpractice, though few in number compared with cases on medical malpractice, point to certain principles which a veterinarian should observe if he wishes to stay out of legal difficulty on this score. Among the rules of good practice which seem advisable are the following:

1. Avoid violence and rough treatment in the handling of animals.
2. Observe strict standards of sanitation. (See section 50.)
3. Be careful and thorough in making diagnoses.
4. Use care in prescribing and administering medicines and drugs.

5. Keep up with advancements in the field of veterinary medicine and surgery—what was good practice ten years ago may be completely outmoded today.

6. Give careful instructions to the client on what he is to do between calls or following the final call.

7. Use care in purchasing, selecting and storing biological products.

8. Do not hold yourself out as a specialist unless you are willing to be held to a higher standard of skill and competency in your specialty than other veterinarians.

9. Be familiar with federal, state and local laws affecting your practice.

10. Whenever possible, secure the owner's consent before doing surgery or making any marked changes in treatment.

11. Keep good records properly filed.

12. Answer calls promptly or by the time promised.

13. Warn the owner of any dangers from infection. (See section 50.)

14. Once a case has been accepted, give it the attention it requires.

15. Follow up on surgery.

50. Standards of Sanitation—Spreading Disease by Carelessness. Veterinarians and physicians, because of their special knowledge of disease and how it is spread, owe a duty to their clients, not only with respect to the manner in which they handle the patient, but also to impart such information as the client ought to have to keep him from unwittingly passing the disease on to others or endangering his own health. This duty is well summarized in an Arkansas case[87] in which the court said:

> It is undoubtedly the duty of physicians who are attending patients afflicted with contagious or infectious diseases not to negligently do any act that would tend to spread the infections. It would likewise be their duty to exercise reasonable care to advise members of the family, and others who are liable to be exposed thereto, of the nature of the disease and the danger of exposure. The relation of a physician to his patient and the immediate family is one of the highest trust. . . . And he owes a duty to those who are ignorant of such disease, and who . . . are liable to be brought in contact with the patient, to instruct and advise them as to the character of the disease.

What is true of a physician is no less true of a veterinarian, particularly since so many contagious diseases of animals are transmissible to persons. Among the things which could easily lead to liability on the part of a veterinarian would be failure to sterilize instruments, failure to sterilize or change items of clothing after treating infected animals, failure to use standard sanitary precautions such as rubber gloves, neglecting to warn a client about the danger to other animals on the farm or to a neighbor's animals when farms adjoin, permitting a layman to assist in treatment without warning of the danger of infection, and failure to inform state sanitary authorities and request quarantine when the need for such is apparent.

51. **Informing Clients about the Law.** Everyone is presumed to know the law. Therefore, the veterinarian may ask, "Why should I owe any duty to explain the law to a client when it is presumed he knows the animal disease laws of his state?" There are some practical answers to this query. Many animal disease laws were drafted by members of the veterinary profession and contain technical terms with which only the veterinary profession is familiar. The veterinarian works with these laws daily and knows how they operate. Quite clearly then, it seems he owes the livestock owner the duty of explaining how he can handle his infected animals without violating the provisions of the law. A failure to disclose such information where the situation demands, or the giving of misinformation about quarantine or movement of animals, for example, would open the way to liability on the part of the veterinarian. Advising a client to disregard or violate a law might lead not only to liability in a suit by the client, but also to criminal prosecution and to revocation of license.

52. **Right to Do Surgery.** When a case is turned over to a veterinarian, there is an implication that he may and shall do everything reasonably necessary to effect a cure, including surgery. However, if surgery did not seem necessary at the time the case arose, and it is possible to consult with the client before operating, consent of the client should be secured. Once an operation has been commenced, there is an implication that all work necessary may be done. Only when an immediate operation is deemed necessary to save the animal and the owner cannot be reached should surgery be performed without the owner's consent.

53. **Survival of Actions.** The law presumes that when one

has suffered a wrong at the hands of another he will seek legal redress within some reasonable period of time after the cause of action arises. If he does not, witnesses will die or move away, evidence will disappear, and the facts will become exceedingly difficult to establish. For these reasons, statutes quite generally prescribed the period of time within which actions of various kinds may be commenced. Torts are limited to a fairly short period, in most states either one or two years. But where the tort consists of damage to property, as distinguished from injury to the person, the action survives for a longer period of time. Claims against a physician are for injury to the person, whereas claims against a veterinarian are for injury to property. Therefore, if the law in a particular state provides different periods of survival for the two kinds of actions, the law affecting veterinarians would differ from that affecting physicians. Also, there is a tendency to view damages resulting from malpractice as arising out of contract so that the limitation period on contracts would apply. This is a longer period than is customarily allowed for personal actions—generally five years for oral contracts and ten years for written—but this depends entirely on the law of each particular state and no general conclusions of a helpful nature may be drawn. In most states it is probably true that the cause of action survives both the veterinarian and the client (in case either die during the running of the limitation period), and may be prosecuted against the personal representative of the veterinarian by the administator of the client.

CHAPTER 8

AGENTS AND EMPLOYEES OF THE VETERINARIAN

54. Principal and Agent. When a man hires another to act for him in any capacity, an agency relation arises. The agent may be given very little authority, or he may be given a great deal. If he has been hired primarily to work and is under the supervision and direction of his employer, the master-servant or employer-employee relation would exist. If he is employed to do buying or selling or to meet and deal with the public on behalf of his employer, more discretion is involved, and the relation of principal and agent, as it is commonly known, arises. This relationship may come about by express agreement in writing, by oral agreement, or, in some cases, through the action of the parties or the nature of the circumstances without any written or oral agreement. One of the prime legal questions in suits involving agency is whether the relation exists and, more particularly, if it existed and the agent was about his principal's business at the time the event giving rise to the lawsuit occurred. For example, it now seems to be well settled that hospital nurses become the agents of a physician when they assist with an operation and come under his direction.[88] This is true though they are not in his employ and are not working under any agency agreement, either written or oral. So it would seem that persons assisting a veterinarian in treating an animal, whether in his employ or not, would become his agents during the time he is directing them and they are following his instructions. This does not mean, however, that all assistance rendered is on an agency basis. If the owner of an animal volunteers to help, and performs acts which he is competent to perform without technical direction from the veterinarian—tying to a manger, throwing a hog, holding a sheep, for example—he would not be regarded as an agent of the veterinarian in the performance of such acts. Likewise, hospital nurses, attendants or technicians who are skilled in doing certain things and who go ahead and do such things while assisting a physician who is not their employer will not be regarded as his agents in the performance of such functions. One test of agency in such cases is whether the particular act complained of was done because it was directed to be done by the physician, or because the attendant or nurse knew or assumed it was necessary and did it without direction. For most veterinarians this question will remain somewhat academic because, ordinarily, the persons assisting him will be his own employees, for whom he is responsible, or the livestock owner or owner's agent.

There is another agency question, however, that may sometimes perplex the veterinarian. This question has to do with responsibility when a case is attended by another veterinarian, at the request of the veterinarian in charge. Whether or not there is an agency relationship depends on the consent of the owner of the animal. If the patient or owner of an animal agrees to accept the services of the person being substituted, the physician or veterinarian in charge would not be regarded as a principal and hence would not be liable for negligent acts of the substitute. In a New Jersey case, Dr. Myers promised to attend the plaintiff's wife during childbirth. However, Dr. Myers was out of town and another doctor came, announcing that he was representing Dr. Myers. The plaintiff's wife raised no objection. The substitute physician treated her, but through his lack of skill caused the death of the child. The husband sued Dr. Myers for damages, claiming that the substitute physician was his agent. The court held that the physician attending the plaintiff's wife at childbirth acted in a separate and distinct professional capacity and that he was not the agent of Dr. Myers. Recovery was therefore denied. Apparently the court considered the failure of the plaintiff's wife to object as equivalent to consent, though there is authority to the effect that "in such a case the jury is not likely to regard the patient's acquiescence as consent, and the substitute will be in the position of the doctor's agent, for whose negligence he (the doctor) is responsible . . . ."[89] There is an Oregon case in which a physician was held liable for the negligent treatment of one of his patients by a substitute he got to look after his patients while he was on vacation. Though it was urged that the substitute was an independent contractor and not an agent of the physician, the court sustained a judgment against both physicians.[90] The moral would seem to be that if a veterinarian wishes to take a vacation, he should have his clients consent to the services of a suitable veterinarian before the latter renders any service. In situations where two or more veterinarians collaborate in surgery or treatment or diagnosis, they may each be held directly responsible for any negligence that may occur. Problems arising out of partnership are discussed in Chapter 18.

55. **"Respondeat Superior."** The idea that a "superior" is responsible for the acts of those under his direction and control is not new. And now that the law has recognized, if not sanctified it, many reasons can be adduced for its existence. Though it probably grew out of Roman law as a method by which a slave owner could redeem a slave who had wronged another and who himself (the slave) would be subject to banishment, it gradually found application to free men in the employ of others. Certainly, the liability of an employer can be justified in instances where the employee performs a mechanical act under the direct supervision of the employer, and where his act can with some truth be regarded as that of his employer. But when the employee is acting independently and exercising his own judgment—driving his employer's truck, for example—the arguments and the logic for holding the employer liable in case of an accident become very weak. But the law says the "superior" is liable if the servant is in the course of his employment at the time of the accident, so the most important question seems to be "Was the agent engaged in doing the principal's work at the time of the incident complained of?" Even telephone companies have been held liable to livestock owners for the loss of animals resulting from negligent failure of the company to connect the owner with the veterinarian.[91] However, if the resulting damage is considered by the court to be too remote and conjectural, no recovery will be allowed.[92]

56. **What Acts May Be Delegated?** One who is not licensed by his State cannot legally practice veterinary medicine and surgery. Therefore, a licensed veterinarian cannot delegate to another, to do for the veterinarian, any act which would be defined as the practice of veterinary medicine and surgery, and it is no defense to a charge of practicing without a license that the person charged was acting under the direction of a veterinarian.[93] However, there are circumstances under which an assistant may properly give shots, apply surgical dressings and do other acts, if he is acting directly under the attending veterinarian. One author-

ity states that "while it is a violation of the medical practice act for a person not duly registered thereby, to inject any fluid or other material whatsoever into the body of a human being, it is permissible for a physician's assistant to inject such medication as ordered by the attending physician. In such situations, the physician is personally responsible for that act of his assistant. His assistant is not practicing medicine, but merely carrying out the order of a licensed physician."[94] When the unlicensed person is skilled in a particular kind of treatment, the physician may properly exercise less direction and control. A medical jurisprudence authority states that:

> When a doctor prescribes expert treatment to be carried out, with the consent of the patient, by a medically unqualified person skilled in that treatment, such as a registered biophysical assistant, he is not responsible for specific acts of negligence by such person if he has good reason to believe that they are competent to carry out the treatment which he has prescribed, and if it is the custom of the profession to delegate such treatment to such persons. If, however, a subordinate is performing a duty in his presence and he is able to exercise control, he may be liable for that subordinate's negligence.[95]

From these authorities it would seem that local custom, the specific nature of the act performed, the degree of direction given by the attending practitioner, and the skill of the unlicensed assistant all enter into the question of whether their acts amount to unlicensed practice of veterinary medicine.

57. **Liability to Third Parties.** Clearly, a veterinarian may be held liable to a client for the negligence of assistants and employees. For example, a dentist has been held liable for his employee's negligent operation of an x-ray machine,[96] and a veterinarian has been held for loss of a client's hogs where the veterinarian's son, acting for his father, gave the client a can of "Lysol" instead of "Mange Oil."[97] But there may be liability to persons other than clients. This is particularly true if trucks or other vehicles are used by employees of the veterinarian. An employee who operates a vehicle negligently and injures others or the property of others, will himself be liable and will also make his employer liable, providing he was engaged in his employer's business at the time of the accident. This latter condition—that the employee be engaged in the employer's business at the time of the negligent action resulting in harm to another—is a very important qualification on the liability of an employer and is

frequently the important issue in liability suits. Since there is no way of avoiding liability to third parties resulting from the negligent acts of employees, the most an employer can do is try to reduce the possibility of liability. This he may do by hiring careful people, giving them safe equipment to work with, and not asking them to undertake anything of a hazardous nature involving third parties.

58. **Liability to Employees.** Veterinarians may be held liable to their employees for injuries received in the course of the employment. If a veterinarian is eligible and chooses to come under the provisions of his state's workmen's compensation act, determinations of liability become relatively unimportant to the veterinarian because insurance carried under the act will pay for the injury according to the schedule of payments set forth in the act: Questions of liability are then of importance to the administrators of the compensation act. But if a veterinarian is not under such an act, his liability is determined by common law rules of negligence. Contrary to an assumption which seems to be current, an employer is not liable to an employee for every mishap that occurs in the course of the employment. Before there can be liability, there must be negligence. If the employer is not at fault, there can be no recovery against him by an employee. Under the rules of the common law, the employer may make certain defenses, even though he is admittedly negligent. One of these defenses, discussed in an earlier chapter, is known as "contributory negligence." This simply means that the employee was also at fault. As a defense it may prevent recovery by the employee or may mitigate the amount recovered. Another defense is called the "fellow servant rule." This means that another employee did something which caused or contributed to the injury of the complaining employee. It is a good common law defense. Still a third defense is known as "assumption of risk." This means that an employee cannot hold the employer liable for an injury caused by a dangerous tool or machine which the employee normally uses in the course of his employment and with which he has had experience. A veterinarian's assistant could not hold his employer liable for injuries received from a knife or needle or dog or horse, unless the veterinarian were himself at fault in contributing to the injury, because these are the kinds of risks a veterinarian's employee assumes when he chooses his occupation. State workmen's compensation acts ordinarily remove these

defenses and permit the employee to recover under the insurance maintained for his benefit, if the injury occurred in the scope of the employment.

59. **Workmen's Compensation Acts and Employment Legislation.** Veterinarians who employ assistants should find out how they are affected by the workmen's compensation act and other employment legislation in their state. With respect to compensation acts, veterinarians may be automatically included, included if they elect to come under the act, or completely excluded, depending on the particular state law. Once under the act, premiums are paid, reports submitted, and other administrative responsibilities discharged as required by those administering the state law. There are many other laws, both state and federal, which may or may not apply to the veterinarian's employees, depending on the nature of the employment, the number of employees, the sex of the employees, and the state in which the veterinarian practices. Federal social security legislation applies, as do any state laws prescribing the hours and conditions of employment for females and minors. Whether or not other state laws such as occupational disease acts, definitions of a legal day's work, wage lien laws, health and safety acts, minimum wage and unemployment compensation laws apply to veterinarians is something that must be determined under the law of the state of residence, by contacting proper state officials.

60. **Insurance.** Several types of insurance may be carried by a veterinarian who employs others. First and foremost—unless he is under the state workmen's compensation act—is liability insurance protecting him from claims of the employees for injuries arising in the course of the employer's business. Included in such a policy, or in a comprehensive liability policy, should be coverage protecting him against personal and property damage claims by clients or third parties who are injured by his employees while carrying on his business. Insurance for the benefit of the employee may be carried if the employer desires. This might include insurance against accident, sickness, medical and hospital expense, surgical expense and loss of time and wages. Federal social security now fills part of the gap.

CHAPTER 9

THE VETERINARIAN AS AN AGENT OR EMPLOYEE

61. Private Employment. Veterinarians are sometimes employed by private corporations such as pharmaceutical houses, medicine manufacturers or others. Such contracts of employment are valid, providing they do not lead to violations of the practice act. Since a corporation cannot be licensed to practice veterinary medicine, a veterinarian employed by a corporation cannot practice as an agent of the corporation, though he may perform other acts for it. This does not mean that he cannot treat animals belonging to the corporation or that he cannot give demonstrations or render free service to animal owners willing to accept such service. It means that if he treats animals belonging to others, the client-veterinarian relation will arise and he cannot purport to act only as an agent. Such an attempt would render the corporation liable for violation of the practice act and the veterinarian guilty of malpractice. In some instances there is a thin line between practice which would be considered that of the veterinarian and practice which would be considered that of the corporation by which he is employed.

Under his contract of employment with a corporation or private company, a veterinarian can acquire the rights usually covered in contracts of employment—the right to his salary, a definition of his working conditions and hours, retirement, accident and leave pay, vacation and other matters.

A modified form of private employment exists when a veterinarian contracts with a herd owner or a kennel owner to take care of the health of all animals in the herd or kennel on an annual basis. Though the relation of veterinarian and client is not affected, the nature of the veterinarian's practice may be affected.

Questions of professional ethics are apt to arise when veterinarians are employed by commercial houses. Advertising of products, demonstrations and other promotional devices, if participated in by veterinarians, may sometimes lead to serious charges against the veterinarian. The fact that he is a member of the profession imposes certain obligations on him, even though he does not engage in active practice.

Companies employing veterinarians have the same responsibility for their acts as such companies have for other employees, and may be held liable for the negligence or want of care of the veterinarian while on the job for the company.

Veterinarians employed by feed companies, biologic products houses, and pharmaceutical houses have come to be known as industrial veterinarians. There are quite a large number of them and they are organized and have their own industrial veterinarians' organization. They recognize many of the problems involved in acting in this capacity—problems involving professional ethics, the practice act, and other provisions of animal disease control laws. One of the primary responsibilities of the industrial veterinarian is to guide his company in doing a thorough research job before a product is released for use. In addition, he is responsible for seeing that the product is properly advertised and that no false or misleading statements are made. Other responsibilities of the industrial veterinarian have to do with the care of animals owned by his company. He should see that humane treatment is accorded them and that they are properly housed and fed. He owes a particular duty to veterinarians with whom he consults because he is expected to have a greater knowledge of the product than they have. Whether or not an industrial veterinarian can engage in practice on the side depends on the terms of his contract. Problems of ethics are involved here also. Since the industrial veterinarian is engaged in a special calling it may be difficult many times for him to keep up on certain phases of the practice. This could very well increase his probability of being involved in malpractice actions, where his knowledge and skill have not kept pace with those of his fellow veterinarians.

62. **Public Employment.** The federal government, the states, municipalities, public health districts, and other units of government employ large numbers of veterinarians to enforce the various federal, state, and local animal disease, meat inspection, food, milk, and similar laws. Sometimes veterinarians are appointed or elected to official government administrative positions. Theoretically, their discharge of such offices is not affected by the fact that they are veterinarians. Whether employed full time, part time, or on a contract basis, they become agents of the govern-

ment and as such are clothed with certain rights. On the other hand, there is a limit to the authority and discretion which can be placed in an agent of the government. Also, the government is not always liable for the acts of its agents. It is not presumed that the government authorizes or condones an illegal act by its agent. Also, it is a principle of law that the federal and state governments cannot be sued without their consent. But the veterinarian may be sued as a private wrongdoer. Some of the specific situations involving veterinarians as agents of the government will be discussed in the sections which follow.

State laws customarily exempt veterinarians from the state civil service, but federal civil service applies to veterinarians in the employ of the federal government. State laws customarily exempt veterinarians from jury service. Also, there is an Arizona case holding that veterinarians employed by a race track are not subject to the state workmen's compensation act.[98] Even veterinarians, though, must pay federal income tax! At any rate, governmental employment as a veterinarian is fraught with enough legal possibilities that a clear understanding of the responsibilities of agents of government—as well as a clear understanding of the job to be done and how to do it—seems to be mandatory for a veterinarian accepting such employment.

63. **Duty of the Veterinarian to Perform.** If a veterinarian fails to perform the functions incident to his public employment, he may be removed from his position, punished according to federal or state laws covering his actions as a public employee, and quite possibly proceeded against by any member of the public who can show direct injury as a result of his failure to perform. If, for example, a veterinarian refused to inspect the meat at a slaughterhouse and the proprietor for that reason is unable to dispose of the meat in accordance with contracts in effect, the proprietor would be injured and could recover from the veterinarian, unless the latter had some valid reason for refusing to inspect. Mandamus—a legal action to force a public official to perform his duties—would ordinarily not be involved. Conceivably it could be used where the veterinarian held an elective position or where he has a tenure status which makes it impossible to remove him before great damage would ensue.

64. **Delegation of Authority to Veterinarians.** State livestock sanitary commissions or divisions of livestock industry are

clothed with certain statutory powers and, in addition, are given
the authority to make such rules as are required properly to administer the laws for which they are responsible. Among the
assorted powers allotted them are the right to inspect, test,
examine, treat, quarantine and destroy. But these powers cannot
be used arbitrarily, and their rule making power cannot be delegated to an agent. In a Texas case,[99] the court held that though
the authority to make rules is given the Live Stock Sanitary
Commission, it does not have authority to transfer this power to
its inspectors, thus giving them the power arbitrarily to discriminate. The court indicated further that if a statute did purport
to confer such authority, it would be opposed to the fundamental
law which forbids the denial of equal protection of the laws. Likewise, it has been held that if the law creating the livestock sanitary board does not authorize an officer or agent of the board to
establish a quarantine of cattle, such authority cannot be delegated to agents or employees.[100] Generally, the courts have held
that any determinations involving judgment and discretion cannot be delegated. This does not mean that the board or commission must itself conduct all investigations, but it does mean that
after its agents have ascertained the facts, it and not the agent
must act on such facts. And in so acting, it must stay within
the bounds of the law. However, once the board or commission
has acted on the facts reported to it, a presumption will arise
that the law has been complied with. For example, in an Iowa
case,[101] the court held that a decision by the secretary of agriculture that sufficient petitions had been received to establish Black
Hawk County as an accredited area could not be attacked col-
laterally in a suit to restrain the enrollment of the county as a
testing unit.

   65. **Liability of Veterinarians as Agents of Government.**
One is not insulated from legal responsibility for his actions
simply because he is working for the government. This proposition is well stated in a Mississippi case[102] where the court said,
"Under the law of this state, the powers of officers, and their
duties, are prescribed by law, and it is the duty of an officer,
upon assuming the duties of an office, to determine what powers
and duties are conferred upon him. He does not become the law
of the land by assuming office, and, if he does an act under color
of office which injures a person, without authority of law, he is
liable to damages therefor."

In line with this view, it has been held that where a testing officer wrongfully destroys a bovine animal not in fact tubercular, the owner has a remedy by suing the officer;[103] that the right to sue the destroying agent at common law for damages if the destroyed cattle were not in fact diseased is essential as a guarantee of due process of law;[104] and that a health officer is personally liable for the destruction of cattle which were not in fact a nuisance or cause of sickness endangering the public health, but were mistakenly adjudged by him to be so.[105] There is some indication, however, that in cases where the destruction of animals is not involved, the courts will protect an officer who is honestly trying to carry out the provisions of the law. In a Utah case,[106] the court held that where a deputy sheep inspector quarantined sheep and prescribed the area in which they could be held and grazed, as provided by statute, he is not liable in a civil action for any damages that may result, in the absence of proof that he acted with malice or through fraud or corruption. The court stated that the acts of inspecting and imposing a quarantine are quasi judicial in nature, as distinguished from ministerial acts for which the inspector may be held personally liable. Along this same line, a Montana case[107] held that a deputy inspector, in selecting and using a dip, acted ministerially and not quasi judicially and was therefore liable for damages arising from his negligence.

66. Liability under Dipping Laws. A large proportion of the cases involving the liability of veterinarians while acting as agents of the state have arisen under statutes authorizing seizure, quarantine and dipping. Unless there is specific statutory authority requiring dipping, it is doubtful if the right exists. In an Alabama case,[108] the court held that under a statute giving the livestock sanitary board authority to make rules and regulations affecting "quarantined livestock" or "quarantined places," the board had no authority to make a regulation requiring all persons having animals infected with or exposed to the infection of ticks to dip animals in an arsenical solution. Likewise, it has been held that the animal disease laws of the state did not confer on the livestock sanitary board or its agents the right to seize cattle without due process of law, dip them for the eradication of ticks, and charge the owner with the costs.[109] Under such circumstances, the officers entering the premises are liable to the owner of the animals. However, when the right is clearly spelled out in the statutes, and regulations adopted are clearly authorized by law, an owner may be required to submit his animals to dipping and pay the costs involved.[110] Under such circumstances, the enforcing officer would be liable to an owner only if he were arbitrary and discriminatory in performing his duties. Where the enforcing officers acted in good faith in detaining animals for dipping, but the law under which the animals were seized is held not to give the right of seizure without a proper writ, the officers may be held for damages arising from the detention of the animals but not for punitive damages.[111] The inspector in charge is responsible for such ministerial acts as preparing the dip, arranging the animals and premises for conducting the dipping, giving instructions to helpers and others, and informing the owner about any precautions he should take after the dipping. Whether or not the inspector is negligent in accomplishing these tasks is a question of fact for a jury to decide. It has been held, for example, that whether the defendant inspector was negligent in permitting the plaintiff's cow to drink some of the liquid which flowed from the vat was such a question.[112] Similar questions may arise regarding the nature and sufficiency of the dip, and the manner in which animals are handled during the dipping process.

CHAPTER 10

FEDERAL ANIMAL DISEASE LAWS

67. **Source of Federal Authority—Interstate Commerce.** One of the cardinal principles of our federal system is that the exercise of the police power is a prerogative of the individual states. The federal government is supposed to have only those powers granted to it by the federal constitution, and the constitution contains no specific grant of any police power. Sometimes the general welfare clause has been urged as such a grant, but thus far the courts have held that it is not. Presumably, therefore, any legislation to protect the general health, morals, safety or welfare of the public must emanate from other public bodies to whom such authority has been delegated by the state. But a search of federal law discloses much animal disease legislation and a sizeable body of regulations, rules and orders for its enforcement. How does the federal government come by this authority? Through the interstate commerce clause in the federal constitution.

Congress, elaborating somewhat on the definition of "commerce" contained in the constitution, has defined it as ". . . commerce between any State, Territory, or possession, or the District of Columbia, and any place outside thereof; or points within the same State, Territory, or possession, or the District of Columbia, but through any place outside thereof; or within any Territory or possession, or the District of Columbia."[113] The right to regulate such commerce has been an increasing source of power and authority for the federal government, and has been augmented by two developments; the great increase in the interstate shipment of goods (this applies with special force to livestock and livestock products) and the tendency of the courts to enlarge the meaning of the term by saying that activities which "affect" interstate commerce may also be controlled.

In Reid v. Colorado,[114] the United States Supreme Court stated that congressional regulation of interstate commerce is paramount throughout the Union, so that when the entire subject of the interstate shipment of livestock is taken under direct national supervision, all local and state regulations of such matters will cease to have any force. The court added, however, that until such time, state and local governments may enact and enforce reasonable regulations over that portion of the field not covered by national regulations. In the later case of Thornton v. United States[115] the court held that passage of diseased cattle from one state to another is interstate commerce, and as such, subject to regulation by the federal government. The court added further: "In the broad provisions of the legislation we have quoted, the authority of the Secretary of Agriculture to direct the employees of the Bureau of Animal Industry to engage in quarantine measures and the inspection of animals suspected of or known to have communicable diseases is not limited to cases in which there is cooperation between the United States and the state authorities in the suppression of the spread of disease among cattle, the one as between the states and the other as within a state. In order to make the action of both more effective, they may co-operate so that their respective purposes may be more effectively carried out, but the power of each to act in its field does not depend upon the consent of the other."

68. **Departmental Organization for Disease Control.** Among the duties of the United States Department of Agriculture is that of investigating and reporting "upon the condition of the domestic animals and live poultry of the United States, their protection and use, and also inquire into and report the causes of contagious, infectious and communicable diseases among them, and the means of prevention and cure of the same, and to collect such information on these subjects as shall be valuable. . . ."[116] The original intent of the law seems to have been that the Department would be mainly a fact finding and information disseminating agency. But it long ago lost this neutral color. It is now the principal agency for the administration of the many federal laws on animal disease. Agencies concerned are the meat inspection, animal disease eradication, and animal inspection and quarantine divisions of the regulatory programs branch of the Agricultural Research Service. The Department has an extensive field organization consisting of stations (some of which handle the work of several divisions) and substations. It also is charged with the responsibility of administering international agreements and compacts

respecting animal diseases—the Mexican-United States Commission for the Prevention of Foot-and-Mouth Disease, for example. To insure that essential work shall not be unduly hampered by objecting livestock owners, a section in the law provides that anyone who impedes or opposes an employee of the Department, while engaged in his work, is guilty of a criminal offense and that threatening such employees with a weapon is punishable by fine or imprisonment or both.[117]

Activities, current organization, personnel changes, and other information about the animal disease activities of the Department are published monthly in *Service and Regulatory Announcements,* a publication available from the Government Printing Office on an annual subscription basis.

69. **Imports and Exports of Animals and Animal Products.** There are several federal laws designed to control the spread of animal diseases and protect the public from unsafe animal products, in so far as these diseases or unsafe products are involved in import or export trade. The importation into the United States of harmful animals or birds is prohibited in the criminal code.[118] The Secretary of Agriculture, upon notification to the Secretary of the Treasury, may prohibit the importation of animals from any foreign country where rinderpest or foot-and-mouth disease exists; and he may prohibit the entry of meat from another country unless it is healthful, wholesome and fit for human food.[119] The Secretary has the power to suspend the importation of any animals likely to bring in an infectious or contagious disease, to quarantine and regulate the interstate shipment of those brought in, to slaughter diseased animals and those exposed to the disease and indemnify the owners of exposed animals not in fact infected with the disease and to inspect all animals for export.[120] He has authority to regulate the importation of milk and cream and prevent importation for good cause, and he has authority to inspect all meat and dairy products for export.[121] Vessels used in the export of livestock are subject to inspection and regulation by the Secretary as relates to their accommodations for livestock.[122] Pursuant to these laws it has been held that the Secretary may designate those ports of entry at which animals will be inspected under quarantine, provide such facilities as are needed to enforce the inspection and quarantine, employ such veterinary surgeons, inspectors and other employees as he deems necessary,

and promulgate such rules and regulations as are essential to the enforcement of the law.[123] Under a proviso giving the Secretary authority to admit into Texas, cattle from Mexico which have been exposed to tick infection, under regulations prescribed by him, the Attorney General ruled that other countries (Colombia in the case at issue) having treaties with the United States containing most-favored-nations clauses must be accorded the same privilege.[124]

70. **Meat and Animal Foods Inspection.** To insure that meat and meat products entering or "affecting" interstate commerce are wholesome and fit for consumption, federal law gives the Secretary of Agriculture authority to do the following:[125]

Inspect animals before they enter the slaughterhouse;
Slaughter suspects;
Examine carcasses of slaughtered suspects;
Inspect all carcasses intended for consumption;
Label all carcasses "inspected and passed" or "inspected and condemned";
Cause the destruction, for food purposes, of all condemned carcasses;
Cause containers to be properly labeled;
Prescribe sanitary standards for slaughterhouses;
Prevent the transportation of uninspected carcasses in interstate commerce;
Inspect for export and give clearance to vessels.

Enforcement of the horse-meat labeling is also a function of the Secretary.[126] Public stockyards and ports of entry are the places where most of the inspection is accomplished, but the Secretary may enter any stockyard, slaughterhouse, packing establishment or other place of business if its activities affect interstate commerce. In practice, federal inspection is coordinated with state inspection, the intent being that state enforcement will take up where federal jurisdiction leaves off.

71. **General Animal Disease Control.** Under federal law the Secretary of Agriculture has a broad authority (limited only by the concept of interstate commerce) to prevent the introduction and spread of contagious animal diseases. He may take such measures and make such regulations as he deems necessary to prevent the spread of animal and poultry diseases from foreign

countries and between the states, including the quarantine, inspection, seizure or destruction of animals, hides, feed, hay, straw, forage or any other likely carrier of animal disease.[127] However, the Attorney-General has ruled (250 A. G. 249) that an order of the Department prohibiting the importation of hay and straw from Europe, to prevent introduction of foot-and-mouth disease, was void as an exercise of legislative power. Included in the law are specific provisions on such subjects as cooperation with the states, cooperation with foreign countries, indemnities to livestock owners, interstate shipment of tuberculin reactors (they may be shipped interstate for immediate slaughter, under regulations of the Secretary) and prosecutions under the law (federal district attorneys are charged with the duty of prosecuting for violations of federal laws and regulations). Authority to impose quarantine and regulate interstate movement has been extended to air transportation,[128] and the right to make rabies, tularemia, and other disease studies and conduct campaigns for the destruction of wild animals that spread these diseases is specifically granted.[129] As in the case of meat inspection, much of the regulatory responsibility is discharged at public stockyards and ports of entry from foreign countries, but the jurisdiction of the Secretary is not limited to such areas.

Though the authority of the federal government is complete, once the subject matter is deemed to fall within its jurisdiction, it is nevertheless bound by the language and intent of the law, by federal constitutional guarantees against illegal searches and seizures, and by constitutional guarantees against the taking of property without due process of law. Under a law giving the Secretary of Agriculture authority to prohibit the movement of diseased animals out of quarantined areas, it was held that the Secretary had no authority to prohibit the movement of any animal out of the area, but that his authority was limited to diseased ainmals.[130] Thus, it is implied that the Secretary must inspect and make a determination concerning an animal, otherwise the application of federal rules or regulations may be regarded as arbitrary as respects such animal. However, if the circumstances under which an animal is held are such as to create a reasonable presumption that it has been or may be exposed to infection, quarantine without inspection of the individual animal would be justified. As a matter of fact, many animal disease laws, both federal and state, operate on this presumption. Provisions on quarantine in the federal law state that "The Secretary of Agriculture is authorized and directed to quarantine any State or Territory or the District of Columbia, or any portion of any State or Territory or the District of Columbia, when he shall determine the fact that cattle or other livestock and/or live poultry in such State or Territory or District of Columbia, are affected with any contagious, infectious, or communicable disease; and the Secretary of Agriculture is directed to give written or printed notice of the establishment of quarantine to the proper officers of railroad, steamboat, or other transportation companies doing business in or through any quarantined State or Territory or the District of Columbia, and to publish in such newspapers in the quarantined State or Territory, or the District of Columbia, as the Secretary of Agriculture may select, notice of the establishment of quarantine."[131]

The federal disease programs in which veterinarians have been most widely involved are bovine tuberculosis and brucellosis control. Through grants-in-aid in the form of a portion of the indemnity to livestock owners for animals destroyed, the federal government has been able to augment the work of the states in such disease control, and, at the same time, control in large measure the nature of the program. Legal control and enforcement, however, except to the extent that interstate commerce is affected, is left to the states. Herd plans for the eradication of tuberculosis and brucellosis, criteria for establishing accredited or disease free areas, and other phases of the program, though set up under state laws and regulations, are patterned largely after standards recommended by the federal government.

72. **Animals in Transit.** The Secretary of Agriculture, as pointed out earlier in this chapter, has a broad authority to control the interstate movement of livestock. In conjunction with the statutory authority, he has a right to make rules and regulations concerning the transportation of diseased livestock and infected materials. In United States v. Pennsylvania[132] it was contended that the law granting authority to make rules and regulations improperly delegated legislative authority to the Secretary. In holding to the contrary, the court said that since new conditions arise from time to time, and prompt and stringent measures may be necessary to stamp out an epidemic, it is proper for Congress to give to executive officers authority to establish

regulations to prevent the spreading of such diseases. But in this same case, the court said the regulations must be taken as applying only to movements of animals in interstate commerce. Despite federal regulations, however, a state may control the admission of diseased animals within its borders, and the Supreme Court of the United States has held[133] that the federal law authorizing every railroad "to carry . . . freight and property on their way from one state to another state . . ." does not authorize such railroads to carry from one state to another, in violation of state law, cattle which are known to be infected with or exposed to a communicable disease. However, when an inspector of the Department has issued a certificate showing that animals have been inspected and passed for interstate shipment, they may be shipped without further inspection or exaction of fees by any other agency. Such animals are regarded as being at all times during transit under the control and supervision of the Department.[134] In view of this provision in the law, a Georgia court held that a shipper was entitled to recover from the railroad, expenses incidental to a second unwarranted dipping of animals certified by the Department as free from communicable disease.[135]

Railroads or other carriers of livestock are bound by both federal and state laws, the latter being held to apply also, unless they constitute an unwarranted burden on interstate commerce or if they are in conflict with federal law.[136] Carriers operating wholly within a state are subject to state and not to federal law. With respect to interstate carriage, the federal government may prescribe standards of sanitation for equipment and premises, procedures to be followed if diseased or exposed animals are being carried (dipping, for example), and rules regarding confinement and quarantine when the animals are unloaded. Federal authority extends, not only to all types of carriage, but also to the driving of animals on foot from one state into another.[137]

Accordingly, it has been held that the federal government has power to require cattle ranging near a state line to be treated in an effort to eradicate Texas fever, since cattle which range across a state line may become infected by those which do not.[138] A regulation establishing a quarantine line across the middle of the State of Tennessee, and prohibiting the transportation of certain cattle from south of the line to any place north of the line, was held void both as to cattle shipped entirely within the state and cattle shipped across state lines.[139] But a state statute making it a misdemeanor to transport into the state, cattle from any point south of the state line except for immediate slaughter, without first having them inspected and passed as healthy by state or federal officials, was held to be a proper exercise of state power.[140] It has been held that when the interstate shipment of baby chicks is regulated by federal authority, state regulation is precluded.[141] A shipper who knew that hogs had been examined by a veterinarian and found to have a fever and who paid much less than market price for them was found guilty of knowingly shipping in interstate commerce hogs afflicted with cholera.[142] A railroad company, innocent of the condition of cattle carried by it, is not liable to a shipper when a government inspector places the cattle in quarantine upon arrival at the destination.[143] An order of the state commissioner of agriculture, prohibiting importation into the state of cattle infected with Bang's disease, was held not invalid as interfering with interstate commerce or with federal quarantine laws.[144] Also, it has been held that a state veterinarian may enforce orders with respect to the bedding materials in cars arriving from tick-infested areas.[145]

Though a railroad may comply with rules and regulations on the shipment of diseased or exposed animals, common law rules of liability still apply. This means that a carrier may be held liable for negligently causing the spread of a communicable disease. Permitting the commingling of diseased and healthy animals[146] or permitting diseased animals to escape[147] has resulted in liability on the part of the carrier.

The Department also enforces the "twenty-eight hour" law which provides that all animals in interstate shipment must be unloaded and fed every 28 hours, unless they can be properly fed, watered and rested without unloading.[148]

73. **The Packers and Stockyards Act.** The primary purpose of the federal law first adopted in 1921 is to insure that unlawful practices enumerated in the act will not be carried on by the meat packing industry, and that stockyards will render adequate and nondiscriminatory service to all who apply for the service. Packers are prohibited from engaging in unfair, discriminatory or deceptive practices; from giving undue or unreasonable preference or advantage to any particular person or locality; from operating in restraint of trade; from trying to manipulate or control prices;

and from conspiring, combining, or agreeing in any way which will act to the detriment of producers and sellers of livestock and the consumers of livestock products. The Secretary of Agriculture can issue a complaint any time he has just reason to believe the law is being violated. Hearings can be held, orders issued and the orders reviewed in court at the instance of either party. There are penalties for violation. Stockyards engaged in interstate commerce must register with the Secretary of Agriculture and abide by the rules and regulations issued by the Department. They are required to provide their services without discrimination and to abide by the rules and regulations having to do with records of livestock yarded, weights, rate schedules, charges and other practices which could lead to discriminatory or inadequate treatment of customers. The Secretary has the right to issue a complaint, conduct a hearing and render a decision regarding charges made against a stockyards company. There is a penalty for violation, and appeal may be had to the courts. Over the years the Packers and Stockyards Administration has become one of the important agencies in the United States Department of Agriculture. It has been a great force in promoting honesty and reliable practices on the part of both packers and stockyards companies and affords a fine example of an efficient federal agency which has gone about its business without ostentation, accomplishing great good for the public without being very much heralded.

CHAPTER 11

STATE AND LOCAL ANIMAL DISEASE LAWS

74. State Administration of Animal Disease Laws. Though the federal government has bitten deeply into the animal disease control field (under the commerce clause of the federal constitution and through grants-in-aid), the state still is vested with the residuum of authority necessary to protect its own citizens and its own industry. There are many statutes on the books in every state designed to give this protection. To be effective these laws must be administered. The chief administering agency is the state department of agriculture or its equivalent—commission of agriculture, board of agricultural commissioners, livestock sanitary board, for example. In administering these laws, the state agency is faced with several important questions: What laws need emphasis at the moment? How far can or should the department go with its enforcement program? How can it maintain the confidence of livestock growers and the veterinary profession? What snarls should be removed from current laws and regulations? What gaps should be filled with additional laws or regulations? How can maximum cooperation be maintained with the animal disease officials of the federal government and of other states? And how can harmony be achieved in the frequently overlapping and illogical allocation of enforcement activities among the agencies of the state? For example, the program of disease control in a department of public health is bound to include some features which are common to the program of a department of agriculture or livestock sanitary board, and at the local level there is always the problem of just how much authority resides in a municipality, public health district, county, parish, or township. Good administration at the state level cannot be achieved unless these problems are kept in mind and conscientious efforts made to solve them. The advisory board provided for in the laws of most states can be a real source of help in working out some of the knotty problems and in keeping the state administration informed of attitudes and feelings in the livestock industry, and in other areas where the public is concerned. Likewise, friendly relations with agriculture committees in the state legislature can do much to expedite the passage of needed laws and the amendment or repeal of laws that are not working right.

Good administration, however, involves much more than policy and public relations considerations at the higher levels. There is such a thing as good business administration within a department of state government! An idea of how excellent this internal organization is can be obtained by a review of the honest answers to such questions as these: Are current copies of all animal disease laws kept on hand and distributed to livestock owners and others who should know what the law is? Are regulations codified and printed in one publication which is kept current? Have good forms for reporting, certification, quarantine and other purposes been developed and are they supplied in adequate numbers to those who need them? Are clear and simple instructions issued for executing such forms? Is a complete and workable filing system in use, from which can be readily obtained all the data on any particular case? Are certificates of health, quarantine notices, releases from quarantine and other communications of official action transmitted without delay? Are inquiries answered promptly and as completely as possible? Are annual or other periodic reports of the activity of the department prepared in such a way as to give an accurate and interesting picture of the current animal disease situation in the state? A "yes" to all of these queries would rate a department fairly high!

75. General Animal Disease Laws. In every state the legislature has clothed the livestock sanitary authority of the state with the power necessary to control, in some measure at least, any dangerous communicable livestock disease that may arise, regardless of the absence of specific legislation on the disease. Among other things, these laws generally do the following:

Place administrative responsibility in the department or board.

Define necessary terms.

Specify the duties of the department.

Grant authority to make necessary rules and regulations.

Empower the department to inspect, test, quarantine, destroy, treat or order the treatment of animals and premises when the situation demands such action.

Prescribe the procedure for the appraisal of animals, submission of claims, and the payment of claims—including a specification of the amounts allowed.

Grant authority to inspect and control the movement of animals into or through the state by public or other carriers, to the extent necessary to prevent dissemination of livestock diseases within the state, and so long as not in conflict with federal laws or regulations.

Prescribe the procedure for review of decisions made by the livestock authority of the state.

Require the reporting of known communicable animal diseases by veterinarians.

Require annual or other reports by the livestock sanitary agency.

Provide for the establishment of entry requirements for animals shipped in from other states, and for the issuance of health certificates.

Authorize the governor to issue proclamations, upon the advice of the state livestock sanitary officials, limiting or prohibiting the entry of animals from particular areas outside the state.

The constitutional right of state legislatures to confer this kind of authority on state administrative agencies is well established by a long line of court decisions from many states. Generally speaking, the only times the courts have not upheld such authority is when it was arbitrary, improperly exercised, improperly delegated, or in conflict with federal law.

Most state statutes contain laws on the following:
Bovine brucellosis
Bovine tuberculosis
Hog cholera
Rabies

Also, laws regulating community sales and dead animal disposal are now widely accepted. Other laws vary more or less by geographical areas—depending on the animal disease problems peculiar to the area: Swine brucellosis and Texas fever laws are examples.

With the passing of time and the occurrence of needs, animal disease laws have simply grown, usually without any reference to an over-all design. There is a real need at the present time for codification of these laws. Furthermore, there is the possibility of adopting uniform state laws on such subjects as dead animal disposal, shipment of animals and entry requirements. A few states have codified their animal disease laws and others are in the process.

76. **Testing and Destruction—Sale for Slaughter.** Questions and controversies frequently arise over the power of state authorities to destroy animals. Generally it may be said that if a diseased animal is a menace—a rabid dog, for example—or has a communicable disease that is incurable, it may be summarily destroyed without compensation to the owner. [149] However, most of the acts that have been adopted make the right of the state to order destruction contingent upon consent, the payment of an indemnity, or the failure of the owner to comply with the requirements of the law.

The federal and state bovine tuberculosis eradication program furnishes the earliest example of the power of the State to destroy upon the payment of an indemnity. In general these laws authorize the State to test all dairy and breeding cattle and require the owner to furnish necessary facilities and render assistance. This requirement of the law has been tested in court on several occasions and has been upheld.[150] Under statutes which do not require assistance by the owner, the courts have held that an owner has a right to be present and participate.[151] Though these laws do not authorize the destruction of healthy animals,[152] they do not need to accord the owner a right to hearing or notice before the tests are conducted, so long as he has legal remedies for determining the correctness of the test and the legality of the procedure.[153] However, the courts consistently hold that since these laws are penal in nature, they must be strictly construed.[154] But an agent acting clearly within his authority under the law will be upheld in his actions. Thus the court in a New Hampshire case held that where the owner refused to unlock the barn and admit an inspecting veterinarian, the latter was authorized to break the inclosure.[155] In a Virginia case the owner sought to enjoin the state veterinarian from making an agglutination test under the Brucellosis law, claiming that his cattle were healthy but that they would react because of a vaccine he had given them. The court held that the law was valid and that it was not within the province of the court to determine if the conditions under which the test was being made were reasonable. The owner's injunction was denied.[156] When diseased animals may safely be used for food or other products, state laws provide for their shipment to slaughter under supervision of the state livestock sanitary authorities. This is a permissible regulation.

77. Quarantine. Along with the power to test, destroy or order animals shipped for slaughter, the power to impose and enforce quarantine is one of the important disease control devices at the disposal of state livestock sanitary authorities. Broadly speaking, it includes actions taken to establish entry requirements for animals shipped into the state, as well as area, herd or individual animal quarantines within the state. Also, some of the regulations imposing duties on public carriers are in the nature of quarantine measures. In quite a wide range of circumstances the courts have found various kinds of quarantine laws valid and enforceable. Only in a few instances have the actions of the state been regarded as invalid.

In cases upholding the power to impose quarantine, the courts have said that the legislature may provide for the quarantine of diseased or suspected animals;[157] authorize the quarantine of any herd when the owner refuses to have his herd inspected and 90 percent or more of the herds in his township have been tested;[158] prohibit the shipment of watermelons from a tick infested area if bedded in pine straw, unless the cars were sealed so none of the straw could escape;[159] prohibit the importation of all livestock from another state in which an outbreak of disease has occurred or is feared;[160] or authorize the sheriff to assume custody of animals suspected of having a contagious disease.[161] However, it has been held that such authority on the part of the sheriff is not conclusive, but is only prima facie.[162]

Though quarantine is supported by the police power of the state, it is nevertheless subject to certain limitations. Persons on whom the quarantine is imposed must be notified, the quarantine must be reasonable, and the discretion to determine if a quarantine should be imposed cannot be delegated to ministerial officers. Diagnosis is important, and if it happens that an owner's animals are not in fact afflicted with the disease for which they are quarantined, the owner is entitled to recover any damages suffered because of the quarantine. In cases of conflict between state and federal laws imposing quarantine, state law must yield to the extent that federal control is constitutionally permissible. State laws authorizing the Governor to proclaim a quarantine against animals from particular areas outside the state do not authorize the issuance of such proclamations without cause.

A quarantine may be imposed with respect to any dangerous infectious disease of animals, and may be as general or as specific as the situation demands: It may apply to all animals or to specific breeds, types or sexes. It may apply over a large area, or over a small area, or to a particular farm, or even to a part of a particular farm. It may apply to carriers, or stockyards, or any place where animals are kept. A valid quarantine lasts until it is officially terminated and proper notice given. All movements of animals may be controlled, whether wholly within the state, from the state to other states, or into the state from outside.

78. Entry of Animals from Other States. A state may control the entry of livestock from without the state, so long as the regulations are necessary, reasonable, and do not conflict with federal law. Such necessary and reasonable control is not regarded as interference with interstate commerce. In a Texas case, the court held that a law giving the state livestock sanitary commission authority to prohibit the importation of cattle from a particular state in which an infectious disease had broken out was not an interference with interstate commerce.[163] The court in this case also said that where the sanitary commission has exercised such authority it will be presumed their judgment and discretion were properly exercised. However, a state inspection law providing that inspection of migratory livestock shall not apply to residents of the state was held unconstitutional by the Supreme Court of Colorado as violative of the federal constitutional provision that the citizens of each state shall be entitled to all privileges and immunities of citizens in the several states.[164]

Though entry requirements of the various states are similar in some respects, the variations are important and the particular requirements of a state into which animals are to be shipped must be studied in detail to determine what must be done prior to shipment. Circular 1 of the United States Livestock Sanitary Association, entitled "Health Requirements Governing Admission of Livestock" contains a digest of the requirements of all the states, territories, the federal government and Canada. The following digest of a portion of the Illinois entry requirements for dairy and breeding cattle is more or less typical (though these are expressed as regulations, they, in part, are simply restatements of the law) :

> All dairy or breeding cattle brought into the State of Illinois or from public stockyards within the State, unless said cattle are consigned to and delivered by the transportation company within the confines of the Union Stock Yards, Chicago, the National Stock Yards, East St. Louis, or the Union Stock Yards, Peoria, or any other like public stockyard, must be accompanied by an official certificate of health showing tuberculosis and brucellosis status of cattle, as follows:
>
> TUBERCULOSIS: Except as otherwise provided—tuberculin test within 30 days previous to shipment, or
> Originate in a tuberculosis-free accredited herd. Accredited herd number must be given and cattle must be identified by either ear tag number or registration name and number, or
> Originate in modified tuberculosis-free accredited area from a herd in which on last complete test of the entire herd no reactors were disclosed and the cattle destined for Illinois were tuberculin tested and negative within one year of date of shipment.
>
> BRUCELLOSIS: All dairy and breeding cattle over 6 months of age must be negative to brucellosis test within 30 days of shipment, or
> Originate in brucellosis-free herd. Certified herd number must be given and cattle must be identified by either ear tag number or registration name and number, or
> Accompanied by certificate of vaccination approved by livestock sanitary authority of state of origin, positively identifying cattle and showing that they were officially vaccinated against brucellosis when between 4 and 8 months of age with an approved vaccine. Serial number and name of manufacturer of vaccine, dosage used, and date of vaccination, must be included in the certificate.
>
> SCABIES: No cattle infested with scabies mites shall be brought into the State of Illinois.
> Cattle recently exposed to scabies mites may enter Illinois when the official health certificate shows the cattle have been sprayed twice at ten-day intervals with a lime and sulphur solution or other spray specified by the Bureau of Animal Industry or the livestock sanitary official of the state of origin, and that upon veterinary examination within ten days of importation were found to be free of scabies.

Entry requirements will not be interpreted so as to impose an unreasonable burden on carriers bringing animals into a state. In an Iowa case, the court held that a regulation requiring carriers to unload horses brought into the state from points west of the Missouri River (when not accompanied by a certificate of health) at the yards nearest the river, did not mean any yards nearest the river, but only those yards on the carrier's line nearest the river.[165] Though a railroad company may wrongfully bring cattle into a state during a prohibited season, it is not liable for the transmission of disease resulting from movement within the state by another party.[166] Likewise, a statute making a railway company liable for injury caused any person, by reason of bringing animals into the state in such condition as to communicate Texas fever, does not make the company's civil liability absolute, but only creates a presumption which may be rebutted by showing freedom from negligence.[167] However, where a railway company maintained a lane or passageway for driving infected cattle from the Indian Territory into the State of Kansas, it was held that the company could be enjoined in an action to abate a public nuisance.[168]

The veterinarian it would seem has but two alternatives with respect to examining and certifying animals for interstate shipment; he must either know exactly what the particular requirements are so the shipper will not be inconvenienced and possibly look to the veterinarian for damages, or he must plead ignorance and refuse to inspect and certify. The first alternative is to be preferred, and is not too difficult to follow if the veterinarian is willing to study the requirements of the other states and call on representatives of the Department for help when necessary.

79. Community Sales and Dead Animal Disposal Laws. Public livestock auctions and the picking up and moving of dead animals by disposal companies are two highly effective ways of spreading contagious livestock diseases throughout a state. State legislatures have generally recognized this and have accordingly adopted legislation to reduce the danger to the livestock industry.

A "community sale" is defined generally as any sale or exchange of livestock at more or less regular intervals, but more often than a stated number of times annually—three, for example. Typical requirements in such laws are the following:

Licensing of the operator

Maintenance of required records by the operator

Examination of all animals by a licensed veterinarian

Testing of animals for tuberculosis, brucellosis, cholera or other specified diseases

The maintenance of certain sanitary standards in the sales barn and sales premises

The posting of fees or commission rates

Typical dead animal disposal laws contain the following provisions:

Licensing of the operator
Periodic inspections by state officials
Truck identification
Sanitary standards for trucks
Sanitary standards for the plant
Regulations on disposing of carcasses within the plant
Restrictions on use of highways
Restrictions on entrance of farm premises
Disinfection of trucks after unloading

There is no question of the validity of either of these types of legislation under the state police power, so long as the laws are reasonable. In a Wisconsin case the court held that within its borders a State may inspect and regulate the business of rendering dead animals, but that such control cannot be extended beyond the jurisdiction of the State.[169] The situation which might otherwise result from this lack of jurisdiction is frequently covered by a reciprocity provision which stipulates that dead animals or parts of dead animals, except green or salted hides, shall not be allowed to enter other states except by reciprocal agreement with the other states. In interpreting the green hide exception, the Florida court held that the livestock sanitary board did not have authority to forbid the shipment of salt-cured hides from a tick-infested area.[170]

In recent years state legislators have adopted laws controlling the operation of dead animal loading platforms and concentration centers for the collection of dead animals. These laws require a license for the operation of such establishments and impose certain sanitary standards. They provide for inspection by the Department of Agriculture or other appropriate agency of state government and require that after shipments of dead animals suspected of having a contagious disease have been handled, the platform, trucks and other equipment belonging to the loading platform operator be thoroughly sterilized. These laws simply represent a further attempt of the state to control the dissemination of contagious animal diseases.

80. **Animal Disease Control by Local Units of Government.** Though state laws may use county boundaries as a means of preventing the spread of diseases (prohibiting the trailing of sheep with scabies across county lines, for example), this is by no means the only significance of the county as a disease control

device. Under its general authority to control disease, both animal and human, and by virtue of legislation applying directly to it, the county as a unit of government has authority to control animal disease through quarantine and the other devices employed by the State, so long as its program does not conflict with that of the State. Particular counties may be vested with additional authority by the State where a distinction between counties is justified for purposes of controlling the spread of a disease within the state.[171] Also, it has been held that it is not unconstitutional to permit a county to determine by an election whether or not certain provisions of a complete state statute shall become operative in the county.[172] Likewise, it is valid to provide that the county board shall enforce a particular law only on petition of a required number of resident cattle owners.[173] In carrying out its disease control functions, a county may appropriate money from its general funds.[174] State fund appropriations generally set up the conditions under which a county veterinarian is to be employed and how his salary will be shared by the county and the state.

Counties may be made liable to a livestock owner for injury caused him in the enforcement of county health ordinances. The extent of such liability depends on several factors, including the methods used by its agents and whether or not state law makes the county liable. In the dipping cases, counties have been held liable to the owner where its agents did not dilute the solution sufficiently,[175] and where the dipping was negligently done, even though in the latter case the county board exercised no supervision over the dipping (state officials supervised).[176] The county is not liable, however, unless the proof establishes the chain conclusively,[177] or in situations where the owner himself supervised the dipping.[178]

Townships have a general authority over public health, including animal diseases. However, the situations with which a township would be called upon to deal are few, after making allowance for authority vested in the state and in the county. Local quarantine measures—rabies, for example—and control of sanitary standards for milk sold within the township, not subject to control by some other unit of government, are examples of the authority which might be exercised.

Municipalities have a rather broad authority to deal with animal disease within their limits. Subject to such regulation are

dogs, cats and other pets, animal products sold within the municipality, and milk. Cities derive their authority from the state and
are regarded as sharing in the police power. Therefore, they are
limited in their regulatory activity by the same tests of reasonableness and necessity that are applied to the state. A muncipal
ordinance cannot conflict with a state law or impose a license
which is simply a revenue measure bearing no relation to the
intended control.

Public health districts are still other entities of local government that have come to mean a great deal in the disease field.
Where organized, they take over many of the disease control
functions of counties and townships within their boundaries. Also,
they may take over some of the health function of municipalities
contained in them—the enforcement of milk ordinances, for
example.

Certainly, the veterinarian should be conscious of the control
of animal disease which may be exercised by these units of local
government, particularly in its relation to human health. More
particularly, he should understand the division of local authority
which exists in his own community and the major problems with
which each entity is attempting to cope.

81. **Common Law Liability for Transmission of Animal Disease.** One of the chief deterrents to the spread of animal disease
is the liability with which one may be charged under ordinary
rules of negligence. Many of these rules have been codified in the
statutory law of the state, but they nevertheless represent the
law, whether codified or not. For example, a statute in Illinois
provides that if any person having sheep known to be affected
with a contagious disease permits them to run at large or keeps
them where other sheep may become infected, he shall be liable
for all damages resulting. This principle does not depend on
statute and is probably a fair statement of the law in practically
every state. Two important elements are necessary to establish
one's liability for causing the spread of an animal disease—he
must have been careless or negligent in some way and he must
have known that his animals had a communicable disease. In
Wirth v. State,[179] the Wisconsin Supreme Court held that to con-
vict a party of keeping a horse affected with an infectious disease
where other animals could have access to it, it must be proved that
he was the owner of the horse so affected, that he knew the horse

to be so affected, and that he kept it where other horses had access to it. Statutes codifying the common law rule generally include the provision that knowledge ("scienter") is essential to liability, and courts hold that it is reversible error for the judge to fail to submit to the jury a defendant's contention that he did not know his animals had a communicable disease.[180] So, if a man is indicted for selling cattle under quarantine, it has been held that facts which tended to create a belief in the defendant that the quarantine had been removed should have been admitted.[181] However, if a statute imposes a penalty on "whoever sells or disposes of any animal infected or known to have been exposed to infection," the courts have held that knowledge is not essential to establish the first named offense, that of " . . . selling or disposing of any animal infected . . . ." A law making it unlawful to sell swine infected with hog cholera, though a criminal statute, may be made the basis for a civil action for damages.[182] If one rents pasture to another, knowing that communicable disease may be harbored in the pasture, and fails to disclose such fact, the owner of the pasture may be held liable for the transmission of disease from the pasture to the animals.[183]

To make one liable to damages as the owner of Texas or Cherokee cattle for infection of other cattle, he must be the owner in the natural and ordinary sense of that term. A conditional ownership growing out of a lien will not make a party liable unless he has the actual possession and control of the cattle.[184]

Where two separate lots of Texas or Cherokee cattle, owned and in the possession of separate owners, contrary to statute were each on the same feeding ground or section where the cattle of the plaintiff were being herded, and the plaintiff's cattle became infected, from which they died, the court, in a suit against the owners of one lot of these cattle, instructed the jury that if plaintiff's cattle took the disease from either lot of the Texas cattle, and the testimony as to which lot communicated the disease was equally balanced, to find for defendants. This instruction was held erroneous. If both lots of cattle contributed to infect plaintiff's cattle, so that it was impossible to say that one lot was more concerned in doing so than the other, it seems that the defendants were all liable.[185]

Where several owners of different droves of Texas and Cherokee cattle drove their respective cattle over the herding ground of another, at different times, and by reason thereof, through one or the other, or both, of such droves, disease was imparted to cattle of the latter, it was held there was no joint liability for such injury.[186]

One who sells hogs infected with cholera renders himself liable for damages if, at the time of the sale, he had knowledge of such infection or notice of such facts as would put a prudent person upon inquiry, and a reasonable inquiry prosecuted by him would have apprised him of the fact, before they were delivered, that they were infected.[187]

The damages suffered by a purchaser of diseased hogs in the loss of his own hogs, with which he placed the diseased animals, were the natural result of the wrong of the persons who originally sold the hogs with knowledge of their diseased condition, and, although the hogs were resold by the immediate purchaser from them before the damage was done, the original sellers were liable for such damages to the ultimate purchaser.[188]

A buyer of diseased animals may ordinarily collect damages from the seller regardless of knowledge on the part of the seller, since there is an implied warranty that animals purchased shall be free from disease. Knowledge becomes important only when the basis of the action is negligence. In the latter case, a defendant may use the defense of contributory negligence. It has been held, however, that where the bringing in of diseased animals is prohibited by law, nothing short of gross negligence on the part of an injured party will prevent his recovery.[189] But if a person learns that he has suspect animals on his premises, where he pastures animals for another, and continues to pasture such animals and mingle his own with them, he cannot then recover from the owner of the diseased animals.[190] On the other hand, the fact that one brings cattle into the state illegally is no bar to his recovery of damages from another for negligently communicating a disease to his animals after they are in the state.[191] The acceptance of a diseased animal from the carrier with the knowledge that it is diseased will ordinarily prevent recovery from the carrier for delivering a diseased animal.[192]

In an action for damages for negligence in permitting sheep afflicted with a disease known as scab to stray and communicate the disease to plaintiff's flock, a showing that a storm on the night of their escape was a "bad one" or "a very severe one," without showing the velocity of the wind, or the temperature, and that five to ten inches of snow and rain fell, did not entitle the de-

fendant to the defense known as the act of God, since to make
that availing it was necessary to show that the escape was due to
an unprecedented storm against which human prudence and
caution could not guard, and that no act of omission or commission on the part of its employees contributed thereto. In this case,
the defendant's sheep escaped from their herders and were found
by plaintiff's herder, who drove them into plaintiff's corral, where
they communicated to plaintiff's sheep the disease of scab with
which they were afflicted at its incipient stage, and which was not
apparent to a casual observer and was unknown to plaintiff. The
court held that where such care of defendant's sheep was not
negligent or a contributing cause of injury, defendant could not
invoke the defense of contributory negligence.[193]

The operation of the negligence rule is exemplified clearly in
a Michigan case where the court held that a person who sold hogs
to a dealer, knowing them to be afflicted with a dangerous and
infectious disease, was liable to one who purchased them of the
dealer, and placed them with other hogs, for the value not only
of the hogs purchased, but also of those which died from the
contagion, where neither the original nor subsequent purchaser
had notice of their diseased condition.[194]

Further information on the amount of damages that may be
recovered is contained in the following cases:

If one wrongfully allows his cattle to mingle with
his neighbor's cattle and communicate fever to such
cattle, he is answerable for all the damages, both direct
and consequential, that result from their trespasses, and
this without regard to his knowledge of their condition.[195] (There are cases that would not permit consequential damage without knowledge.)

He who has the care and custody of sheep, for the
purpose of pasturing them, is liable for damage done by
them, in the same manner and to the same extent, as the
owner.[196]

One who sells hogs infected with cholera renders
himself liable for damages if, at the time of the sale, he
had knowledge of such infection or notice of such facts
as would put a prudent person upon inquiry, and a
reasonable inquiry prosecuted by him would have apprised him of the fact before they were delivered that

they were infected. But the mere negligent failure to follow up such notice and ascertain the fact does not justify the imposition of punitive damages, such damages being properly awarded only when the defendant is shown to have acted in wanton disregard of the plaintiff's rights.[197]

In a suit by the keeper of a livery stable to recover damages for an injury done to two stallions of his own by the communication of a distemper to them by a horse of the defendant, which the plaintiff had been induced to receive into his stable by the defendant's representation that the horse had recovered from the distemper and could not communicate the disease to other horses, the court permitted the plaintiff to prove the profit he would probably have derived from the services of one of the stallions during the foaling season, but for his incapacity from the disease. It was held, on appeal, that the evidence, though not admissible definitely to fix the measure of damages, was proper for the consideration of the jury as an aid in estimating them.[198]

Where defendant's agent, authorized to sell a flock of sheep, sold a portion of the flock, knowing that the sheep were diseased, and the purchaser mixed the sheep purchased with a flock before owned by him, and the disease was contagious and was communicated to the other flock, the purchaser's claim to damages was not limited to the loss of the sheep purchased, but extended to the other sheep to which the disease was communicated.[199]

The position of carriers and transportation companies with respect to liability for spreading disease is fairly well set out in the following cases:

Where a railroad company, transporting through a state, upon a train of cars, cattle diseased with the Texas fever, has its train wrecked within the state, so as to make it necessary to unload the cattle, and thereupon is notified that the cattle are from Texas, and will spread disease among the domestic cattle if permitted to run at large, or if driven upon the public highway, —it should *corral* the cattle at or near the wreck, or otherwise prevent them from running at large, or getting upon the public highway, until reloaded. If, however, it drives the cattle, after receiving notice of their diseased condition, upon the public highway, it does so at its own peril, and is liable, under the statute, for the damages arising by the communication of the disease or fever to domestic cattle from the cattle so diseased, provided the owners of the domestic cattle are not guilty of contributory negligence.[200]

A railway company is not liable for the death of stock from disease contracted from stock which escaped from its cars while being shipped through the state, unless negligence on its part be shown.[201]

The defendant railroad company negligently permitted cattle infected with Texas fever to escape from its right of way to the adjoining highways, one of which led to a pasture from which plaintiff derived profits, which were thereafter lost when the state veterinarian placed the highways under quarantine without lawful authority. From the fact that the diseased cattle had been thereon, plaintiff's patrons would not permit their animals to be driven to the pasture, there being no way by which it could be reached, except over the highway. The court held that the injury was not a natural and probable consequence of the negligent acts which might have been foreseen by a man of ordinary prudence and plaintiff could not recover.[202]

A railway company which negligently allows Texas cattle to escape from its cars, and run at large, thereby affecting native cattle with Texas fever, is liable for the resulting loss.[203]

Where quarantine restrictions on cattle north of a quarantine line were limited to pastures in which infected cattle had been or were running, a railway company was not liable for damages caused by a quarantine declared against a pasture north of the line resulting from southern cattle being negligently permitted to escape while in transit and go into the pasture, where it did not appear the escaping cattle were actually infected, or that any of the cattle therein were thereafter infected.[204]

A railroad which negligently diverted to plaintiffs, cattle infested with ticks instead of plaintiff's cattle, was held liable for loss of plaintiff's land, which was quarantined, and for wages paid to employees to ride the lines of the quarantined land to prevent cattle from going upon it.[205]

In an action by the owner of land (across which infected cattle were driven) against a railroad for resulting damages, the complaint alleging railroad's receipt of infected cattle, its duty to transport them to their destination and to exercise ordinary care to prevent their being diverted to a different place and delivered into territory free from infection of fever ticks, and that county in which plaintiff resided was not subject to quarantine regulations, was held to permit recovery, not solely on the railroad's breach of contractual duty relative to shipment of cattle, but for railroad's negligence in permitting infected cattle to be diverted into territory free from quarantine.[206]

82. The Zoonoses—What They Are, and How They Are Being Studied. Zoonoses are diseases transmissible between animals and man. The word is fairly new (since about 1870) in medical circles, but the problems it represents are old and continuing ones.

Research on and treatment of the diseases of man and animals have been thought of separately since the Middle Ages. Zoonoses may do little or no harm in one host (man or animal) but may injure or kill the other species. Better organization is needed to control inapparent as well as obvious zoonotic diseases of wild and domestic animals and man.

More than 100 zoonoses are found throughout the world. Among them are yellow fever, plague, tuberculosis, sleeping sickness and many protozoan and helminthic diseases. At least 40 of these diseases are known to occur in Illinois. People, birds, fish and migratory insects and even jet streams of air can spread these diseases from one country to another.

Throughout the entire world the zoonoses take a major toll in terms of human health and happiness and animal welfare.

They and their control are, therefore, and will continue to be, of major importance.

Because many of the factors involved in zoonoses are not known, we find them emerging and receding without clear reasons. Scientific teamwork will be required to add to present knowledge before many of our zoonotic problems can be solved.

A major step was taken by the University of Illinois when the Center for Zoonoses Research was established by action of the Administration and Board of Trustees of the University of Illinois in 1960 to meet the need for research on zoonotic diseases.

A major purpose of the Center for Zoonoses Research is to improve the means of carrying on interdisciplinary research on the zoonoses. Not only physicians and veterinarians, but also many other scientists, zoologists, ecologists, epidemiologists, microbiologists, anthropologists, meteorologists, climatologists, biometricians and other specialists are working on the zoonotic research team. Private citizens, businesses and foundations are also assisting.

CHAPTER 12

FOOD AND FEED LAWS

83. Why the Veterinarian Is Concerned. The federal government, the states and municipalities all have exerted an extensive control over food products of animal origin. This control is meant to accomplish two objectives—protect the public and improve the marketing of such products. The formulation of standards and inspection of products under these laws require trained help. Veterinarians have long been relied upon as the principal source of such trained help. Also, veterinarians are frequently called as expert witnesses in cases involving the purity and fitness of foods and feeds.

84. The Federal Food, Drug and Cosmetic Act. This law[207] prohibits the introduction or delivery for introduction into interstate commerce of any food, drug, device or cosmetic that is adulterated or misbranded, the receipt of any such food, drug, device or cosmetic in interstate commerce, and the adulteration or misbranding of any food, drug, device or cosmetic while in interstate commerce. "Food" is defined as any article used for food or drink for man or other animals. The Secretary of Health, Education, and Welfare is authorized to ". . . promulgate regulations fixing and establishing for any food, under its common or usual name so far as practicable, a reasonable definition and standard of identity, a reasonable standard of quality and reasonable standard of fill of container. . . ."

Under this act, a food is considered to be adulterated "if it bears or contains any poisonous or deleterious substance which may render it injurious to health; . . . if it bears or contains any added poisonous or added deleterious substance except a pesticide chemical in or on a raw agricultural commodity, which is unsafe . . .; if it consists in whole or in part of any filthy, putrid, or decomposed substance, or if it is otherwise unfit for food; . . . if it has been prepared, packed, or held under insanitary conditions whereby it may have been rendered injurious to health;

100

... if it is, in whole or in part, the product of a diseased animal or of an animal which has died otherwise than by slaughter; or if its container is composed, in whole or in part, of any poisonous or deleterious substance which may render the contents injurious to health." The law further provides that a food shall be considered adulterated, "if any valuable constituent has been in whole or in part omitted or abstracted therefrom; if any substance has been substituted wholly or in part therefor; if damage or inferiority has been concealed in any manner; if any substance has been added thereto or mixed or packed therewith so as to increase its bulk or weight, or reduce its quality or strength, or make it appear better or of greater value than it is," or " ... If it bears or contains a coal-tar color other than one from a batch that has been certified in accordance with regulations ... provided by ... (law) ..."

A food is regarded as misbranded if its label is false or misleading in any particular. The law lists these particular acts as violations:

1. "If it is offered for sale under the name of another food."

2. "If it is an imitation of another food, unless its label bears, in type of uniform size and prominence, the word 'imitation' and immediately thereafter, the name of the food imitated."

3. "If its container is so made, formed, or filled as to be misleading."

4. "If in package form unless it bears a label containing (1) the name and place of business of the manufacturer, packer, or distributor; and (2) an accurate statement of the quantity of the contents in terms of weight, measure, or numerical count: *Provided*, that under clause (2) of this paragraph reasonable variations shall be permitted, and exemptions as to small packages shall be established, by regulations prescribed by the Secretary."

5. "If any word, statement, or other information required by or under authority of this chapter to appear on the label or labeling is not prominently placed thereon with such conspicuousness (as compared with other words, statements, designs, or devices, in the labeling) and in such terms as to render it likely to be read and understood by the ordinary individual under customary conditions of purchase and use."

6. "If it purports to be or is represented as a food for which

a definition and standard of identity has been prescribed by regulations. . ., unless (1) it conforms to such definition and standard, and (2) its label bears the name of the food specified in the definition and standard, and, insofar as may be required by such regulations, the common names of optional ingredients (other than spices, flavoring, and coloring) present in such food."

7. "If it purports to be or is represented as . . . (1) a food for which a standard of quality has been prescribed by regulations . . ., and its quality falls below such standard, unless its label bears, in such manner and form as such regulations specify, a statement that it falls below such standard; or (2) a food for which a standard or standards of fill of container have been prescribed. . ., and it falls below the standard of fill of container applicable thereto, unless its label bears, in such manner and form as such regulations specify, a statement that it falls below such standard."

8. If it does not purport to be or is not represented as a food for which a definition and standard of identity has been prescribed, "unless its label bears (1) the common or usual name of the food, if any there be, and (2) in case it is fabricated from two or more ingredients, the common or usual name of each such ingredient; except that spices, flavorings, and colorings other than those sold as such may be designated as spices, flavorings and colorings without naming each . . ."

9. "If it purports to be or is represented for special dietary uses, unless its label bears such information concerning its vitamin, mineral, and other dietary properties as the Secretary determines to be, and by regulations prescribes as, necessary in order fully to inform purchasers as to its value for such uses."

10. "If it bears or contains any artificial flavoring, artificial coloring, or chemical preservative, unless it bears labeling stating that fact . . . ."

These provisions on adulteration and misbranding are the heart of the Act. There are innumerable court decisions and administrative decisions involving an interpretation of the law or of regulations promulgated under it. Among the important questions to arise are, "Was the food in interstate commerce? Did the federal inspector have the right to seize? Is the food in fact unfit for human consumption? Were the proper tests conducted to determine the condition of the food? Did the condition exist while the food was in interstate commerce? Is the particular regulation, definition or standard reasonable?"

85. **Other Federal Laws.** There are many federal laws which in a sense supplement the Food, Drug and Cosmetic Act. The most important of these are listed below, together with pertinent language from each.

Meat. " . . . the Secretary of Agriculture shall cause to be made by inspectors appointed for that purpose a post mortem examination and inspection of the carcasses and parts of all cattle, sheep, swine, and goats to be prepared for human consumption at any slaughtering, meat-canning, salting, packing, rendering, or similar establishment in any State, Territory, or the District of Columbia for transportation or sale as articles of interstate or foreign commerce; and the carcasses and parts thereof of all such animals found to be sound, healthful, wholesome, and fit for human food shall be marked, stamped, tagged, or labeled as 'Inspected and passed'; and said inspectors shall label, mark, stamp, or tag as 'Inspected and condemned' all carcasses and parts thereof of animals found to be unsound, unhealthful, unwholesome, or otherwise unfit for human food; and all carcasses and parts thereof thus inspected and condemned shall be destroyed for food purposes by the said establishment in the presence of an inspector, and the Secretary of Agriculture may remove inspectors from any such establishment which fails to so destroy any such condemned carcass or part thereof, and said inspectors, after said first inspection, shall, when they deem it necessary, reinspect said carcasses or parts thereof to determine whether since the first inspection the same have become unsound, unhealthful, unwholesome, or in any way unfit for human food, and if any carcass or any part thereof shall, upon examination and inspection subsequent to the first examination and inspection, be found to be unsound, unhealthful, unwholesome, or otherwise unfit for human food, it shall be destroyed for food purposes by the said establishment in the presence of an inspector, and the Secretary of Agriculture may remove inspectors from any establishment which fails to so destroy any such condemned carcass or part thereof. . . . No person, firm, or corporation engaged in the interstate commerce of meat or meat food products shall transport or offer for transportation, sell, or offer to sell, any such meat or meat food products in any State

or Territory or in the District of Columbia or any place under
the jurisdiction of the United States, other than in the State or
Territory or in the District of Columbia or any place under the
jurisdiction of the United States in which the slaughtering, packing, canning, rendering, or other similar establishment owned,
leased, or operated by said firm, person, or corporation is located
unless and until said person, firm, or corporation shall have complied with all the provisions of this title. . . . The provisions of
. . . (this) . . . title, requiring inspection to be made by the Secretary of Agriculture, shall not apply to animals slaughtered by
any farmer on the farm and sold and transported in interstate
or foreign commerce, nor to retail butchers and retail dealers in
meat and meat food products, supplying their customers. . . ."[208]

Meat and meat food products. "For the purpose of preventing
the use in interstate or foreign commerce of meat and meat food
products which are unsound, unhealthful, unwholesome, or otherwise unfit for human food, the Secretary of Agriculture, at his
discretion, may cause to be made, by inspectors appointed for
that purpose, an examination and inspection of all cattle, sheep,
swine, and goats before they shall be allowed to enter into any
slaughtering, packing, meat-canning, rendering, or similar establishment in which they are to be slaughtered and the meat and
meat-food products thereof are to be used in interstate or foreign
commerce; and all cattle, swine, sheep, and goats found on such
inspection to show symptoms of disease shall be set apart and
slaughtered separately from all other cattle, sheep, swine, or
goats; and when so slaughtered, the carcasses of said cattle,
sheep, swine, or goats shall be subject to a careful examination
and inspection, all as provided by the rules and regulations to be
prescribed by the Secretary of Agriculture, as herein provided
for."[209]

Meat and meat products. "The foregoing provisions shall
apply to all carcasses or parts of carcasses of cattle, sheep, swine,
and goats, or the meat or meat products thereof which may be
brought into any slaughtering, meat-canning, salting, packing,
rendering, or similar establishment, and such examination and
inspection shall be had before the said carcasses or parts thereof
shall be allowed to enter into any department wherein the same
are to be treated and prepared for meat food products; and the
foregoing provisions shall also apply to all such products, which

. . . [have] been issued from any slaughtering, meat-canning, salting, packing, rendering, or similar establishment where such inspection is maintained."[210]

Inspection of agricultural products. "The Secretary of Agriculture is directed and authorized: . . . To inspect, certify, and identify the class, quality, quantity, and condition of agricultural products when shipped or received in interstate commerce, under such rules and regulations as the Secretary of Agriculture may prescribe, including assessment and collection of such fees as will be reasonable and as nearly as may be to cover the cost of the service rendered, to the end that agricultural products may be marketed to the best advantage, that trading may be facilitated, and that consumers may be able to obtain the quality product which they desire, except that no person shall be required to use the service authorized by this subsection. Any official certificate issued under the authority of this subsection shall be received by all officers and all courts of the United States as prima facie evidence of the truth of the statements therein contained. . . ."[211]

Sanitary inspection. "The Secretary of Agriculture shall cause to be made, by experts in sanitation or by other competent inspectors, such inspection of all slaughtering, meat canning, salting, packing, rendering, or similar establishments in which cattle, sheep, swine, and goats are slaughtered and the meat and meat food products thereof are prepared for interstate or foreign commerce as may be necessary to inform himself concerning the sanitary conditions of the same, and to prescribe the rules and regulations of sanitation under which such establishments shall be maintained; and where the sanitary conditions of any such establishment are such that the meat or meat food products are rendered unclean, unsound, unhealthful, unwholesome, or otherwise unfit for human food, he shall refuse to allow said meat or meat food products to be labeled, marked, stamped, or tagged as 'inspected and passed.' "[212]

Inspection of animals for export. "The Secretary of Agriculture shall cause to be made a careful inspection of all cattle, sheep, swine, and goats intended and offered for export to foreign countries at such times and places, and in such manner as he may deem proper, to ascertain whether such cattle, sheep, swine and goats are free from disease."[213]

Transportation of diseased animals. "No railroad company within the United States, or the owners or masters of any steam or sailing or other vessel or boat, shall receive for transportation or transport from one State or Territory to another, or from any State into the District of Columbia, or from the District into any State, any livestock and/or live poultry affected with any contagious, infectious, or communicable disease, and especially the disease known as pleuropneumonia; nor shall any person, company, or corporation deliver for such transportation to any railroad company, or master or owner of any boat or vessel, any livestock and/or live poultry, knowing them to be affected with any contagious, infectious, or communicable disease; nor shall any person, company, or corporation drive on foot, or transport in private conveyance from one State or Territory to another, or from any State into the District of Columbia, or from the District into any State, any livestock and/or live poultry, knowing them to be affected with any contagious, infectious, or communicable disease, and especially the disease known as pleuropneumonia.

"Cattle which have reacted to the tuberculin test may be shipped, transported, or moved from one State, Territory, or the District of Columbia, to any other State, Territory, or the District of Columbia, for immediate slaughter, in accordance with such rules and regulations as shall be prescribed by the Secretary of Agriculture. The said Secretary of Agriculture may, in his discretion, and under such rules and regulations as he may prescribe, permit cattle which have been shipped for breeding or feeding purposes from one State, Territory, or the District of Columbia to another State, Territory, or the District of Columbia, and which have reacted to the test subsequent to such shipment, to be reshipped in interstate commerce to the original owner."[214]

Prevention of contagion among animals. "The Secretary of Agriculture shall have authority to make such regulations and take such measures as he may deem proper to prevent the introduction or dissemination of the contagion of any contagious, infectious, or communicable disease of animals and/or live poultry from a foreign country into the United States or from one State or Territory of the United States or the District of Columbia to another, and to seize, quarantine, and dispose of any hay, straw, forage, or similar material, or any meats, hides, or other animal products coming from an infected foreign country to the United States, or from one State or Territory or the District of Columbia in transit to another State or Territory or the District of Columbia whenever in his judgment such action is advisable in order to guard against the introduction or spread of such contagion."[215]

Meat and animals for export. "The Secretary of Agriculture shall also cause to be made a careful inspection of the carcasses and parts thereof of all cattle, sheep, swine and goats, the meat of which, fresh, salted, canned, corned, packed, cured, or otherwise prepared, is intended and offered for export to any foreign country, at such times and places and in such manner as he may deem proper."[216]

"No clearance shall be given to any vessel having on board any fresh, salted, canned, corned, or packed beef, mutton, pork, or goat meat, being the meat of animals killed except as hereinbefore provided for export to and sale in a foreign country from any port in the United States, until the owner or shipper thereof shall obtain from an inspector appointed under the provisions of . . . this title a certificate that the said cattle, sheep, swine, and goats were sound and healthy at the time of inspection, and that their meat is sound and wholesome, unless the Secretary of Agriculture shall have waived the requirements of such certificate for the country to which said cattle, sheep, swine, and goats or meats are to be exported."[217]

"No clearance shall be given to any vessel having on board cattle, sheep, swine, or goats for export to a foreign country until the owner or shipper of such cattle, sheep, swine, or goats has a certificate from the inspector authorized to be appointed, stating that the said cattle, sheep, swine, or goats are sound and healthy, or unless the Secretary of Agriculture shall have waived the requirement of such certificate for export to the particular country to which such cattle, sheep, swine, or goats are to be exported."[218]

Suspension of importation. "Whenever the President is satisfied that there is good reason to believe that any importation is being made, or is about to be made, into the United States, from any foreign country, of any article used for human food or drink that is adulterated to an extent dangerous to the health or welfare of the people of the United States, or any of them, he may issue his proclamation suspending the importation of such articles from such country for such period of time as he may think necessary to prevent such importation, and during such period it shall be unlawful to import into the United States from the countries designated in the proclamation of the President any of the articles the importation of which is so suspended."[219]

86. **State Food Laws.** There is a certain amount of consistency in state laws on food. In all instances the counterpart of the Federal Food, Drug and Cosmetic Act has been established with provisions against adulteration and misbranding. The right to inspect premises, equipment, raw materials for food preparation, storage rooms, and all food handling and serving establishments is given by statute and supported by court decisions. "Food," as used in such laws, customarily includes food, drink, confectionery, condiment, whether used by man or animal.

Among the provisions ordinarily found in these laws are the following:

Definitions of many foods, including standards of strength and purity.

Meat inspection by the State, to supplement federal inspection.

Milk and milk products inspection and control.

Veal, when it is immature and unsalable.

Restaurant inspection and the inspection of all food-handling establishments.

Health regulations for personnel working in food processing or handling establishments, including the requirement of physical examinations.

Sale and use of preservatives.

Egg regulations on purity, fitness for consumption, candling and grading.

Regulation of drug sales.

Cold storage and food locker plants, regulations on food, packaging and temperature control.

Oleomargarine laws, regulating its coloring, labeling and sale.

The labeling, mixing and sale of specially designated products such as vinegar, extracts and baking powder.

Lard and lard substitutes regulations.

87. **The Regulation of Milk and Milk Products.** Milk is beyond doubt the most likely medium among all the foods for the spreading of disease. Because of this fact, there are many laws, federal, state and local, to reduce the danger. Needless to say, some are more effective than others, and none of them help very much unless they are enforced. Following is a summary of federal laws dealing with the health aspects of milk distribution.

The Filled Milk Act, adopted in 1923, was one of the earliest federal laws on milk. It defines filled milk to mean: "any milk, cream or skimmed milk, whether or not condensed, evaporated, concentrated, powdered, dried or dessicated, to which has been added, or which has been blended or compounded with, any fat or oil other than milk fat, so that the resulting product is in imitation . . . of milk, cream, or skimmed milk, . . ." This definition shall not include any distinctive proprietary food compound not readily mistaken for milk or cream or for evaporated, condensed, or powdered milk or cream where such compound (1) is prepared and designed for feeding infants and young children and customarily used on the order of a physician; (2) is packed in individual cans containing not more than sixteen and one-half ounces and bearing a label in bold type that the content is to be used only for said purpose; (3) is shipped in interstate or foreign commerce exclusively to physicians, wholesale and retail druggists, orphan asylums, child welfare associations, hospitals, and similar institutions, and generally disposed of by them."[220] The law declares filled milk to be an adulterated article of food, injurious to the public health. Its sale constitutes a fraud upon the public and its sale or shipment in interstate commerce is unlawful.[221] However, the United States Supreme Court, in U. S. v. Carolene Products Co.[222] stated that the statutory characterization of filled milk as injurious to health and as a fraud upon the public is not to be considered as more than a declaration of the legislative findings deemed to support and justify the action taken as a constitutional exertion of the legislative power, and not as precluding proof to the contrary.

Imitation or adulterated butter or cheese. This law provides that "All articles known as oleomargarine, butterine, imitation, process, renovated, or adulterated butter, or imitation cheese, or any substance in the resemblance of butter or cheese not the usual product of the dairy and not made exclusively of pure and unadulterated milk or cream, transported into any State or Territory or the District of Columbia, and remaining therein for use, consumption, sale, or storage therein, shall, upon the arrival within the limits of such State or Territory or the District of Columbia, be subject to the operation and effect of the laws of such State or Territory or the District of Columbia, enacted in the exercise of its police powers to the same extent and in the same manner as though such articles or substances had been produced in such State or Territory or the District of Columbia, and shall not be exempt therefrom by reason of being introduced therein in original packages or otherwise."[223] Its purpose is to give full effect to state laws on the same subject, and remove the objection that such state laws may interfere with interstate commerce.

Dairy products for export. This law gives the Secretary of Agriculture the same inspection and regulatory authority with respect to dairy products intended for export to a foreign country, as he has with respect to live cattle and meat.[224]

The import milk act. The purpose of this law is to empower the Secretary of Agriculture to deny entry to milk or cream unfit for importation into the United States. It provides that "Milk or cream shall be considered unfit for importation (1) when all cows producing such milk or cream are not healthy and a physical examination of all such cows has not been made within one year previous to such milk being offered for importation; (2) when such milk or cream, if raw, is not produced from cows which have passed a tuberculin test applied by a duly authorized official veterinarian of the United States, or of the country in which such milk or cream is produced, within one year previous to the time of importation, showing that such cows are free from tuberculosis; (3) when the sanitary conditions of the dairy farm or plant in which such milk or cream is produced or handled do not score at least fifty points out of one hundred points according to the methods for scoring as provided by the score cards used by the Bureau of Dairy Industry of the United States Department of Agriculture at the time such dairy farms or plants are scored; (4) in the case of raw milk if the number of bacteria per cubic centimeter exceeds three hundred thousand and in the case of raw cream seven hundred and fifty thousand, in the case of pasteurized milk if the number of bacteria per cubic centimeter exceeds one hundred thousand, and in the case of pasteurized cream five hundred thousand; (5) when the temperature of milk or cream at the time of importation exceeds fifty degrees Fahrenheit."[225]

Quite apart from the regulatory program enforced by the Department of Agriculture, the federal government, mainly through the United States Public Health Service, has been instrumental in improving the conditions under which milk is produced and sold. Of special note is the widespread adoption of local milk ordinances, many of which are based on a standard recommended by the Service.

At the state level there is a multiplicity of laws dealing with the sanitary aspects of milk production, sale and distribution. Probably the most universal and earliest laws are provisions in the criminal code making it a misdemeanor to adulterate or "water" milk or to offer for sale milk unfit for human consumption. Frequently there are legislative determinations of "unfit for human consumption"—the Illinois law, for example, which declares that milk from a cow fed on distillery waste, or from a cow that is diseased, is unwholesome and unfit for human consumption.[226] Following is a brief summary of state milk laws which seem to have been rather generally adopted.

Grade A milk laws. These prescribe the conditions under which milk and milk products can be produced and sold as "Grade A," or as unpasteurized milk. Authority is granted to inspect dairy farms and prescribe standards.

Dairy plant licensing and inspection laws empower an agency of the state to inspect, prescribe standards for, and license dairy plants.

Pasteurization laws prescribe acceptable pasteurization processes. These are generally quite detailed. Most of them permit alternative methods of pasteurization.

Laws prohibiting the sale of unclean and unhealthful milk or cream by the producer, and prohibiting the use of unclean or unsanitary containers.

Laws prohibiting the manufacture of articles of food from unclean or impure milk or cream.

Marks and brand laws to prevent fraud and imitation.

Container laws specifying what is acceptable, requiring that containers be sanitary and that they come within the prescribed tolerance of holding the quantity of fluid they are supposed to hold.

Milk or cream testing laws prescribing the tests which may be used and the qualifications of testers. Licensing may be required.

Oleomargarine laws.

Skim milk laws requiring the proper identification of skim milk when offered for sale.

Laws establishing standards of purity and strength for dairy products.

Dry milk products laws.

There are many other state laws on milk, but they deal with marketing, trade practices, advertising and certain economic phases of production and sale.

Local laws on milk are mainly in the form of milk ordinances, and are generally those of a municipality, though counties and townships do have some public health authority. Also, in many states the public health district has come to be an important agency in the enforcement of milk ordinances.

88. **State Feed Laws.** Legislation on commercial feeding stuffs has two aims; to require labeling of a kind which will enable the buyer to determine its composition, and to require a statement of net weight of contents. A typical provision on labeling requires that the tag or other label shall certify the minimum per cent of crude protein, the minimum percent of crude fat, and the maximum percent of crude fibre. Reference may be made to the methods adopted by the Association of Official Agricultural Chemists of the United States for determining these percentages. Whole grains, unmixed meals, hay, hulls, stalks and straw are excluded from the definition of feeding stuffs. A statement of mineral content may be required, together with the specific name of each ingredient used. State Departments of Agriculture are required to take samples, make tests and take action against any feed manufacturer who is not complying with the law. Penalties for violation are customarily provided.

89. **Liability in the Sale of Foods and Feed.** There are two general principles or theories of law under which persons may be held liable to others for sickness or injury caused by food or feed. One theory, that of implied warranty, operates to make any seller of food or feed liable to a purchaser, regardless of knowl-

edge or fault on the part of the seller. The other theory involves negligence and permits an injured person to sue the manufacturer or any other party through whose fault the food or feed became deleterious.

An implied warranty of fitness for consumption accompanies any food or feed sold to members of the public, and if it turns out to be unfit, the right for breach of warranty is more or less automatic. For example, where a grain dealer sold decayed and adulterated bran to a purchaser who did not examine it, and the purchaser's horse died and his mule became sick when it was fed to them, a recovery for damages was allowed.[227] And in Chapman v. Roggenkamp,[228] a retail dealer was held liable on implied warranty for illness and suffering of the purchaser of peas which caused ptomaine poisoning. In Gray v. Pet Milk Co.[229] the company was held liable where through its alleged negligence a mouse was sealed in a can of condensed milk and subsequently caused illness in the plaintiff. Recovery was on the theory of negligence or fault. There must be adequate proof, however, to sustain a finding of negligence. In Wiehardt v. Kreg Packing Co.,[230] the court held that a purchaser of meat seeking recovery from the manufacturer has the burden of proving the diseased state of the meat and lack of due care on the part of the manufacturer. Also, the person claiming injury may not be able to recover from the manufacturer if he was himself at fault. This same principle holds in suits against retailers based on breach of warranty, and recovery can be had only if the purchaser can show that he exercised due care for his own health.[231] For example, if one detected a doubtful condition in food, and ate it anyway, he would probably be barred from recovery. It is possible, of course, for both the manufacturer and the retailer to be held liable on grounds of negligence.[232]

The principles of common law liability—particularly liability for breach of warranty—may be altered by statute. For example, if a statute prohibits the sale of food preservatives containing boric acid or sodium sulphite, a purchaser could claim breach of warranty if he purchased a preservative containing such.[233]

90. **Chemicals and Antibiotics in Feed.** It may fairly be said that the addition of chemicals and antibiotics has created a whole new legal area in the realm of feed and food law. Among

the problems presented are safety of the consumer, safety to the animals themselves, and the threat of economic loss or the hope of economic gain in the producers. Speaking to the American National Cattlemen's Association Convention in January, 1963, George P. Larrick, Commissioner of Food and Drugs, said:

As the environment changed, problems upon problems became evident and the scientists throughout the country have performed outstanding services in the solution of these problems. It is not at all uncomplimentary to add, however, that in many cases the solution to one problem often presented a new difficulty which in turn had to be resolved.

With all these changes and developments it has been essential that laws dealing with our food and drug supply had to keep pace. The Federal Food, Drug, and Cosmetic Act of 1938 was hailed as an outstanding law—and it was—but it could not stand still. Particularly over the last decade, we have had a number of real improvements, especially the Pesticide Chemicals Amendment of 1954, the Food Additives Amendment of 1958, the Color Additive Amendments of 1960, and now the Kefauver-Harris Drug Amendments enacted by the last Congress. Fundamentally, all of these amendments play their part in providing ground rules whereby, in our present environment, there can be not only an assurance of the safety of our food and drug supply, but perhaps equally important, an assurance that there will be public acceptance of the food and drug products produced.

Much has been said and written about the evils of additives; whether they involve pesticide chemicals on crops or our food-producing animals, or the so-called food additives including drug items which are deliberately added to animal feed and human foods. There is no question but that most of the substances in these categories cannot properly be used indiscriminately, but to us it is a mistake to try to categorize these as "good" or "bad" on a group basis. Instead, we think that each individual product and proposed usage must be evaluated on its own merits or lack of them.

Why is it not sound to devote the utmost intelligence to any determination of using or not using a pesticide or another type of additive in a particular situation? Then, when we have done this and the answer is in the affirmative, we should be sure there are enough safeguards in the particular operation to insure safety. Of course, when we do this in matters involving your industry we evaluate, in close cooperation with our colleagues in the U. S. Department of Agriculture, not only safety as far as the animals are concerned, but also the safety of the edible products of those animals. We are convinced that we can do this, but in any such operation we must be ever alert to avoid operating in a vacuum, considering additive after additive without regard to the entire problem.

We should also recall that in both the food additive and pesticide field the evidence has in many instances disclosed that safety can be assured only if there is a withdrawal period before slaughter. In those cases our regulations and other authorizations for using the additives, including the pesticide labels registered by U.S.D.A., clearly specify such withdrawal periods. I cannot emphasize too strongly the need for complying precisely with the instructions which you will find on the labels of the additives and pesticides. While we can invoke the sanctions of the law by seizure, criminal action or injunction against the careless or deliberate violator, it should be obvious that this will not work if there is widespread disregard of the rules. Where such occurs, we will, in our judgment, have no alternative but to withdraw the original authorization.

It is obvious that the use of chemicals and antibiotics imposes duties on several people. It imposes a duty on the drug companies to make thorough tests and checks and be certain of the product before it is released, it imposes a duty on the Food and Drug Administration to see that such tests are made, and to exercize such surveillance as is necessary to assure the safety of the drug. It is the duty of the veterinarian to inform his clients about how the feed may be used. It is the duty of the feed company to abide by the rules which have to do with mixing, labeling, and advertising. It is the duty of the owner to abide by any regulations which require a cessation in feeding the substance before the animals are offered for sale or slaughter.

CHAPTER 13

NARCOTICS, DRUGS, MEDICINES, BIOLOGICS AND SERUMS

91. Professional Use of Narcotic Drugs. Both the federal government and the individual states have laws regulating the manufacture, production, compounding, sale, dealing in and dispensing of narcotics. Included in the list of persons privileged to use and dispense such drugs are veterinarians. The federal law of greatest importance is the Harrison Act.[234] A summary of its provisions follows:

1. Veterinary surgeons are lawfully entitled to distribute, dispense, give away, or administer to patients; but on or before July 1 of each year, they must pay a tax of $1.00 and register with the Secretary of the Treasury or his delegate.

2. Employees of registered veterinarians are not required to register, so long as they are acting solely in the course of employment. (Also exempt are governmental officials who have possession of such drugs by reason of their official duties.)

3. A duly qualified veterinarian is not required to pay an additional tax on account of the sale of narcotics for legitimate medical purposes to his bona fide patients; but if he operates a drug store and sells narcotics pursuant to prescriptions written by other practitioners, he incurs additional liability as a retail dealer.

4. A veterinary surgeon may distribute, dispense, give away, administer, or prescribe narcotics in any revenue district where he is lawfully engaged in practice, if he is duly registered with the director of the district in which his office is located, and if his complete stock of narcotics and all narcotic records are kept at his office location.

5. A partnership is subject to the same tax liability as an individual.

6. Hospitals, colleges, medical and dental clinics, sanatoriums, and other institutions not exempt as public institutions

are subject to the same tax as other persons similarly dealing in or handling narcotic drugs or preparations.

7. Nurses are considered agents of the veterinary surgeon or institution under whose supervision or direction they act; they are not permitted to register, nor to have narcotics in their possession except as such agents.

8. Narcotics must be ordered in writing, on a form issued for the purpose. The order must be prepared in duplicate, and preserved for two years, readily accessible to inspection. The Director of Internal Revenue may require any registrant to furnish "a true and correct statement or return, verified by affidavit, setting forth the quantity of drugs received by him in his internal revenue district immediately preceding the demand of the collector, not exceeding three months, as the said collector may fix and determine; the names of the persons from whom the said drugs were received; the quantity in each instance received from each of such persons, and the date when received."

Further information on compliance with federal narcotics laws is contained in a rather comprehensive publication of the Bureau of Narcotics known as *Regulation No. 5.*

Additional regulations and detailed instructions are issued from time to time by the Bureau.

The federal law defines "limited narcotic content" and provides that such preparations shall not be subject to the general provisions of the law regarding drugs and narcotics.

Many states have now adopted the provisions of the "Uniform Narcotic Drug Act," thus integrating the state laws and regulations with those of the federal government.

92. **Sales of Drugs and Medicines by Veterinarians.** Many people are concerned about complaints of the indiscriminate sale of veterinary products, antibiotics, biological products, hypodermic needles and like items to lay persons. The laws of all states provide that veterinarians may use and sell such items, and sometimes there are very few safeguards with respect to the kind of distribution a veterinarian can make. The purpose, of course, is to enable him to prescribe and dispense drugs and other medicines and products for the purpose of curing animals. However, the evidence shows that there is a considerable carry-over into the human disease field. This can obviously become unsafe because in the first place the products are not always

designed for human beings and in the second place the veterinarian may not have the knowledge essential to make proper prescription. At any rate, under the laws of most states he would be violating the practice acts in prescribing for other than the kinds of patients he is licensed to treat. The American Veterinary Medical Association has been concerned about this problem and has been attempting to formulate policies under which there can be a general tightening of controls in this regard.

Though the client has some protection under the theory of implied warranty, through statutes and regulations which have been adopted by both federal and state governments, and through his right to sue for negligence on the part of the veterinarian, he is nevertheless left partially vulnerable as long as veterinarians are able to procure and sell these products for human use. Among the suggestions has been a model or uniform state law spelling out the needed control. The Food and Drug Administration and the United States Department of Agriculture bear a heavy responsibility in developing a regulatory program which on the one hand is reasonable and does not impede the use by the livestock industry and by veterinarians of needed products, but which on the other hand does protect both the livestock producer and the consumer.

It would appear that under both federal and state law a veterinarian is subject to criminal prosecution if he knowingly sells adulterated drugs or medicines.

Apparently no distinction is drawn between sales of food and other articles of personal property in the application of rules giving rise to an implied warranty of quality or fitness of goods sold for particular purposes.[235] Furthermore, it has been held that

> The rule of caveat emptor is not applicable to a sale of drugs by either a retail or manufacturing druggist. Thus a druggist undertaking to sell a certain drug to a customer impliedly warrants the good quality of the drug sold, that the article sold and delivered is of the kind he contracted to sell, and if the sale is on a prescription, that he used due and proper care, and that the proper medicines, and none other, were used in mixing and compounding it.[236]

These rules of implied warranty undoubtedly apply to a veterinarian dispensing drugs to his patients.

93. **Viruses and Serums.** The federal government has long pursued the policy of regulating as closely as possible the manu-

facture, distribution and use of serums, viruses, toxins and similar products. A summary of these laws follows:

Inspection of imports. The Secretary of Agriculture is authorized to cause the Bureau of Animal Industry to examine and inspect all viruses, serums, toxins, and analogous products, for use in the treatment of domestic animals, which are being imported or offered for importation into the United States, to determine whether such viruses, serums, toxins and analogous products are worthless, contaminated, dangerous, or harmful, and if it shall appear that any such virus, serum, toxin, or analogous product, for use in the treatment of domestic animals, is worthless, contaminated, dangerous, or harmful, the same shall be denied entry and shall be destroyed or returned at the expense of the owner or importer.[237]

Interstate and foreign trade. No person shall sell, barter, or exchange, or offer for sale, barter, or exchange in the District of Columbia, or send, carry, or bring for sale, barter, or exchange from any State or possession into any other State or possession or into any foreign country, or from any foreign country into any State or possession, any virus, therapeutic serum, toxin, antitoxin, or analogous product, or arsphenomine or its derivatives (or any other trivalent organic arsenic compound), applicable to the prevention, treatment, or cure of diseases or injuries of man, unless (1) such virus, serum, toxin, antitoxin, or other product has been propagated or manufactured and prepared at an establishment holding an unsuspended and unrevoked license, issued by the Secretary as hereinafter authorized, to propagate or manufacture, and prepare such virus, serum, toxin, antitoxin, or other product for sale in the District of Columbia, or for sending, bringing, or carrying from place to place aforesaid; and (2) each package . . . is plainly marked with the proper name of the article contained therein, the name, address, and license number of the manufacturer, and the date beyond which the contents cannot be expected beyond reasonable doubt to yield their specific results . . .

This same law also provides that

No person shall falsely label or mark any package or container of any virus, serum, toxin, antitoxin, or other product aforesaid; nor alter any label or mark on any package or container of any virus, serum, toxin, antitoxin, or other product aforesaid so as to falsify such label or mark.[238]

Regulation. The Secretary of Agriculture is authorized to make . . . such rules and regulations as may be necessary to prevent the preparation, sale, barter, exchange, or shipment . . . of any worthless, contaminated, dangerous, or harmful virus, serum, toxin, or analogous product for use in the treatment of domestic animals, and to issue, suspend, and revoke licenses for the maintenance of establishments for the preparation of viruses, serums, toxins, and analogous products, for use in the treatment of domestic animals . . .[239]

Permits and licenses. The Secretary of Agriculture is authorized to issue permits for the importation into the United States of viruses, serums, toxins, and analogous products, for use in the treatment of domestic animals, which are not worthless, contaminated, dangerous, or harmful.[240]

All licenses issued under authority of this chapter to establishments where such viruses, serums, toxins, or analogous products are prepared . . . , shall be issued on condition that the licensee shall permit the inspection of such establishments and of such products and their preparation; and the Secretary of Agriculture may suspend or revoke any permit or license issued under authority of said chapter, after opportunity for hearing has been granted the licensee or importer; when the Secretary of Agriculture is satisfied that such license or permit is being used to facilitate or effect the preparation, sale, barter, exchange, or shipment, as aforesaid, or the importation into the United States of any worthless, contaminated, dangerous, or harmful virus, serum, toxin, or analogous product for use in the treatment of domestic animals.[241]

Hog cholera. It is declared to be the policy of Congress to insure the maintenance of an adequate supply of anti-hog-cholera serum and hog-cholera virus by regulating the marketing of such serum and virus in interstate and foreign commerce and to prevent undue and excessive fluctuations and unfair methods of competition and unfair trade practices in such marketing. . . . The Secretary of Agriculture shall have the power, after due notice and opportunity for hearing, to enter into marketing agreements with manufacturers and others engaged in handling of anti-hog-cholera serum and hog-cholera virus only with respect to such handling as is in the current of interstate or foreign commerce or which directly burdens, obstructs, or affects interstate or foreign commerce . . . The making of such an agreement shall not be held to be in violation of any of the antitrust laws of the United States, and any such agreement shall be deemed lawful.[242]

In an interesting case involving the Associated Serum Producers, it was held that a restriction of sales to licensed veterinarians was not a violation of the Sherman Anti-trust Act.[243] However, a Nebraska law,[244] which provided that

No person, firm or corporation shall sell, barter, exchange, carry, give away, ship or deliver for shipment any anti-hog-cholera serum or virus within the state of Nebraska unless such person, firm or corporation shall first hold an uncancelled, unexpired United States government veterinary license, issued by the United States Department of Agriculture, and a permit from the Live Stock Sanitary Board

was held to be an attempted restriction on the power of the citizen to buy and sell anti-hog-cholera serum, and thus unconstitutional, for the reason that any person has the right to adopt and follow any lawful industrial pursuit, which is not injurious to the community.[245]

In an Iowa case, the court held that a statute giving the state department of agriculture control of tuberculin, and providing that it shall formulate rules for its distribution and control, and that only licensed veterinarians shall apply tuberculin tests to cattle, does not create an unlawful monopoly, but is within the police power. The court also held that it is not arbitrary to provide that only those possessed of requisite skill and knowledge shall be permitted to practice.[246] In another Nebraska case, the court held that in the exercise of its police power the State may create agencies and provide means for scientific research on behalf of the public in an effort to aid in the production and preservation of food, and to that end may make experiments and manufacture and distribute remedies for the purpose of eradicating diseases among domestic animals.[247]

It has been held that the manufacturer and seller of anti-hog-cholera serum is not precluded from recovering the value of such serum because he gratuitously administered it to the plaintiff's hogs, merely because he was not an authorized veterinarian under the statute, the statute expressly exempting from its application those persons "who gratuitously treat diseased animals."[248]

94. Nonmailable Materials. It is the policy of the federal government to prevent the use of the mails for materials which might injure the mail, persons or property. Following is the pertinent federal law:

All kinds of poison, and all articles and compositions containing poison, and all poisonous animals, insects, and reptiles, and explosives, inflammable materials, infernal machines, and mechanical, chemical, or other devices or compositions which may ignite or explode, and all disease germs or scabs, and all other natural or artificial articles, compositions, or material, which may kill or injure another, or injure the mails or other property, whether or not sealed as first-class matter, are nonmailable matter and shall not be conveyed in the mails or delivered from any post office or station thereof, nor by any letter carrier.

The Postmaster General is authorized and directed to permit the transmission in the mails, under regulations to be prescribed by him, of live scorpions which are to be used for purposes of medical research or for the manufacture of anti-venin . . .

The transmission in the mails of poisonous drugs and medicines may be limited by the Postmaster General to shipments of such articles from the manufacturer thereof or dealer therein to licensed physicians, surgeons, dentists, pharmacists, drug-gists, cosmetologists, barbers, and veterinarians, under such rules and regulations as he shall prescribe.[249]

95. Stock Remedies. Most of the states do not have a special stock remedies law, but all of them do have some laws on the subject. These are generally included in the state pure food act and in other laws on drugs and narcotics. Most of the laws in this category concern human remedies rather than livestock remedies, though many of the basic principles are the same. In some foreign jurisdictions comprehensive stock or pest remedies laws have been passed. South Africa, for example, has had such a law since 1925.[250] One authority asserts that:

> The states may control the sale and use of livestock remedies under the police power. Some states recognize however that abuses may arise in administration and specifically restrict the administrative official from issuing regulations unless definitely permitted. . . . These officers and commissions must not make regulations which are unreasonable or unjustly discriminatory. . . . The United States Supreme Court permits States to legis-late in fields not covered by Congressional acts so long as they do not enact laws in conflict with federal laws. . . . The United States Supreme Court has opened the way for the Congress to regulate the manufacture, sale, and use of livestock remedies by reaffirming the power of the Federal Government to regulate interstate commerce.[251]

Another authority states that

> The Administration (federal) has not adopted the policy of restricting over the counter sales of veterinary medicinal prepara-tions to the same extent as for medicinal preparations for human use. The propriety of such sales, however, depends entirely on whether or not adequate directions can be prepared to enable livestock and poultry raisers to treat their own animals safely and intelligently with the drug purchased. Therefore, the labeling of potent drugs for veterinary use should bear a forthright statement to the effect that the safe and efficacious use of such products as directed depends on an adequate diag-nosis obtained from a qualified diagnostic laboratory or prac-ticing veterinarian . . . With the exception of Section 502 (d) of the Federal Food, Drug, and Cosmetic Act, which deals with habit forming drugs, all provisions of the Act dealing with adulterated or misbranded drugs and devices are applicable to veterinary medicinal preparations and devices. Likewise, all food provisons of the Act are applicable to foods for animal feed-ing.[252]

"Domestic remedies," as defined in a state pharmacy act, which provided that nothing contained therein should in any manner interfere with the sale of "domestic remedies by retail dealers," are not confined to harmless concoctions of teas and herbs, which those unlearned in medical and scientific lore can prepare at home, but may include a drug, although prepared by skilled chemists and scientific apparatus, which has come into such common use and is so well understood in its effects, by people without medical knowledge as to make it a domestic remedy.[253]

Though a person may recover damages for the negligent sale by a druggist of extract of belladonna, a dangerous and deadly poison, in the place of extract of dandelion, a mild and harmless medicine,[254] the failure of a druggist to place labels upon drugs sold, as required by statute, would not relieve a customer from exercising reasonable care on his part in using the drugs.[255]

In summary, it is fair to say that legislation to control the sale of stock remedies is not very effective; that it should be more effective; and that uniform state legislation to supplement appropriate federal legislation is the logical answer.

CHAPTER 14

LIVESTOCK AND FENCE LAWS

96. **Livestock as Property.** An animal has been defined as any living thing besides man, endowed generally, though not necessarily, with the power of self-locomotion. Due to certain characteristics of farm animals, a large body of "livestock" law has developed. This has to do with trespass, fences, grazing, branding, marketing, diseases, injuries to persons, and many other problems.

Livestock laws differ from state to state in the United States, owing largely to variations in the predominance of different kinds of livestock and to the manner in which they are handled. In the western range country, laws on grazing and brands are important, whereas in the corn belt, laws on fences and animal trespass become important.

According to the common law, dogs and cats were never considered property. Therefore, the usual rights in case of theft and injury by others did not exist in owners of cats and dogs. This rule is no longer recognized. Captured wild animals are subject to property rights only so long as they are retained in confinement or are pursued and kept within the possibility of recapture. There is a theory that if a wild animal shows a will to return, or an *animus revertendi,* it can be retaken as the property of the owner.

One famous old case held that a fox hunter who, with his hounds, had practically overtaken the fox had no right against an interloper who happened along, shot the fox, and carried it away. The court said the hunter had never had the fox under his control, consequently, it had never been his property.

Killing or mortally wounding, along with taming, confining, and domesticating, have generally been held sufficient acts to create property interest in wild animals.

All the useful domesticated farm animals are regarded as property and can be recovered wherever found, subject to laws on estrays and animals at large.

97. Liability for Injury to Persons. In his book, "The Common Law," Justice Holmes says in effect that if a man keeps a ferocious animal, he is bound to know at his peril that the object is a continual threat to his neighbors. Unless a person injured by such an animal is himself negligent, the owner can be held liable for injuries caused. It has been held, however, that if one torments a bear until the latter accomplishes revenge, there can be no recovery from the owner of the bear.

The strict rule of liability applicable in the case of wild animals does not hold in the case of domestic animals. An owner of domestic animals may be held liable for personal injuries caused by them in two general situations:

a. When he negligently allows or causes them to commit the injury.

b. When he is aware that an animal owned by him is vicious, and when such an animal bites, strikes, kicks, or gores someone who was not acting negligently.

When hunters or other persons come on farm property without the consent of the owner, they are classed as trespassers and cannot be heard to complain if they are injured by the owner's animals. He owes such persons no duty other than not willfully to injure them. But if a hunter asks for permission to hunt and it is granted, and the owner fails to warn him of a bull or some other animal of a vicious nature, liability for injury may result. Also, under certain circumstances, the law views trespass by children in a different light. If, for example, an owner knows that youngsters from a nearby school or village, or even from a neighboring farm, are in the habit of playing in his pasture, and he keeps a mean animal in the pasture, he may very well be liable for injuries which result. On the other hand, adults who have a right to be on the farm, but who know of the vicious nature of the animal (a hired man or a neighbor, for example) may not be allowed to recover if they are injured.

98. Transportation of Livestock. Public carriers (railroads, trucks, trucking companies, steamship lines) are charged with certain duties in the transportation of livestock. They must see that the animals receive adequate feed and water on long hauls, and that reasonable precautions have been taken against physical injury, suffocation, and similar mishaps. Under the federal "28 hour law," animals moving in interstate commerce must be unloaded, and fed and watered every 28 hours unless such can be done without unloading. Many states have similar laws, some of which permit carriage for a longer period without unloading. The courts say public carriers must exercise "due diligence" to prevent delay. Since they are a semipublic agency, they cannot, under ordinary circumstances, refuse to carry livestock.

Carriers are not insurers, however; they cannot be held liable for damage caused by peculiar propensities of the animals carried (vicious horse, mean bull), nor are they liable for damage caused by acts of God (flood, lightning, earthquake). Rates of carriage in interstate shipment are determined by federal regulations and must not be discriminatory. State law regulates contracts of carriage within the state.

Regardless of the nature of the carrier—whether a railroad or a private trucker—certain duties are owed the shipper. It would be a breach of duty to overload animals and cause loss of injury, to mix animals so that injury is likely to result (lambs and hogs, for example), to use bedding which may be injurious (cinders, for example), to use cars or trucks with weak or broken flooring or siding, or to be careless or cruel in handling the animals. It is customary for carriers to insure animals consigned to them. Some states require such insurance.

99. **Joint Ownership of Animals.** There are many possible arrangements under which two or more persons share the ownership of livestock. The most usual is a livestock share lease under which the tenant and landlord have an undivided interest. Sometimes fathers and sons have such arrangements. Also, it is possible for a man with capital to buy livestock and place it on another's land under an agreement which creates an undivided ownership in the animals. Where animals are jointly owned, certain problems are created. Who has authority to sell and buy? Who determines when to sell? Who is responsible for feeding, care and management? Who has authority to subject the animals to a chattel mortgage? Though the answers may be spelled out in the lease or other agreement, such an agreement is not necessarily binding on innocent third parties. As a matter of law, one joint owner may be regarded as the agent of the others, capable of binding all of them, at least to any agreement which it would be reasonable to make in the course of the business. As a matter of caution, those who buy or sell or make chattel mortgage loans

on livestock should determine if a joint ownership is involved
and then take such steps as are necessary to protect themselves—
securing the signature of the other joint owners, for example,
or getting a livestock share tenant and landlord to both sign a
chattel mortgage or an agreement to divide the property in case
of necessity.

100. Trespass by Animals. The courts have repeatedly held
that an owner of animals has a duty to keep them fenced in to
avoid trespass: Other landowners have no duty to fence them out.
So, if one does not properly confine his animals, he can be held liable for the damage they cause another, regardless of whether the
injured party has his own property fenced. Exceptions to this
rule occur in some of the western states where the "open range"
principle is recognized. In those states there is no duty on the
part of a livestock owner to fence his animals in, though he may,
nevertheless, be held liable for negligent range handling resulting
in injury to others.

If animals driven along a road get out of control and enter
adjoining fields, their owner can be held liable, even though the
road is not fenced. The courts have said that "animals" includes
"poultry" and that there is a duty on the poultry owner to confine
them so they will not trespass. Dogs and cats are in a different
category so far as trespass laws are concerned, though by municipal, county, or township ordinance one may, under certain
conditions, be required to confine them. But dog and cat owners
may, nevertheless, be held liable for actual damages caused by
their pets, though technically there is no trespass.

When animals wrongfully enter the property of another,
their owner can generally be held liable for the damages which
may reasonably be expected to result. Crop injury, injury to
persons, injury to other livestock, injury to property, spreading
disease and service of female animals by trespassing male animals
are the most frequent types of damages. The courts have allowed
recovery for all of these, the amount being based on the best
evidence of actual loss—impairment of crop yield, difference in
value of progeny, value of an animal killed or injured, for example. With respect to liability for the spread of disease, there is
good authority for the proposition that the owner of the trespassing animals is not liable for such damage unless he knew or
had reason to believe that his animals were afflicted with a com-

municable disease. However, if animals are permitted to run at large, an owner may be held liable for the transmission of disease, regardless of knowledge.[256] As in all injury cases, negligence or fault on the part of the injured party (commonly called "contributory negligence") may prevent recovery, or at least reduce the amount of the damages. Also, when an owner is himself completely free of negligence or fault, he may not be held liable. If, for example, a highway commissioner wrongfully tears out an owner's fence or a storm blows it down, the owner of the animals could not be held liable unless he failed to make "immediate pursuit" after discovering the breach in his fence.

When animals escape through a division fence, their owner may not be held liable if they escape through the adjoining owner's portion of the fence and the facts show that such portion of the fence is not in good repair. It has been held, however, that if an owner turns his animals out knowing that his neighbor's portion of the fence will not restrain them, he may be held liable for their trespass. The court's reasoning was based on the fact that the owner of the animals has a statutory right to make the adjoining owner repair the fence or pay for having it done. This was the remedy he should have used.

Those who take care of animals for others ("agisters" or stablekeepers, for example) are liable for trespass as though they were the owner, and the actual owner of the animals is not liable. However, if an owner fails to tell the agister about a particularly breachy animal, he may be held liable not only by the injured party, but also by the agister. As a general rule, landlords are not liable for the trespass of the tenant's livestock. However, a livestock-share landlord might be held liable if the arrangement creates a legal partnership and thus makes the tenant an agent of the landlord. This is a fairly remote possibility. However, under the principle that an employer is liable for the acts of his employees while engaged in the employer's work, a livestock owner may be held liable for trespass resulting from the negligence of a hired man.

State laws quite generally provide that the owner of land on which animals are trespassing may do anything reasonably necessary to terminate the trespass. He may drive them back into their own fields or call their owner and ask him to do so. Necessary force may be used to drive the animals, and if injury results from the application of such an amount of force, the owner of the animal cannot complain. However, the law does not tolerate greater force than is needed, so if hogs are beaten with clubs and their backs or legs are broken, the owner of the hogs may have a right of recovery against the person on whose land they were trespassing.

An additional right accorded by most state laws is that permitting the confinement, watering, feeding, and caring for trespassing animals until the owner comes and takes them, making good any damage suffered. Generally a landowner is not privileged to do this unless he himself is free from fault or negligence. The "taker-up" must notify the owner immediately and give him an opportunity to come after his animals. The cost of feed and care during the confinement must be paid by the owner.

Estrays (domestic animals of unknown ownership running at large—except dogs, cats, or poultry) may be confined and cared for by an injured party. A reasonable attempt must then be made to locate the owner. Some laws specify a public posting and the giving of notice in local papers. If the owner comes for the animals, he must satisfy the claims of the taker-up for feed, housing, care, and any other costs involved. If the owner does not claim his animals, they become the property of the taker-up. Some state laws provide for sale, reimbursement of the taker-up, and transfer of the balance to county funds. One taking up estrays is entitled to make a reasonable use of the animal while in his custody—if it is a horse, he may work it, or if a cow in lactation, he may milk it.

Estrays may be impounded by local (generally township) authorities when state law so provides. In this case, the animals are sold at public auction on failure of the owner to appear and claim them.

101. **Fence Laws.** A fence has been defined legally as "an enclosing structure of wood, iron, or other material, intended to prevent intrusion from without or straying from within." Early in the history of agriculture, conflicts arose between grain and livestock farmers over the right of the latter to permit unrestrained grazing. In localities where grain farming predominates, land owners have been successful in securing legislation prohibiting unrestrained grazing and requiring the owners of livestock to keep the stock fenced in. In some of the western states where

grazing is more important than grain farming, the opposite rule exists and the owner of livestock is not required to fence in his animals. This latter rule existed in some of the corn belt states for a time during the middle of the nineteenth century, and was contrary to the earlier common law. Many statutes requiring fencing are simply reversions to the old common-law rule.

In the absence of statutes fixing the responsibility of adjoining owners for the building and maintenance of division fences, each owner is required to fence his own land. This is the old rule established by common law and custom. State legislatures realized that this was not satisfactory, however, for when parties could not agree to use one fence, two fences would be built alongside each other. This not only doubled the cost of fencing and upkeep, but made useless the strip of land between.

The law of one midwestern state provides that "when two or more persons shall have lands adjoining, each of them shall make and maintain a just proportion of the division fence between them. . . ." Owners ordinarily assume the responsibility for a designated one-half of the fence, usually the half on their right as they face the division line when standing on their own property. When owners cannot agree on the proportion of fence which should be maintained by each, the township fence viewers can mark and define the proportion to be built or maintained by each. Frequently town assessors and commissioners of highways are ex officio fence viewers except in counties not under township organization, in which case fence viewers may be appointed by the county board or otherwise designated.

The same law mentioned above provides further that when a person who has let his land lie open (unused for agricultural purposes) afterward encloses it upon the enclosure of another, he shall contribute to the latter a just proportion of the value of the fence as it stands. If the parties cannot agree on the value of the fence or the share which each owner should bear, they may call in the fence viewers, or the aggrieved party may bring an action before a justice of the peace.

In interpreting this section, the courts have said that an adjoining landowner is bound to maintain his share of the partition fence, and that he cannot escape this duty unless he chooses to let his lands lie without cropping or use for farm purposes. An action may be taken, under the provision of this act, to compel the building of a fence by one obligated to share in a division fence. Similarly, one who lets his part of a division fence fall into disrepair may be compelled to repair it. When repair is urgent, the other owner may give written notice that repairs are necessary and after that do the work himself. He is then entitled to recover from the adjoining owner the expense of repairing and other costs incurred.

No one has a right to remove his portion of a division fence unless he gives notice of his intentions to the adjoining owner, and after the removal of the fence allows his land to lie open. In such cases, the adjoining owner may be able to buy out the other's interest in the fence.

In some states the legislatures have provided that the residents in a locality may, through the medium of a fence district, determine the legality of fences and the areas that must be fenced. Districts are organized according to procedure established by law, and generally correspond to the boundaries of townships, counties, or other local political subdivisions. The officers of such districts are empowered to enact regulations providing that certain lands may lie open and unfenced and that other lands on which livestock is kept must be fenced. District officers may also settle certain types of fence problems arising within the district, and exercise such other powers as are given to them by state law.

The condition of fences on an owner's land, and also on the land subject to animal trespass, has an important bearing on liability for damage done by trespassing animals. The predominant views of state courts on various factual situations involving livestock, fences, and disgruntled owners may be expressed as follows:

a. When an owner of livestock maintains good fences (legal fences, if state law defines these), is not aware that his animals are in the habit of breaking out, does no negligent act causing them to break out, and makes an immediate attempt to retake them when they do break out, he is not liable for damage caused by them. However, the courts of some states have held that he is liable, even under these circumstances. This rule makes him an "insurer" and is not as equitable, in the writer's opinion, as the foregoing rule. Also, some states distinguish division fences and other fences, holding that he is an "insurer" as to the latter but not as to the former.

b. When animals break through an adjoining owner's part of a division fence, and such fence is not in good repair or is not legally sufficient, the owner of the animals cannot be held liable for their trespass.

c. An owner of trespassing animals may be held liable:
   (1) When his animals are in the habit of breaking out, regardless of the condition of his fences.
   (2) When his fences are defective or insufficient.
   (3) When negligence causes the trespass (frightening animals until they break out, or leaving a gate open).

Some states have statutes forbidding the use of barbed wire in a division fence, unless the adjoining owner consents. An owner who does not abide by such a law may be held liable for injuries caused to animals of an adjoining owner.[257]

Public officials such as highway or drainage commissioners must give notice to a landowner before fences are impaired. If they fail, they may be held liable by an owner for damages resulting from the escape of animals.[258] Ordinarily, however, highway, drainage, or irrigation commissioners have no duty to fence their own canals, ditches, drains or roads.[259]

102. **Animals on Highways.** Farm animals, particularly calves and hogs, often get out on highways. If a user of the highway runs into a loose animal, is injured, or has his vehicle damaged, he frequently turns to the owner of the animal for compensation. Although it is not possible to predict with accuracy what damages, if any, may be recovered in particular instances, there are certain general rules which apply:

a. If a farmer is negligent in maintaining his fences and his animals escape, he can be held liable for damage resulting to persons using the highway.

b. If a farmer maintains his fences in good repair but has one or more animals which he knows are in the habit of breaking out, he may be held liable for damages caused by such animals.

c. If adequate fences are maintained in good repair and animals not in the habit of breaking out get through the fence and onto a highway, the owner of the animals may be held liable for damages caused if he knew the animals were out and made no reasonable effort to get them back in. The law is not always clear with respect to a farmer's liability when he is not negligent in any way. The better rule would be to exclude liability when there is no negligence.

When animals are being driven across or along a highway, particularly a paved highway, the owner should use the degree of care necessary to keep them under control. Naturally, if animals are being driven at night or if visibility is poor, more care is necessary in order that motorists will be properly warned and the animals kept under control. Also, the amount and nature of the traffic will affect the care that is necessary. When a road is jammed with traffic, it might be negligent to try to drive a herd of cattle across it, no matter how much caution were exercised. When animals are being driven along or on a highway, the basis of a farmer's liability is negligence, and if he is careful, he is much less likely to suffer liability.

In all of the situations listed above, a farmer may use the defense of contributory negligence. In other words, if motorists are themselves at fault, they may be precluded from recovering anything from the farmer. On the contrary, it may be possible for the farmer, if he is not negligent, to recover the value of his animal from a negligent motorist.[260]

Some states give statutory recognition to a livestock owner's right to move animals on a highway. For example, Illinois law provides that "Any person . . . who shall ride or drive faster than a walk, into or through a herd . . ." is guilty of a misdemeanor and may be fined.[261] Stockcrossing signs do not excuse a farmer from using due care in driving his animals on the highway—such signs simply increase to some degree the care which motorists must exercise.

Laws in some states provide that a farmer may, under the supervision of and with varying amounts of financial assistance from highway authorities, construct an underpass for his animals and for general farm use.

103. **Injuries to Animals by Railroads.** By the laws of many states, every railroad company is required to erect and maintain fences on both sides of its road sufficient to prevent cattle, horses, sheep, hogs, or other stock from getting on the tracks. Railroads are also required to maintain at road crossings cattle guards sufficient to prevent cattle, horses, sheep, hogs, and other stock from getting on the railroad. When such fences or cattle guards are not made or not kept in good repair, the railroad corporation

may be liable for all damages which may be done by its agents, engines, or cars to stock on its tracks.[262]

The following facts are important in connection with these laws:

a. They vary by states and if relied upon must be thoroughly understood for the state in question.

b. If the railroad company maintains adequate fences and guards and keeps them in good repair, it is not liable for injury to livestock unless negligently or willfully done.[263]

c. Some courts have interpreted this law as imposing an absolute duty on railroads to maintain adequate fences and guards. The policy of law and of court decisions is expressed in this statement from one case:

The design of the statute was to require and compel railroad companies to fence their tracks so as to prevent animals from getting upon them, thus affording safety and protection to the traveling public as well as to the owners of stock. Reported decisions show a great deal of variation, however, and some points seem to be unsettled.

d. Some laws provide a penalty for the following: Driving livestock down a railroad right-of-way (within its fences) without the consent of the railroad; damaging railroad fences or guards; leaving gates at farm crossings open; leaving horses or other animals standing on farm or road crossings.

e. When a railroad company neglects to build or repair its fences and farm crossing gates, some laws provide that the owner of the land adjoining the railroad may give written notice to the company to build or repair, as the case may be, and if the company fails to comply, the owner may do the work himself and recover all expense.

It has been held that if a railroad or other public corporation negligently causes the death of an animal, the owner may include veterinary fees in the damages recovered.[264] However, an agent of the railroad apparently has no authority to call in a veterinarian[265] or engage someone to care for animals.[266]

A railroad may be liable for "consequential" as well as direct damage to livestock. For example, the Iowa Supreme Court held that the negligence of the defendant in setting a railroad right-of-way fire was the proximate cause of injuries received by one who, having no interest in certain horses, nor employment with reference to them, attempted their rescue from a burning barn, the court saying:

> It is the duty of everyone, according to the requirements of an enlightened and just public sentiment, to use reasonable efforts to preserve the property of others from destruction; and, as is well-known, it is the duty which people generally are quick to discharge. The defendant could have foretold, with almost absolute certainty, when it set the fire in question, that plaintiff, being near, would use every reasonable means in attempting to save Ortman's horses from the flames, and there was nothing surprising or unusual in the attempt he made. Under the circumstances of the case, it was the natural and probable result of the wrong of the defendant.[267]

Interestingly enough, however, a Michigan court held precisely opposite on this same point. It held that where a burning shed, negligently set on fire by the defendant owner, flamed so brightly at night as to awaken plaintiff and her husband, the injuries she received in attempting to rescue the husband's horse from the shed were too remote for recovery, the court saying: "The act in which she was engaged may have been such as she may have thought proper, and laudable, and worth some risk, but defendant's responsibility cannot be created or increased by such independent and voluntary conduct of plaintiff in putting herself in harm's way."[268]

104. **Marks and Brands.** In the range country it is necessary that some means be provided for determining the ownership of animals. The function of a brand law is to provide a method whereby cattle carry with them prima facie proof of ownership.[269] It has been stated that the primary purpose of such a statute is to protect persons in their honest dealings with livestock.[270] The legislatures of all the states in which open grazing is practiced have enacted comprehensive laws relative to the recording and inspection of brands and the transfer of branded animals. These laws generally contain the following provisions:

a. A requirement that each owner of certain kinds of livestock (generally cattle, horses, and mules) adopt a brand and have it recorded. The brand must differ from any already recorded. When approved, it must be applied to the owner's livestock.

b. When animals are sold, a bill of sale or other written evidence of the transfer must be signed by the seller and given to the purchaser. The purpose of the bill of sale is to overcome presumptions of wrongful possession by someone who has animals with different brands.

There are exceptions to this requirement in the laws of some states.

c. Local brand inspectors, usually working under authority of the state department or commissioner of agriculture, must inspect all animals leaving their district to determine if any are being sold by a person other than the owner.

d. An inspection of hides at slaughter houses is frequently required as a further means of disclosing theft and wrongful sale.

e. Usually there is a provision that animals shall not be skinned in remote locations which make difficult the detection of theft.

f. Penalties of a substantial nature are provided for violation of this law and especially for attempted defacing or changing of brands.

A recorded cattle brand is prima facie, but not conclusive, evidence of ownership.[271] Though a statute may require branding, failure to do so does not give another the right to affix his brand. In a Montana case, the court held that a bill of sale was not sufficient proof of ownership where the animal in question bore the uncancelled brand of a third party, and a chattel mortgage including this animal and executed by the third party was on file in the office of the Montana Livestock Commission.[272] A brand owned by a partnership cannot be used by any of the partners on animals belonging only to him, unless the right is assigned to him by the other partners.[273] Under a statute penalizing the misbranding of livestock belonging to another, or the willful defacing or obliterating of any brand upon "any livestock," the quoted words were held to include all livestock, regardless of ownership.[274] However, in prosecutions under such a statute, the intent to claim an animal belonging to another must be proved beyond a reasonable doubt.[275]

105. **Cruelty to Animals.** Some think of cruelty to animals in terms of external violence and picture the members of societies for the prevention of cruelty to animals as the only persons seriously concerned about maltreatment. As a matter of fact, the law on the subject is extensive. Many people, including authorities in the field of animal husbandry, have pointed to the failure of some farmers to afford adequate feed, shelter, and footing for

farm livestock, especially during bad weather, as a cause of economic loss, and in the worst cases, as a species of cruelty to animals.

Some state legislatures have given counties the power to take necessary measures and institute proceedings to enforce laws for the prevention of cruelty to animals. Criminal codes quite generally provide that persons guilty of cruelty to any animal in any of certain specified ways shall be subject to criminal penalty. The usual forms of cruelty designated by statute are: overloading, overdriving, overworking, cruelly beating, torturing, tormenting, mutilating, cruelly killing; cruelly working any old, maimed, infirm, sick, or disabled animal; unnecessarily failing to provide any animal with proper feed, drink, and shelter; abandoning any old, maimed, infirm, sick, or disabled animal; carrying or driving in an unnecessarily cruel manner.

Although such laws were aimed primarily at abuses of horses in the pre-automobile and pre-tractor days, they are sufficiently comprehensive to cover cruelty to other animals.

Legislatures have also made it unlawful for railroads or common carriers to allow animals to be confined for more than a specified number of hours without being fed and watered unless the carriers are delayed by storm or accident.

The keeping of pigeons to be killed for sport, the artificial coloring of baby chicks, the mutilation of horses' tails, and the maintenance of a place for, or the paying of admission to see, the fighting of bulls, bears, dogs, cocks, or other creatures, are prohibited in many states, and also by federal law.

The courts have rendered many decisions involving certain of these laws. Most important are those decisions stating that killing an animal out of mercy may not be cruelty, and that incidental injury to trespassing animals is not cruelty if reasonable means have been used in driving them off.

In some of the European countries cruelty statutes are much more comprehensive than they are in the United States. In Norway, for example, the law provides as a general principle that animals shall be treated with care and not exposed to unnecessary suffering. Feed and water must be sufficient and stable accommodations adequate. Except for very young calves, pigs or lambs, all castration must be done by a veterinarian with the use of a general or local anaesthetic. Hog rings are outlawed in Norway —also caponizing, the force feeding of poultry, the use of live fish for bait, and the use of ear notches that remove more than one-third of the ear.

Congress and many state legislators have become involved in the enactment of laws intended to impose certain minimum standards on the care, feeding, and treatment of animals maintained for experimental purposes. The intent of these laws is sound, but in some instances the requirements have been made unreasonably burdensome without any significant benefit to the animal. Laws and regulations requiring humane methods of slaughter are now becoming more and more common. There are many cases from higher courts supporting both the statutory and common law intent that animals should not be treated in a cruel and inhumane fashion. For example, it has been held that cruelly confining dogs in a vehicle not of sufficient size, cruelly neglecting to provide food and water, and tying a dog behind a car and dragging it until it is wounded and bleeding are all actionable.

106. **Stallion and Jack Registration and the Sire Owner's Liens.** It is accepted policy for legislatures to protect farmers against damage resulting from breeding to sires advertised with bogus or fraudulent pedigrees, and secure to the owners of sires payment for the service of their sires. Though many of these laws were designed to protect the owners of stallions and jacks, by requiring registration with some agency of the state—ordinarily the department of agriculture—there are other laws applying to sire owners generally. In either case, the lien against the dam or get-of-sire (sometimes it applies to both) is effective only after the owner has filed a verified statement with the state department of agriculture, giving the name, age, description, and pedigree of the sire, together with the terms and conditions upon which the sire will be advertised for service. The department, upon payment of the required fee, issues a certificate of pedigree. Also, the law may require the posting and recording of a copy of the certificate of pedigree.

The lien upon the get-of-sire, for nonpayment of the service fee, exists for a specified time after the date of birth of the progeny and may be enforced in any court of competent jurisdiction. If the statute does not state the method of enforcement, the general law on foreclosure of liens applies.

Obtaining the registration of a sire with a breed association by false pretenses or issuing a false pedigree is a criminal offense.

Regardless of statute the parties may by contract create a lien or mortgage in favor of the sire owner.[276] Also, it has been held that so long as the owner of a stallion retains possession of a mare, he has a lien for services regardless of statute.[277] This is not a practical consideration however, since sire owners ordinarily do not have possession of the dams more than temporarily. If proper action is taken under a lien statute, the claim will follow the animals into the hands of purchasers from the one engaging the service, regardless of knowledge on the part of the purchaser.[278] Though one of the purposes of these lien laws is to improve the quality of sires, it has been held that a statute which prohibits the use of sires simply because they are grades is unconstitutional.[279]

107. Horseshoers, Stablekeepers and Agisters' Liens. One who pastures, feeds, or cares for the livestock of another, for hire, is an agister. The term is borrowed from English law, and the occupation has been recognized by the legislatures of most states in the form of lien statutes in favor of agisters. These laws provide that the person pasturing, yarding, feeding, or otherwise caring for livestock for hire, shall have a claim against the animals for agreed or reasonable charges, and that such claim may be enforced by retention and sale of enough animals to satisfy it. State law may provide that the lien can be enforced even if the animals have left the custody of the agister, but unless the law so states, the lien dies when possession terminates.

In interpreting these laws the courts have established at least three important rules:

a. To be entitled to this statutory lien, the person claiming it must have the animals in his charge and under his control. Elevator companies or feed companies are not entitled to a lien simply because they supply feed to another on credit.

b. There must be at least an implied agreement for the pasturing, feeding, or care before the lien can attach. One who wrongfully keeps the livestock of another is not entitled to a lien.

c. An agister's lien does not take precedence over a chattel mortgage unless the chattel mortgagee consents to an arrangement whereby persons other than the mortgagor feed and care for the animals. However, a mortgage executed while animals are under agistment would be subject to the lien.

To enforce this lien, the one entitled, while still in possession of the animals and after requesting reasonable or agreed compensation from the owner, must give the owner written notice of a time and place at which the property will be sold. After due publication of notice, as required by law, the animals may be sold and the amount claimed for feed, keep or pasture, together with procedural costs, retained. The balance, if any, is paid to the owner.

Attendant upon the undertaking of an agistment are certain duties: the agister must keep his premises properly fenced, take reasonable precautions against injury to the animals, and provide suitable feed, water, and shelter. In case of loss due to poisoned feed or pasture land harboring disease organisms, the agister is liable if he knows or should have known of the circumstances.

Though the existence of the lien depends upon possession of the animals, the lien is not lost if the animals are wrongfully removed from the premises. However, a wrongful use of animals by the agister may terminate the agistment and constitute a "conversion" of the animals in violation of the owner's rights.[280] It has been held that an owner is liable to an agister for damage to the latter inflicted by animals after expiration of the period of agistment and failure of the owner to retake possession.[281]

Most states have lien laws in favor of horseshoers and stablekeepers. Generally, the former may be preserved by filing, whereas the latter depends upon possession. Horseshoers must ordinarily be licensed to practice, and in the absence of a license may not qualify under a horseshoer's lien statute. Veterinarians can legally shoe a horse as a part of their treatment; though a strict interpretation of some state laws would seem to prohibit even this invasion of the horseshoeing profession.

108. **Chattel Mortgages of Livestock.** Farmers use a large amount of short-term credit to finance crops, purchase equipment and supplies, and buy lambs, feeder cattle, and breeding animals. State laws relative to the use of personal property as security for such loans are, therefore, of importance to the farmer.

The chattel mortgage is the most common form of security for such loans. It is an instrument developed for the purpose of allowing the debtor (mortgagor) possession and use of mortgaged chattels (personal property) and, at the same time, giving to the seller or lender (mortgagee) a security interest superior to the rights of purchasers or transferees of the mortgagor, regardless of the actual knowledge of such persons concerning encumbrances on the chattel. As a credit device it enables farmers to obtain loans because it gives the lender a high type of security. Production credit association loans for feeder cattle, seed, feed, and other purposes are secured by chattel mortgages.

When a note secured by a chattel mortgage is paid and satisfied, whether at the time it is due or later, the farmer is entitled to a release. This should be filed or recorded immediately so the borrower's record will be clear and also for his protection in case doubt ever arises as to his having satisfied the indebtedness.

There are few limitations on the type of personal property used as security. Chattel mortgages on farm property may include livestock, grain, growing crops, machinery and equipment, feed to be fed to livestock included in the mortgage, and even household furniture if necessary.

The following facts about chattel mortgages are important:

a. They are ineffective unless recorded within the time and in the manner provided by state law.

b. They must be prepared and signed in accordance with state law.

c. They become ineffective when not renewed or foreclosed within the time specified by law.

d. They must contain an accurate description of the property included.

e. In most states mortgages on female animals attach to progeny born while the mortgage is in effect.

f. Unless state law provides that chattel mortgages may attach to crops before planting, they do not attach to crops until the seed is in the ground.

g. A chattel mortgage on feed, seed, or fertilizer is good if the same mortgage includes the animals to which the feed is fed, or the crop on which the seed and fertilizer are used.

h. In some states a chattel mortgage on household goods must be signed by husband and wife.

i. Although the rule is not well settled, the better view is that the statutory lien given landlords for their rent takes precedence over chattel mortgages on the same property (generally crops), regardless of the time of execution of the chattel mortgage.

j. Mortgaged chattels cannot be sold without the consent of the mortgagee. If they are sold without consent, the buyer does not acquire title. The mortgagee then may recover the property from the purchaser or the purchaser's transferee, and may recover damages from the mortgagor.

k. Partial payments may be made on notes secured by a chattel mortgage, and a partial release of the security endorses on the mortgage instrument.

l. Although all states have laws on chattel mortgages, these laws differ in some very important respects, such as time for recording, place of recording, duration, and renewal. Therefore, the appropriate state law must be studied thoroughly by those whose business requires the use of chattel mortgages.

In chattel mortgages of livestock, especially of feeder animals, adequacy of description is an important consideration. However, the courts have recognized the practical problem involved and have taken what seems to be a sensible view. For example, in a Nebraska case,[282] a chattel mortgage covered 482 head of steers, two and three years old past, all dehorned, and all branded with a certain brand, and recited that all of said cattle were owned by the mortgagor and in his possession on certain described premises. The court held, it being shown that the mortgagor had on the premises described but 471 head of steers of the ages specified, that the mortgage was valid as to all of said 471 head, although some of them were not dehorned nor branded, the description being sufficient, aided by such inquiries as the mortgage itself suggested, to enable a third party to identify such steers as those intended to be conveyed.

109. Contract Feeding, Pasturing, and Maintenance of Livestock. A grower and a feeder may enter into a contract whereby the grower agrees to supply the livestock, and the feeder the feed, pasture, equipment, and labor for finishing the animals. These contracts specify how the animals will be handled and marketed, and how freight, marketing expense and the proceeds of sale will be divided. Many times there is no provision for shrinkage, loss, or other contingencies. In such cases the feeder is generally the loser. These contracts cannot be set up after any rigid form and still be equitable. In each circumstance it is necessary to fit them to the particular situation. A contract for grazing or maintaining breeding cattle or ewes would be quite different from one for fattening steers or lambs. A division of profits may be worked out in various ways—on the basis of the investment by each party, gain put on the animals, or by a custom contract in which the grower furnishes the animals and pays the feeder for his feed, labor, use of equipment, and other expense. Any of these methods is fair if intelligently applied. One common practice is for one party to supply the animals and the other party the land, equipment, labor and feed, with the offspring divided equally.

110. **Hatcheries and Poultry Flocks.** Hatchery inspection is standard procedure in all the states, the primary objective being to control coccidiosis and other virulent and transmissible poultry diseases. In addition to general regulatory laws, state legislatures have in many cases provided that departments of agriculture may formulate plans and rules for the inspection, culling, and supervision of hatcheries and poultry flocks supplying eggs for hatching. Cooperation in such a program is voluntary. The stated purpose of these laws is to promote the health of poultry, increase production, bring about breed improvement, and classify hatcheries and poultry flocks supplying eggs for hatching, in accordance with conditions ascertained by inspection. It is a misdemeanor for a hatchery or flock owner to represent falsely that he is operating under such an act. Likewise, it is a misdemeanor for one who elects to operate under regulations of a department of agriculture to violate them.

111. **License Laws.** Many activities involving farm animals are subject to license and regulation. Some of them have been mentioned. Following is a list of additional activities and individuals subject to license and regulation:

a. The operation of a public stockyard
b. The operation of a slaughterhouse
c. Livestock dealers
d. Poultry dealers
e. Egg buyers
f. Hatchery operators
g. Veterinarians
h. Horseshoers

i. Owners of sires for public service
j. Meat dealers
k. Meat and produce peddlers
l. Public carriers of livestock
m. The keeping of a dog
n. Commission merchants handling meat, poultry, livestock, and livestock products
o. Public weighing of livestock
p. Auctioneers
q. Operators of livestock sales rings
r. Itinerant horse and mule traders

CHAPTER 15

DOG LAWS

112. Dogs as Property. At common law dogs were either not considered as property,[283] or were considered as property of an inferior sort entitled to less protection than other types of personal property.[284] In accordance with this view, it has been held that dogs are not subjects of larceny or of taxation and that they are not to be inventoried or appraised as assets of an estate. Needless to say, these views have changed quite markedly,[285] and both court decisions and statutes have placed dogs in the property category along with other domestic animals.[286] They have been held to fall within the statutory definition of " chattel,"[287] to be a thing of value,[288] and to be entitled to constitutional protection against the taking of "property" without due process of law.[289] Statutes making dogs subjects of taxation probably make them property in the fullest sense, though it may be argued that such statutes are just a form of control. The intent of such a statute and its mode of application would make some difference. Certainly, a state legislature has some discretion in deciding how dogs should be treated from the standpoint of property. In an Indiana case, for example, there was a complaint in replevin to recover the body of a dead dog. The complaint alleged a wrongful taking and detention, and that the body was of the value of two dollars, in that the hide was of the value of one dollar, and the carcass, exclusive of the hide, of the value of one dollar for fertilizing purposes. The court held that this stated a cause of action, under Burns' Rev. Stat. 1894, §1286, since dogs are property, and ownership is not lost by death of the animal, especially if the body is of value.[290]

113. Liability for Trespass. The mere presence of a dog on another's property does not constitute a trespass for which damages are recoverable. The courts recognize the roving nature of dogs and do not impose the tests of trespass that would be used in the case of animals which are generally supposed to be confined by their owners. This does not mean that a dog owner cannot be held liable for damage caused by his dog while on the property of another; it simply means that the trespass itself is not actionable.

The courts are not uniform in their holdings regarding one's liability for damage caused by his dog on the property of another. Some hold that there is no liability unless the owner had knowledge of his dog's inclination to commit the injury complained of.[291] Others hold that knowledge is unimportant and that the owner is liable for any damage caused.[292] In any case, contributory negligence on the part of the injured person—inciting the dog, for example—could be used as a defense. State legislatures and municipalities undoubtedly have the right to restrict the freedom with which one may permit dogs to roam, where considerations of public health or livestock protection seem to demand.

114. **Liability for Injury to Persons.** The general rule, apart from statute, is that the owner or keeper of a dog is not liable for bodily injuries inflicted by it unless he knew, or should have known, that it had dangerous propensities; or unless his own negligence or fault in some way contributes to the injuries.[293] If one chooses to keep a vicious dog, he does so at a rather high risk of liability to others. Some courts have even gone so far as to indicate that an owner should kill such a dog.[294] The better view, however, is that an owner may keep a vicious dog for the necessary protection of life and property, providing it is kept under circumstances which do not make it a threat to innocent persons.[295] If a dog is trained not to molest people unless they tamper with his owner's property—a dog in an automobile or by your clothes at the beach, for example—the owner is not likely to be held for injuries incurred by others in attempting to molest his property. A statute imposing liability generally for injuries inflicted by dogs, which is silent with respect to knowledge of the owner as a condition of liability, impliedly eliminates the necessity of proving knowledge.[296] In cases arising under such a statute, where there was no knowledge of a dangerous propensity, only compensatory damages could be recovered—as distinguished from punitive—and consequential damages.

In an action for injuries inflicted by a dog, it is not essential that the defendant be the actual owner, since the "harborer" of a dog is charged with the same duty to restrain it that is imposed on an owner.[297] One who "keeps" a dog is liable under a statute imposing liability on dog owners, but a wife cannot be held liable for damages caused by her husband's dogs.[298] Knowledge by one's agent or servant of the habits of a dog may be imputed to the owner under the general principles of agency,[299] but a servant's knowledge of the vicious character of a dog accustomed to follow him around, but not put in his charge by the owner, is not imputable to the owner.[300]

While one may keep a vicious watchdog, he must take precautions to see that friends, business callers and others with a right to enter the premises are not injured. Warning signs are of some effect, especially with regard to strangers, but may constitute no protection against liability to persons who have habitually ignored the signs, or to children. It has been held that one is not justified in keeping a vicious dog untied on his premises in the daytime.[301] However, loosing dogs at night has been considered proper.[302] When a person is misconducting himself, and calling a dog is under the circumstances a necessary use of force to assist in expelling him, he cannot recover for injuries received.[303] Contributory negligence is a good defense, where the facts show that the negligence of the injured party played a material part in producing the injury.[304] The assumption of risk doctrine might be a good defense also under certain circumstances. However, it has been held that a veterinarian summoned to examine a dog that had been acting queerly did not assume the risk of injury arising from the owner's negligence in not properly restraining the dog in bringing it for examination.[305]

Recovery for injuries inflicted by a dog include all the direct and necessary results of the injury, including physical pain and mental anguish, nursing, medical attendance and loss of employment.[306] If the injury is caused by a dog known to be vicious, the owner may be held for punitive as well as compensatory damages.[307]

115. Liability for Injury to Livestock. The liability of dog owners for livestock losses caused by their dogs is recognized, both by court decision and statute. However, the fact that most damage, particularly to sheep, is done at night, and the difficulty of proving that a particular dog was involved, leaves the livestock owner with means which are ineffective to solve the problem. Some courts have held that if any one dog in a pack can be identified, the dog's owner can be held for all the damage done by the pack,[308] but there is authority to the contrary, holding that each dog owner is liable only for the mischief done by his dog.[309] The joint liability theory seems to be the most practical. Some states have laws making it illegal to keep a dog which is a known sheep-killer. The measure of damages is actual loss caused—not simply recovery for animals killed. Recovery may be had for crippling, loss of weight, abortion, or any other impairment of animals which can be traced to a dog's attacks: For example, frightening horses on the highway (a bow to the past) was actionable. As a general rule, however, a dog owner cannot be held liable for losses caused by rabies unless he knew his dog was rabid.

Finally, just so the main idea is not lost, let us recapitulate: Unless changed by state law or local ordinance, a dog or cat owner is (a) not bound to confine his pet; (b) not liable simply because his pet sets foot on or crosses the property of another; (c) liable for actual damages caused to others or their property (in the case of disease transmission, however, his liability would depend on knowledge); (d) entitled to recover damages from anyone who without good cause detains, injures, or kills his dog or cat; (e) not liable for damage caused when his pet escapes from a competent custodian—a small animal hospital or boarding kennel for example—but the custodian may be liable to anyone injured and also to the owner if there is negligence.

116. License Laws and Indemnity Funds. Municipalities and counties may require persons keeping dogs to register them, procure tags and pay a license fee.[310] The fee collected is considered a license for the purpose of regulating dogs rather than as a revenue measure. So long as these ordinances or statutes are reasonable, they will be held constitutional as a valid exercise of the police power.[311] Likewise, it has been held that a dog license fee imposed for the purpose of building a county indemnity fund out of which livestock owners can be paid for losses caused by dogs is a valid exercise of the police power and not a tax.[312] Most states provide for these county indemnity funds. Generally, they contain the following provisions:

The manner in which the claim is to be made and the officer to whom it shall be made.

The amount which may be recovered for different types of animals.

The time of payment. Many laws require payments from the fund once annually, so if there is any shortage, it can be prorated. This is likely to be the case if enforcement of the license law is lax.

A provision "subrogating" any right the owner has against a dog owner or requiring that the fund be reimbursed if the owner is able to recover from the dog owner.

117. **Rabies.** Annually, thousands of dollars worth of live-stock are destroyed and human lives endangered by rabid dogs. It is true that lives can be saved, but the hazard and inconvenience to persons bitten and the economic loss frequently resulting when rabid dogs bite valuable animals make the eradication of rabies an important public problem.

Many states have passed effective laws aimed at the eradica-tion of rabies. One type of law provides that when a case of rabies has occurred in a locality, the state department of agriculture shall have power, and it shall be its duty, to prevent the spread of rabies among dogs and other animals. The department of agri-culture has authority to order that all dogs in the locality be:

a. Kept confined within an enclosure from which escape is impossible, or

b. Kept muzzled and restrained, or

c. Subjected to such prophylactic measures as the depart-ment may deem necessary.

The department has the power to determine the area and the period of time during which these requirements apply.

It is generally provided that expense involved in any action taken by the state department of agriculture shall be borne by the owner or keeper of the dog. Officers failing to carry out pro-visions of the law are subject to penalty.

Another type of law is one requiring that all dogs be vac-cinated annually or kept confined, and providing for enforcement, either by counties or by agents of the State. This is by far the most effective kind of legislation.

A question often arises as to the liability of the owner of a rabid dog. As a rule, unless the owner or keeper of a dog is aware of its rabid condition, he may be held liable only for direct acts of destruction or damage and not for any damage resulting from the spread of disease. However, it has been held that the owner of a known vicious dog, who permits it to live, is liable for injuries inflicted by it when it suddenly becomes rabid, although he had no time after learning of its condition, and before the injuries were inflicted, to kill or confine it.[313] Upon submission of adequate proof, the owner of an animal destroyed after being bitten by a rabid dog may usually be indemnified from the county dog license fund, as in other cases.

118. Pounds. The purpose of a public pound is to protect the public, prevent the destruction of lost pets and provide a central facility through which to locate stray animals. Townships, counties and municipalities may operate such pounds. Though laws vary from state to state, there are certain common features: They all provide for a poundmaster, for notification of the pound by private persons confining or picking up an animal, for destruction or sale if not claimed in a specified time, and for payment to redeem an animal taken up by the pound. Some laws permit private persons to retain animals, providing they advertise in accordance with the law, and yield possession to owners who claim their animals and offer a reasonable amount for feed and care. Private individuals or organizations have no right to dispose of animals by killing.

119. Right to Kill. With few exceptions, state laws allow anyone to kill a dog caught in the act of chasing, killing, or wounding sheep or other livestock on land not owned by the owner of the dog. Other conditions under which some of the states permit dogs to be killed by anyone are:

When found at large unattended and without a collar bearing the license number.

When found at large after having been proved to be sheep killers.

When found at large and unattended between sunset and sunrise.

A few states have added to these the right to put out poison for sheep killing dogs.

Apart from statute, however, there are well established common law justifications for killing a dog. Among them are the right to kill a rabid dog or one justly suspected of being rabid;[314]

a known vicious dog running at large;[315] in self-defense;[316] and to prevent further damage to livestock or property, when killing seems to be the only possible way of terminating the injury.[317] Killing for scientific purposes may be permitted by law, subject to any conditions expressed in the law.

120. **Dogs on Highways.** It is apparently an accepted rule that a dog, unless vicious, has a right in the highway. In an Iowa case, the owner of a dog was held not liable for the overturning of an automobile when his dog at night jumped from the road bank into the path of the car.[318] But if one has a dog which he knows is in the habit of running out and barking at cars, or at pedestrians, he may be held liable for any damage which results. This principle was well established in the day of the horse, and recovery was common.[319] Thus, liability does not hinge on the vicious character of the dog, but on its proclivity to annoy by barking and chasing. Conceivably the same would be true of friendly dogs who habitually plant their front feet on people's legs or midsections—depending on the size of the dog. It has been held, however, that a pedestrian who was tripped and knocked over by a dog could not recover from the owner, even though the dog was running at large without a muzzle, contrary to law.[320] The court held that violation of the law was not the proximate cause of the injury to the pedestrian.

CHAPTER 16

SALES AND WARRANTIES OF ANIMALS

121. **"Caveat Emptor."** Purchasers always assume some risk. No article is likely to be so clothed with implied and express warranties that the purchaser is relieved of all the burden of decision—he at least must decide which national advertiser to favor. In the sale of animals, the application of "caveat emptor"— let the buyer beware—has had some interesting applications. Generally, the term means that when one examines and chooses, he is bound by his choice, unless there is some hidden defect, or unless he has been intentionally misled by the seller. There have probably been more cracker-barrel than court interpretations of the term. At any rate, it remains a vague concept until there is some application to a particular set of facts.

122. **Statute of Frauds.** Oral contracts are as valid and binding as written contracts, save for limitations imposed by statute. The most common limitations—generally contained in a law known as an act to prevent frauds and perjuries, or by some similar title—are the following:

(a) That contracts for the conveyance of real estate must be in writing.

(b) That contracts to answer for the debt of another must be in writing.

(c) That contracts which cannot be performed within one year from the time they are made must be in writing.

(d) That contracts involving goods valued at more than some specified amount ($500, for example) must be in writing.

With respect to the limitation on contracts that cannot be performed within one year, or that involve goods valued at more than the stipulated amount, it has been held—sometimes it is provided by statute—that they are validated if the goods or a part of them are delivered, if the purchase price or a portion of it is paid, or if something else has been done which amounts to performance or part-performance of the contract. The idea of part-performance has no bearing on oral contracts not subject to the statute of frauds, where an exchange of promises is enough to make a binding contract. For example, where a person agreed to take and break a pair of mules for a year's use of them and it was intended that he should take immediate possession, the fact that he did not remove them at once because of fear that they would not lead behind his buggy but returned for them several days later, did not invalidate the agreement under the statute.[321]

A more practical application of the statute arises when feeder animals or breeding animals are sold over the telephone or through personal conversation, and their value exceeds the amount specified in the statute of frauds. Technically, neither party would be bound, but custom, usage, the preservation of good will and reputations, and other considerations generally impel the parties to stand by their agreement. Also, the law has developed a theory known as "equitable estoppel" which may sometimes be used to keep one clearly in the wrong from hiding behind the statute of frauds. No particular form of instrument is necessary to constitute the writing required by law (except in the case of deeds), and notes, letters, memoranda or other signed promises may be sufficient.

123. **Express Warranties.** The Uniform Sales Act—a law on sales adopted by most of the states—defines an express warranty as any affirmation of fact or any promise by the seller relating to the goods, the natural tendency of which is to induce the buyer to purchase the goods. It follows that the buyer must purchase the goods relying on the affirmation or promise before the express warranty can arise. No affirmation of the value of the goods, nor any statement of the seller's opinion only shall be construed as a warranty.

No particular form of words is necessary to make a warranty. The word warrant need not be used, but there must be some language used to indicate the intention of the party to oblige himself that the article shall be of the quality stated.[322]

To make an affirmation at the time of sale constitute a warranty, the evidence must show it to have been so intended, and not to be a mere matter of opinion and judgment.[323] For example, a statement that a young stallion, sold before he had been used as a stock horse, would "make his mark as a foal getter" does not amount to a warranty that he will prove an ordinarily sure foal getter.[324] The vendor of a mare and a mule had them both in a single stall, where defects were not easily discoverable. When the buyer called to examine them, he was assured that the mule was sound, and, being inexperienced, he made the purchase, relying on the assurance given. The court held there was a warranty of soundness, which extended even to visible defects.[325]

Also, where cattle were bought, warranted to be in sound health, the purchaser notifying the seller at the time that he designed to ship them directly to New York to sell for beef, and he did so ship them, the purchaser may recover for loss and expenses incurred on those that showed disease or died on the passage.[326]

If a warranty is made after the sale is completed, it is not effective unless there is some additional payment or consideration to support it.[327]

Contracts of warranty imply an agreement to indemnify or make payment of money to the vendee in the event of a breach of warranty.[328] The amount would ordinarily be the difference in value of the animal as warranted and as it turned out, together with damages which may have resulted from the breach of warranty. Another remedy a purchaser has is to rescind the sale, return the animal, and get a refund of the purchase price plus any other cost or damages which might have resulted.

124. **Implied Warranties.** An implied warranty is one which accompanies goods as a matter of course, without any specific promises having been made.

The Uniform Sales Act contains the following provisions on implied warranties:

> Subject to the provisions of this act and of any statute in that behalf, there is no implied warranty or condition as to the quality or fitness for any particular purpose of goods supplied under a contract to sell or a sale, except as follows:
> (1) Where the buyer, expressly or by implication, makes known to the seller the particular purpose for which the goods are required, and it appears that the buyer relies on the seller's skill or judgment (whether he be the grower or manufacturer or not), there is an implied warranty that the goods shall be reasonably fit for such purposes.
> (2) Where the goods are bought by description, there is an implied warranty that the goods shall be of merchantable quality.
> (3) If the buyer has examined the goods, there is no implied warranty as regards defects which such examination ought to have revealed.

(4) In the case of a contract to sell or a sale of a specified article under its patent or other trade name, there is no implied warranty as to its fitness for any particular purpose.

(5) An implied warranty or condition as to quality or fitness for a particular purpose may be annexed by the usages of trade.

(6) An express warranty or condition does not negative a warranty or condition implied under this act unless inconsistent therewith.

In view of this section, in an action on a check given for the purchase price of hogs, the buyer could set up a breach of warranty by way of recoupment, where the buyer requested that the hogs be taken back on learning of a breach of warranty, but the seller refused, and advised the buyer to ship the hogs elsewhere to be sold on the market; as against the contention that it was the buyer's duty to reject the hogs on learning of the breach of warranty.[329] Under this section, when the buyer made known to the seller that he desired to buy a carload of stock hogs for feeders which would be vaccinated and pass government inspection, there was an implied warranty that the hogs would be reasonably fit for the purpose.[330]

Where a sale is made of breeding cattle, an implied warranty arises that the animals are fit for breeding purposes.[331] This is the general rule with respect to sales of animals for breeding purposes.

Where the proposed buyer of cows informed the seller that he was purchasing them for breeding purposes and for use in his dairy business, there was an implied warranty under the Uniform Sales Act of their fitness for breeding purposes, the buyer relying upon the judgment of the seller as to the suitability of the animals for his use. This implied warranty is breached as to an animal which was proven sterile after being repeatedly bred, there being evidence sufficient to take the case to the jury as to whether or not the animal was sterile at the time of the sale.[332]

It may be shown that there is a general custom among people dealing in registered breeding cattle which are sold at public sale to the effect that if a cow sold does not get with calf, she may be returned to the seller and bred to the seller's bulls; that if she does not come with calf then, the seller will either return the money to the buyer or give him another animal of like value which shall be satisfactory.[333]

Upon the purchase of a number of bulls for breeding purposes, the seller was bound to select and deliver such only as were then suitable for that use, and the tender of animals too young for breeding purposes was not a compliance with the contract.[334] An implied warranty that an animal sold is merchantable and reasonably suited to the use intended arises upon the sale thereof, and is breached where it is infected with the germs of a disease unknown both to the seller and the buyer, which subsequently develops, causing the death of the animal.[335] On the assumption that there was an implied warranty that a horse was merchantable and reasonably suited for the purpose intended, such warranty was not breached by the existence of defects discoverable by ordinary care, such as deafness, blindness, or spavin.[336] A warranty of soundness does not of itself imply that the subject matter of the warranty, a cow, will give milk.[337]

But if the seller knows the use the buyer intends to make of the property, the sale for such use at a sound price carries an implied warranty that the animal is free from hidden defects which would impair its usefulness for such purpose.[338] Where a competent judge of cattle, especially dairy cows, purchased such a herd, and had full and ample time to inspect the herd before he bought them, there was no implied warranty, although the purchase was made for that particular purpose to the knowledge of the seller.[339]

The sale of a car of live hogs, described as stock hogs, raises an implied warranty that the hogs shall be fit for stock purposes, which is breached by the hogs being unsound and apparently infected with a fatal disease.[340]

An implied warranty of the merchantable quality of foxes to be delivered in the future, which is not inconsistent with the description thereof in the contract of sale, is not excluded by an express warranty based upon the description of the foxes, which is ambiguous, being only as to the delivery of registered and pedigreed silver foxes to be selected by the seller.[341] A provision in a contract for the sale of a horse to the effect that the seller does not warrant the health, life, and soundness of the animal, but only the title thereto, does not exclude an implied warranty that the horse is merchantable and reasonably suited for the use intended.[342]

125. Warranty of Title. When one sells something, there is an implication that he owns it and can convey good title, unless he voluntarily discloses facts to the contrary. The Uniform Sales Act covers this proposition as follows:

> In a contract to sell or a sale, unless a contrary intention appears, there is:
> (1) An implied warranty on the part of the seller that in case of a sale he has a right to sell the goods, and that in case of a contract to sell he will have a right to sell the goods at the time when the property is to pass.
> (2) An implied warranty that the buyer shall have and enjoy quiet possession of the goods as against any lawful claims existing at the time of the sale.
> (3) An implied warranty that the goods shall be free at the time of the sale from any charge or encumbrance in favor of any third person, not declared or known to the buyer before or at the time when the contract or sale is made.
> (4) This section shall not, however, be held to render liable a sheriff, auctioneer, mortgagee, or other person professing to sell by virtue of authority in fact or law goods in which a third person has a legal or equitable interest.

Prior to the Sales Act, however, it had been held that there being upon the sale of personal property an implied warranty of title, the vendee had his action against the vendor, if his title proved deficient. The buyer must then take care that he is not deceived by dealing for a pretended title, or—if he is—that his vendor is able to respond in damages for any loss which may happen to the vendee.[343] Also, it had been held that upon the sale of personal property there was an implied warranty of title, and if, in such case, the rightful owner should take the property out of the possession of such purchaser, he might recover its value upon that warranty.[344]

In the case of mortgaged animals, both the purchaser and the mortgagee are by most state laws given further protection against wrongful sales by a mortgagor in the form of penalties.

126. Elements of Damage. Ordinarily, the difference in actual value and the value as warranted is the measure of damages for breach of warranty in the sale of animals. However, other factors may enter in, such as care and feeding, infection of other animals with disease, losses arising from inability to perform, and others. For breach of express or implied warranty of the soundness of animals, one of the elements of damage which may be recovered by the buyer is the amount expended by him for veterinary service and medicine in his efforts to cure the animal, or animals, of the disease with which they were infected at the time of their purchase, or with which they became infected from the animals purchased.[345] There is some departure from this rule however, for in a Minnesota case the court held that special damages compensating the buyer of a horse for expenses incurred for medical attention and treatment, due to its diseased condition at the time he purchased it, are not recoverable in addition to the general damages based upon the difference between its actual value and its value if it had been as warranted.[346]

In cases expressing the majority view, the courts have said that the seller must have contemplated at the time he sold the horse that if it turned out to be worthless and diseased, the buyer would have to incur expenses in attempting to cure it, and, if he failed in his attempt, he would lose not only the expenses thus incurred, but the price of the horse.[347] In a Pennsylvania case, the court held that the seller of a cow which had tuberculosis was liable to the buyer, in addition to the ordinary damage, for loss to him occasioned by other cattle becoming infected with the disease, including the necessary expense incurred in caring for and doctoring such animals.[348]

In an action to rescind an oral agreement to exchange plaintiff's albino stallion for defendant's mare and recover the value of the stallion, the mere fact that no other sales of such horses or other stallions of the same kind were made in the immediate vicinity did not disqualify an experienced veterinarian, acquainted with plaintiff's stallion, from testifying as to value when the exchange was made.[349]

127. Auction Sales. The Uniform Sales Act provides that in the case of a sale by auction:

(1) Where goods are put up for sale by auction in lots, each lot is the subject of a separate contract of sale.

(2) A sale by auction is complete when the auctioneer announces its completion by the fall of the hammer, or in other customary manner. Until such announcement is made, any bidder may retract his bid; and the auctioneer may withdraw the goods from sale unless the auction has been announced to be without reserve.

(3) A right to bid may be reserved expressly by or on behalf of the seller.

(4) Where notice has not been given that a sale by auction is subject to a right to bid on behalf of the seller, it shall not be lawful for the seller to bid himself or to employ or induce any person to bid at such sale on his behalf, or for the auctioneer to employ or induce any person to bid at such sale on behalf of the seller or knowingly to take any bid from the seller or any person employed by him. Any sale contravening this rule may be treated as fraudulent by the buyer.

Although at an auction sale of sheep it was announced that the right was reserved to resell any goods as to which a dispute arose, the seller had no right to resell sheep under this section merely because he wanted them sold in a different manner.[350] An auction sale of cattle constitutes an executed contract complete when the cattle are knocked down to the buyer with nothing to do on the buyer's part but to give a note and take the cattle. After such sale, the cattle are held by the seller as bailee for the buyer.[351] Prior to the Sales Act, it was held that where an auctioneer at an administrator's sale sold a horse not belonging to the estate, a buyer who refused to take the horse on learning its ownership was not liable for the purchase price, under the rule that everyone has the right to select the person with whom he shall contract. [352]

Evidence that the crier at a public sale announced, and that the owner upon being questioned asserted, that the mare being offered for sale had a bruised shoulder and was offered "just as she was" and that she was not being offered as sound would not warrant the jury in finding there was a warranty of the mare's condition at the time she was offered for sale.[353] When the auctioneer at an auction sale stated in the presence of the buyer that the reason for cattle being in thin condition was that they had been on a short pasture, when in fact they were diseased, and the owner did not correct the statement of the auctioneer although he was present, there was active fraud on the part of the owner warranting recovery for damages.[354]

Where a sales catalogue distributed to bidders at an auction sale of cattle contained a recital, under the heading "Tuberculin Guarantee," that all animals over six months of age had been tested by authorized state veterinarians, and made specific warranty that such animals had been tuberculin tested within twenty days of sale and found free from tuberculin, certificate of which would be furnished with each animal, the buyer of a bull, who left the bull with the seller for four or five days after sale with seller's consent, during which period the state veterinarian notified the seller that the bull should be held in quarantine for sixty days on the ground that it was infected with or had been exposed to tuberculosis, could, within a reasonable time, rescind the purchase for breach of warranty; and he was, therefore, entitled to rescind when the seller refused to make delivery before the expiration of the sixty day period.[355]

Where a credit of nine months was to be given to a purchaser if he gave approved security, and one purchased a mule without complying with the terms of sale, or taking possession of the mule, it was held that the vendor, after the credit expired, might recover the price of the mule without a delivery or offer of delivery to the purchaser, the law giving the vendor a lien which he was not bound to relinquish, unless the terms of the sale were complied with.[356]

An auctioneer can maintain a suit in his own name for goods sold and delivered by him, whereon he holds a lien for his charges.[357] Persons operating an auction may be held to a reasonable standard of care with regard to the health and safety of patrons. If the grounds are not safe, animals are not properly confined, or unsafe food is served, for example, liability may result.

128. **Conditional Sales.** In common terminology, a conditional sale is a contract under which the buyer takes possession of, and the seller retains title to, personal property until paid. For example, if a farmer does not have sufficient cash to buy an animal and the seller is willing, the purchaser may sign a conditional sales contract reserving title in the seller until all installments have been met. Failure to meet an installment when due is generally such a breach of contract as will entitle the seller to retake the property. Automobiles, tractors, machinery, refrigerators, furniture, and electrical appliances are common subjects of conditional sales contracts. Farmers in the United States annually buy millions of dollars worth of equipment under such contracts. Livestock is not ordinarily purchased in this manner, but it may be.

Whether or not a purchaser should use this method depends upon his available supply of cash, the urgency of his need, and the kind of conditional sales terms he can get. Interest rates are generally quite high, and a substantial service charge is frequently made. Anyone who becomes a party to such a contract should bear in mind the following points:

a. The total cost will be more than the cash purchase price because of interest and service charges. The buyer should know before signing the contract what the interest rate and service charges will be and what his responsibility will be with respect to insurance on the property purchased.

b. Payments are ordinarily in installments. Failure to pay an installment when due is grounds for terminating the contract, in which case the property is returned to the seller and all payments made to the seller are retained by him. The buyer should know what the contract states on this point.

In some states conditional sales contracts must be recorded to be valid. In others they need not be. In any event, it is a breach of contract with the seller for a purchaser to dispose of the property without the consent of the conditional seller. There are exceptions to this, as in the case of a conditional sale of goods for resale. Whether or not a purchaser from the conditional vendee acquires a right superior to that of the conditional vendor depends on several factors—his knowledge of the conditional sales contracts, whether or not there is a recording statute, or if not, what the courts in the particular state have said about these so-called "hidden liens."

CHAPTER 17

LOCATING AND ORGANIZING
A VETERINARY PRACTICE

129. **Zoning.** Both municipalities and local governmental units have the power to zone. In most states counties can zone; in some instances towns have the power to zone. Zoning is simply the process through which an agency establishes geographical limits determining what kind of buildings or enterprise can be constructed, improved or carried on in particular described areas. This purpose of course is to protect property values, to protect citizens in the use of their own property, to prevent undesirable growths in areas of the city or county and to promote the general well-being of all concerned by the kind of land use control which zoning affords.

Veterinarians are concerned because in many municipalities certain areas of the city will be denied to the practice of veterinary medicine or to small animal hospitals because these are deemed undesirable in such areas. This is generally true of residential areas and may be true also of certain areas designated for a small business. Before establishing a practice, the veterinarian should learn what zoning regulations if any exist. He can then determine whether his practice will fit the requirements of the law; if not he may be able to get a modification of the zoning act permitting him to establish his practice where he desires. In the case of a small animal hospital or a veterinary practice already in existence when zoning laws are adopted, such business may continue to be carried on because it has been held unconstitutional for zoning laws to be retroactive. However, if the business ceases it cannot again be established; also there are limitations on how much repair or expansion one can do after zoning applies to an area in which he is carrying on business.

130. **Nuisance.** Regardless of zoning, a veterinary establishment may so affect the people living nearby that they will be

162

able to recover damages, enjoin the operation of the establishment, or both. Although some states have statutes further defining the things which constitute nuisance, the theory is a common law innovation, and applied regardless of statute. If one so uses his property that he causes undue harm to another, either through noise, smoke, dust, odors or otherwise, he may be enjoined or damages may be recovered. Obviously, a small animal hospital may create conditions of this kind giving rise to causes of action by surrounding property owners. The veterinarian or small animal hospital or kennel owner can do many things to avoid the likelihood of nuisance, and with a closed establishment and strict sanitary standards it is not likely that people will complain.

131. **The Corporation and Veterinary Practice.** It is a general rule that the corporation cannot practice a profession. This seems rather obvious, since only an individual can acquire the skills essential to the carrying on of a profession. However, if this same argument were extended, it might be said that a corporation really can't do anything since it is an artificial person. However, the law does not adopt this view, because it has said that a corporation can do many things in the same manner an individual can do them; but with varying degrees of interpretation it can be safely said that a corporation cannot practice veterinary medicine. That is, the corporation cannot substitute itself for a licensed veterinarian in establishing veterinarian-client relationships or in preventing a client from suing an individual professional man for malpractice. Furthermore, in many states it is illegal for a veterinarian to associate himself with a corporation in such fashion as to permit non-licensed persons to do acts which are defined as practice. If all members of the corporation are licensed individuals, then the objection to the corporation would seem negligible because it would be operating very much as a partnership, except that it would have a corporate structure. Certainly, the corporation could not insulate the veterinarian from his private liability to the client. It is likely also that if more than one veterinarian were employed by the corporation, an agency relation could very well exist among them. This relation would be similar to that existing among partners in which they are liable for the contract and tort actions of each other while they are carrying on their professional busi-

ness. There is an urge to use a corporation because of tax advantages, particularly in the establishment of retirement plans. Also, the corporation can purchase and own property and render services for the veterinarians who create it. Many human hospitals and clinics are established with this principle in mind. If a veterinarian is interested in the possibility of corporate organization he should explore the laws of his own state and be well advised before entering into this kind of enterprise. Some states have passed laws which attempt to straddle the fence between a partnership and corporation, the intent being to give professional men the advantages of the corporation for income tax and retirement purposes but to destroy the veterinarian-client relationship which would exist in a partnership. These are sometimes referred to as professional association laws. As an example, the Illinois law provides that:

> Any 2 or more persons duly licensed to practice a profession under the laws of this State may form a professional association, as distinguished from either a partnership or a corporation, by associating themselves for the purpose of rendering professional services and dividing the gains therefrom as stated in articles of association; provided that no professional association organized pursuant to this Act shall engage in more than one type of professional service. All members of the association shall be licensed to perform the type of professional service for which the association is formed.
>
> . . . Any type of personal service to the public which requires as a condition precedent to the rendering of such service the obtaining of a license, and which service by law cannot be performed by a corporation. The term "license" includes a license, certificate of registration or any other evidence of the satisfaction of State requirements.

The law further provides that the association:

1. May adopt a name to be followed by a term signifying association.
2. May own property and make investments in its own name.
3. Shall be governed by a Board of Directors or an Executive Committee.
4. Shall have a president, vice-president, secretary, treasurer and such other officers as it may determine—but any one person may hold more than one office, except those of president and secretary.

Shares of stock can be held only by licensed professional members, and the existence of the association does not alter the veterinarian-client relation or relieve the veterinarian from his professional responsibilities under the Practice Act.

Whether or not these laws prove to be of benefit to veterinarians remains to be seen. The Treasury Department has expressed the view that a professional association organized under the Illinois law would not be considered as having the corporate attributes essential to qualify it for the desired special tax treatment.

Federal law now makes possible the establishment of voluntary pension plans by self-employed individuals and at least a partial tax reduction. However, the federal law has not as yet gone all the way in giving self-employed professionals the same kind of treatment a corporation can give its employees.

132. Convenants Not to Compete. It is quite common when an older veterinarian employs a younger one for the older veterinarian to insert a provision in their partnership or employment agreement that the young veterinarian, in case he quits the partnership or employment, shall not establish a practice which will compete. The main elements of these covenants not to compete are the limitations imposed on geographical area and time. Generally, they provide that the veterinarian who quits another shall not practice within a certain defined locality, within a certain period of years. As long as these two conditions are reasonable the courts will uphold the validity of a covenant not to compete. If the provision is unreasonable, either in terms of the geographical area in which practice is prohibited—a whole state for example—or with regard to time—a limitation of 25 years for example—the courts say the covenant is void and unenforceable. The remedy for the enforcement of such a covenant is injunction. The courts have upheld such a covenant against practicing in the same county for five years, for example. This would most certainly be upheld in most state courts.

133. Disaster and the Veterinarian's Liability. What duty does a veterinarian owe to his clients when conditions beyond his control make it impossible for him to render his usual service? The answer is based upon the same principles of contract, bailment, and negligence that apply in all such situations, and there is a considerable accumulation of legal doctrine surrounding this subject. Let us examine the probable application of this doctrine by posing a number of specific situations.

1. Destruction or Partial Destruction of an Animal Hospital

Certainly the veterinarian is not liable for loss of animals or injury to animals in his custody immediately resulting from a bombing, fire, explosion, or other cause beyond his control. But if there are surviving animals, he would then owe the owner the duty of providing such care and taking such steps as would be reasonable to preserve the lives and health of such animals. This duty might be discharged in a number of ways—placing the animals in another hospital, finding temporary quarters, notifying owners and asking them to take the animals. If X-ray and other equipment essential to the treatment of animals are destroyed, then there would be no liability for failure to conduct such treatments until such time as the veterinarian could, with reasonable alacrity, make arrangements for their continuation. The veterinarian's legal duty might be altered considerably by the application of civil defense rules. If, for example, he is required to look after human patients, his duty to animal owner clients would be discharged by leaving the animals with the best kind of help he is able to find and notifying owners of the situation. Even the duty to notify would be altered by the destruction of communication facilities—telephones, highways, vehicles, the local press. Countless factual situations can grow out of disaster, so that it is impossible to rationalize all of them. For example, what is the duty of the veterinarian—

> to recapture escaped animals?
> with respect to the spread of disease by escaped animals?
> to sheep owners whose sheep are killed by escaped dogs?
> to people who are attacked by escaped animals?
> for damage caused by the negligent acts of the employees or agents he procures to look after the animals?

If we were to coin a rule or guide, it might say, "The veterinarian in charge of an animal hospital is not liable to animal owners or the public generally in case of disaster, so long as he moves with reasonable speed to take the next logical step to protect the interests of both." As we have already indicated, this next logical step will depend on a number of variables and cannot very well be predicted in advance. Some of the steps will be covered by civil defense rules, but even these cannot allow for all contingencies.

2. Death or Incapacity of the Veterinarian

The veterinarian's death would ordinarily terminate any liability against his estate arising out of his failure to care for patients. Likewise, he would be relieved of liability if he were seriously injured and could not make arrangements for follow-up. If he is able to attempt to make arrangements by telephone or through members of his family or other agents, there would be some duty on his part, but it might not extend beyond seriously ill animals for which he knows some arrangements must be attempted. If he has one or more uninjured partners, then of course the partnership is still liable for "carrying on," and the immediate responsibility would devolve on his partners. If he has an animal hospital and animals in his custody, then his employees would be expected to protect the animals unless they are likewise excused by circumstances beyond their control.

3. Destruction of Veterinary Facilities

Since veterinarians are not legally bound to accept cases, the decision to accept no more following destruction of their offices, supplies, and equipment is clearly within their right. But they would still owe a duty to clients whose animals they were attending at the time of the disaster. As indicated under situation 1, their duty will depend on what they are able to do through reasonable efforts. If they cannot find a vehicle to use, they would not be negligent in failing to follow up on a sick animal 10 miles distant from their place of business. Here, again, the law will have to rely on a "rule of reason" and perhaps our statement about "taking the next logical step" in view of particular circumstances and possibilities is as close as we can come to answering the question—"What is the veterinarian's duty to his clients in case of a disaster?"!

4. Treatment of Human Patients

It is the obvious intent of both the federal and state laws in case of emergency to provide for the care of patients and casualties by other than the professional people who would ordinarily care for them.

Veterinarians, dentists, laboratory technicians, biologists—anyone with some special knowledge of physiology or medicine would be expected to take over roles in preference to a layman with no learning or special knowledge of any kind. This, of course, will raise questions about negligence, malpractice, degree of skill and care, and other subjects which in normal times could very well become the basis for law suits. Certainly, the presence of such an emergency and the policy of both state and federal governments would go a long way toward excusing the non-professional in the care of human patients. For want of a better generalization, perhaps one could say such care is justified and would not be subject to action of any kind so long as professional care is not available for patients and casualties requiring attention, and the person in attendance is not wanting in the skill of his calling and is not careless or negligent. Conceivably, this could be for quite a long period if the number of casualties were great and all the professional people in medicine were needed to take care of the most serious cases and to man emergency hospitals and other units.

CHAPTER 18

ANIMAL HOSPITALS

134. **Location of Hospitals.** Many considerations besides the legal ones enter into a decision on the location of an animal hospital or clinic. But there are at least three important legal considerations—municipal or county zoning ordinances, restrictive covenants in deeds, and the nuisance theory.

The purpose of a zoning ordinance is to control the development of a municipality so that maximum use and enjoyment of property can be had by all. Zones are established within which only certain kinds of structures and enterprises are allowed. For example, one zone may permit only residential structures, another may permit residential structures and business establishments, another light industry and another heavy industry. The veterinarian may find that in a particular city he cannot operate a hospital or clinic in the residential zone. Therefore, before one buys or leases property, he should ascertain whether his intended use of it will be permitted. For information, one should contact the zoning enforcement officer or the city attorney. It may be that if the question of animal hospital location is not settled by existing regulations, one can get the municipality to adopt a regulation favorable to him: Zoning regulations must meet the test of reasonableness and necessity, and if there is no good reason for excluding a business from a particular zone, the regulation doing so may be successfully challenged. Also, zoning ordinances cannot be retroactive. That is, they cannot prevent the continuation of a business already located in a zone, though they may operate to prevent any material expansion or change in character. In most states, counties also have the power to zone. Though a veterinarian is not likely to be affected by such ordinances, he may be in cases where the county and municipality have cooperated, and through the use of the county's authority, restrictions have been carried beyond the city limits and into suburban areas.

Deeds of property located in or near municipalities frequently contain restrictive covenants on the use which may be made of the property and on the type and location of structures erected on the property. When a veterinarian purchases property, he should be certain there is nothing in the deed which will interfere with his right to carry out his plans with respect to the use of the property. In a Missouri case, for example, the use of a residence by a veterinarian as a cat and dog hospital was held in violation of certain restrictive covenants in deeds to lots in the subdivision, even though the restrictions excepted maintenance of an office by a physician or dentist in a residence.[358]

Though one may not be subject to zoning regulations or restrictive covenants, he may, under certain circumstances, nevertheless be limited in his right to keep animals. The gist of the nuisance theory is that one should not so use his property as to interfere unreasonably with the surrounding owners' enjoyment of their property. Noise is probably the most frequent complaint, but odors and the maintenance of a health hazard may also give rise to complaints. A veterinarian should consider the possibility of creating a nuisance when he picks a location, and after locating should take reasonable steps to keep his business from creating a nuisance. This is good business and good public relations as well.

135. Obligation to Accept Animals. In one treatise on medical jurisprudence, the writer states that "the board or other governing body may prescribe all reasonable rules for the proper supervision, management and control of a hospital, and may determine the conditions under which patients are to be admitted, retained and discharged."[359] It has been held that a private hospital need not assign a reason for its refusal to accept a patient.[360] An animal hospital is not a public institution in any sense, and is under no obligation to accept animals unless it has voluntarily entered into a contract, either with private persons or public agencies, which obligates it to do so.

136. Bailment—Duties of Bailee. Veterinarians, trainers, stablekeepers, and others with whom animals are left for care, are known as bailees. The owner who leaves them is known as a bailor. If the bailee is paid for his service, the arrangement is called a bailment for hire—if he is not paid, it is known as a gratuitous bailment. Bailees for hire are responsible for the custody and safe care of animals left with them. They are not insurers. But, on the other hand, the fact that they receive pay implies, at least, that they will exercise ordinary care. In some respects, veterinarians are probably charged with more than ordinary care, since they are presumed to know more about the nature of animals and disease transmission than the average person: It would certainly be a breach of the bailment contract for a veterinarian negligently to mingle healthy and diseased animals. Among the duties owed the bailor would be proper feed and care, secure confinement, sanitation to prevent the spread of disease within the hospital, and reasonable precautions against loss by theft or fire. Also, it is implied that the veterinarian will do anything the condition of the animal seems to require. When an animal is released to someone other than the bailor, the veterinarian should make certain that the person to whom the animal is released is an authorized agent of the owner, a transferee of the owner, the true owner, or someone who has authority to receive the animal. Otherwise, the bailor may hold the bailee responsible. Bailment does not imply any right to use the animal, except insofar as certain use may be beneficial to the animal (milking a cow or exercising a horse, for example). Generally, the courts construe contracts of bailment rather strictly. In a Tennessee case, for example, where an owner turned a disabled horse over to an agister with orders to kill it in order to end its suffering, and instead the agister preserved the horse and ultimately sold it; on learning the facts, the owner recovered in assumpsit for use and conversion of the mare. The jury found that he had not abandoned the horse, since the owner's order to kill the animal did not constitute an abandonment as a matter of law.[361]

137. Duties of Bailor. When one places animals in the custody of another, he has a duty to warn the bailee about any unusual or dangerous habits of the animals. If he fails to do so, and the bailee or any of his servants are injured, liability may follow. Also, one bringing an animal to a hospital has a duty to restrain it until custody or control has passed to the hospital or veterinarian. When the contract has been completed, it is the duty of the bailor to take and remove his animals. If he fails to do so, the bailee may recover for feed, care and other expenses, including damages for injuries inflicted by the animals after termination of the contract.[362]

138. Liens against Animals. It has already been stated that a veterinarian not in possession of animals treated has no lien or prior claim for his services. (See Section 45.) The veterinarian who operates an animal hospital is in a different position: He acquires possession, and under one provision of law or another may generally retain possession until paid. The only exception would be in a state that has no statutory agister's lien and that recognizes no common law lien either for care, feed and housing or for veterinary services. Most states have an agister's lien statute, however, and the general rule seems to be that a veterinarian in possession of an animal has a common law lien against it for his professional services.[363]

A lien against female animals would attach to progeny born while the animal was in an animal hospital. Also, it has been held that if any part of the animals are retained, the lien may be enforced against them for the total amount due.[364] Chattel mortgages duly filed or recorded prior to the rendering of services by an animal hospital would take precedence over the lien of the hospital.[365] A lien may be lost by voluntarily surrendering possession, by making an unauthorized use of the animals, or by the tender of a proper amount for services rendered. A temporary surrender of possession or possession gained by the owner through fraudulent statements does not extinguish the lien. If a veterinarian surrenders possession, and at a later date the animal is again returned to him, he may hold it for all that is due on the animal for past as well as present services. However, if the animal is sold and a new owner returns it to the veterinarian, the lien for past services no longer holds.[366] When a lien is created by statute, it must be enforced in the manner provided by statute —generally by notice, advertising and sale.

139. Contracts with Clients. Though written contracts are not necessary to establish the validity of a veterinarian's claim for his professional services, they should be used as a matter of course in the operation of an animal hospital. The contract can take the form of an admission card or form, signed by the owner, and containing pertinent facts regarding the animal admitted, services to be rendered, date of admission and time and method of payment for services. Such an instrument may contain language creating a lien against the animal, and stating the method of enforcement. This should be made in duplicate and a copy given to the owner. The instrument should give the veterinarian maximum latitude in determining the need of animals left with him so that clients will have fewer objections as to the kinds of services rendered. Even so, it is still important to get separate written contracts for euthanasia or for major surgery. Insistence on the use of an admission form or contract may, to some degree, alleviate the problems created when kindly persons leave sick or injured animals not belonging to them, with no intention of paying for the service.

140. **Abandoned Animals.** One of the problems of a veterinarian, and especially of a veterinary hospital, is what to do with abandoned animals. The problem may be difficult or simple, depending on circumstances. If the person who left the animal is unknown or cannot be found, and the ownership of the animal is likewise unknown, the veterinarian has no one to turn to for remuneration. He may dispose of the animal, to a pound or otherwise, but he is out his services and care unless the animal has some value. At the opposite extreme is the owner whose residence is known and who signed a contract, but who simply fails to come and retake the animal. In this case the veterinarian may enforce his lien and dispose of the animal as prescribed by law or as provided in the contract. This emphasizes the importance of having a written contract except in those cases where, for humane reasons, the veterinarian is willing to render service to an animal and take a chance on being paid. Some states have statutes specifying what one can do when he has lost or abandoned property in his possession.

141. **Disposal of Dead Animals.** Death of an animal terminates a bailment,[367] and the animal hospital would ordinarily have no further obligation except to notify the owner and dispose of the body. However, the owner still has a property right in the body if he cares to exert it. In disposing of dead animals, an animal hospital should make certain that a neighborhood nuisance is not created and that sanitary standards are maintained. Disposal may be to a rendering plant or a dead animal service. Care should be taken not to violate any state laws prohibiting the movement on public highways of animals that have died of a contagious disease.

142. **Sanitary Standards.** What was said in Chapter 7 regarding sanitary standards to be observed by the veterinarian holds also for the animal hospital. In addition, there is the problem of maintaining the hospital so it does not become a source of dis-

ease to animals brought in for treatment, and so that it does not create a nuisance. Though there may be no special law on the licensing or inspection of animal hospitals, most states could probably inspect and enforce certain standards under their general authority to control animal disease. Any client who could prove that his animal became diseased or was injuriously affected by failure of an animal hospital to maintain adequate standards could recover any damages suffered by him.[368]

143.   Hospital Employees. The rules of responsibility and liability which generally apply in the employment of help by a veterinarian are covered in Chapter 8. The principles discussed there apply as well to an animal hospital. However, in an establishment employing several persons, different situations are likely to arise. Jobs are apt to be delegated to certain people, for example, and less control exercised by the veterinarian. This may increase the likelihood of liability to a client, and emphasizes the importance of having well-trained and reliable helpers. Also, injuries to employees themselves may sometimes result from the negligence of other employees. In such instances, the employer would be excused from liability under the "fellow-servant" rule, unless the law of the particular state has removed it as a defense. Also, whether or not workmen's compensation acts or other employment legislation applies to a particular employer sometimes depends on the number of persons hired by him.

144.   Liability to Callers. Anyone who operates a business establishment to which the public is "invited" owes a duty to the public to see that his premises are safe. He is not an insurer—that is, he is not liable for every mishap that may occur on his premises—but he must eliminate obvious sources of injury if he is to avoid liability. Dangerous steps, sidewalks or doors, insufficient lighting, unsafe furniture or slick floors, for example, are hazards which should be eliminated. A business caller is in a sense a trespasser, however, when he goes beyond the reception room without having been invited. In such situations, the duty owed by the hospital is very small. People who regularly enter any part of a hospital as a matter of routine (deliveries and pickups, for example) are entitled to assume that the premises are safe. However, as a result of their regular visits, they may be deemed to have assumed certain risks which they know to be present.

CHAPTER 19

VETERINARY PARTNERSHIPS

145. What Is a Partnership? The Uniform Partnership Act, a law operative in most states, defines a partnership as "an association of two or more persons to carry on as co-owners of a business for profit."[369] Further definition has been frequently made by the courts. In an Illinois case, a partnership was described as a contract of mutual agency with each partner acting as a principal on his own behalf and as an agent for his co-parties, and with each partner possessed of a joint interest in the wealth but not owning any separate part of the partnership property.[370] Written articles of agreement are not necessary—a partnership may be created orally or may result from activities carried on by the persons associated.

Both the livestock share lease and various father-son or manager-operator agreements are frequently referred to as "farm partnerships." In a sense, they are partnerships; that is, they are joint arrangements between an owner and his tenant or son to cooperate in carrying on the farm business and to receive income from the farm proportionate to their contribution of land, equipment, livestock, feed, seed, fertilizer, machinery, labor and operating expenses. However, the general assumption is that few of these arrangements are partnerships in the legal sense. This is important because, if an owner and his tenant or son are partners, either of them may make contracts for the business, sell partnership property, or create partnership debts without the consent of the other. Also, an income tax return would have to be made for the partnership, and, in case of death, a partnership accounting would be necessary.

Certain enterprises in which the son or manager contributes only labor would not be considered partnerships, even though they may receive a percentage of the income. The usual crop-share lease, under which the machinery, equipment and livestock are all owned by the tenant, would not create a partnership. The

175

problem arises under livestock leases, with joint ownership of livestock and some equipment. However, the partnership act states that "joint property, common property, or part ownership does not of itself establish a partnership . . . the sharing of gross returns does not of itself establish a partnership, nor does the receipt of a share of the profits if it is received as . . . rent to a landlord."

Whether or not a partnership exists between individuals depends largely upon their intentions. A person dealing with farm owners and tenants is not bound by their intentions, however, and may judge from their actions and business setup as to whether there is a partnership. Each case must be considered by itself. If parties do not wish to create a partnership, they should: 1. Have a written lease or agreement stating that no partnership is intended and specifically designating the owner's or landlord's share as rent. 2. Agree that mutual consent is necessary for major purchases and sales, or specify who shall have authority to handle various kinds of transactions. This is not absolute insurance that the arrangement will not be considered a partnership, but it will add weight to the negative side.

146. **Reasons for Establishing a Partnership.** There are many circumstances under which two or more persons may be able to increase their income and gain other advantages by associating as partners. The plan has been widely used by professional men. Among the advantages or reasons for associating are the following:

1. More capital can be put into the business.
2. The risks are shared.
3. A better division of work can be effectuated, with free time and vacations more certain.
4. Specialization is possible.
5. The business is more likely to be perpetuated.
6. Losses which generally result when a deceased person's property must be sold are minimized.
7. Income for older partners can be prolonged.
8. Younger partners can earn a livelihood while they acquire skill and experience.
9. Older partners can work less without running the risk of losing clientele.

10. Younger members are busy from the outset and gain skill and experience more rapidly.

147. The Agency Relation of Partners. The Uniform Act states that "every partner is an agent of the partnership for the purpose of its business, and the act of every partner, including the execution in the partnership name of any instrument, for apparently carrying on in the usual way the business of the partnership of which he is a member binds the partnership. . . ."[371] However, a partner cannot bind a partnership under the following circumstances:

1. When he in fact has no authority and the one with whom he is dealing is aware of his lack of authority.
2. When his act is not apparently for the business and his partners have not given him authority.
3. Unless joined by all the other partners (except when they have abandoned the business) he cannot:
   a. Assign partnership property for the benefit of creditors.
   b. Dispose of the goodwill of the business.
   c. Do any act which would make it impossible to carry on the ordinary business of the partnership.
   d. Confess a judgment.
   e. Submit a partnership claim to arbitration.

Another consequence of the agency relation is that notice to one partner constitutes notice to the partnership.

It is obvious that one irresponsible partner can virtually ruin a partnership. The more or less unlimited agency authority possessed by each partner is one of the chief deterrents to the establishment of partnerships. Certainly, caution should be exercised in the choosing of one's partners—in some respects it parallels the choosing of a wife or husband.

148. Contractual Liability of Partners. From what has been said about the agency relation, it is obvious that one partner can make contracts binding the partnership. This raises the next question: "How far can a party go in pursuing his contractual rights against a partnership?" The answer to this question discloses one of the basic differences between a partnership and a corporation. In the case of a corporation, the creditor cannot ordinarily look beyond the assets of the corporation itself—it is a legal person. But in the case of a partnership, creditors can pursue their claims against any or all of the partners themselves. So, if a contract cannot be satisfied out of partnership assets, the creditor may then proceed against the personal assets of the partners. Of course, any partner who had to satisfy a partnership obligation would then have a claim against partnership assets, but this might be worth very little unless the partnership is still a going concern. Thus, another reason is disclosed for picking partners with care.

149. Tort Liability of Partners. Brown and Jones are partners in veterinary practice. Brown answers an urgent call from a client. On his way he fails to slow down at a county road intersection and crashes into a tractor. The operator is killed. A lawsuit follows. Who can be sued, and for what? The Partnership Act states that

> Where, by any wrongful act or omission of any partner acting in the ordinary course of the business of the partnership, or with the authority of his co-partners, loss or injury is caused to any person, not being a partner in the partnership, or any penalty is incurred, the partnership is liable therefor to the same extent as the partner so acting or omitting to act.

Brown can be sued. The partnership can be sued. If a recovery of $12,000 can be had against Brown, it can be had against the partnership. If a judgment is entered against the partnership, its assets can be taken in satisfaction. If they are insufficient, the personal assets of the partners may be taken. Automobile accidents are not the only ways in which a partner may create such liability. Malpractice, negligence in handling animals, lack of care in handling biologics, in fact, any fault or omission which might bring liability to the veterinarian, can bring it to the partnership, and ultimately, to all the partners. The best antidotes are insurance and due care.

150. The Partnership Agreement or Articles. Persons contemplating a veterinary partnership should settle several major questions involving their relations in the business, and should reduce their conclusions to writing. This, then, will become the "core" of a written partnership agreement. Though each case should be worked out to suit the partners, there are some elements common to all veterinary partnerships. These have been very well set forth by an experienced veterinarian in a review article.[372] His suggestions are as follows:

ARTICLES OF CO-PARTNERSHIP

THIS CONTRACT is made and entered into on the _____ day of _____, 19___, by and between Dr. _____, hereinafter known as the Senior Partner, and Dr. _____, hereinafter known as the Junior Partner.

WITNESSED: Both of said parties have agreed, and by these presents do agree to associate themselves for a period of _____ years from the date hereof as co-partners in the profession and practice of veterinary medicine in all its branches under firm name of _____ and, during such period, to devote their entire time severally to the professional business of said firm to the best of their ability and skill and for the mutual advantages and benefits thereof.

First: The said co-partnership is to continue for the period specified herein from the date hereof and is to exist during that time. It may be terminated upon the expressed desire of either party in writing or notice within sixty days of the termination thereof.

Second: In case of death of either party, this contract becomes wholly binding and the clauses herein incontestable.

Third: Senior Partner shall be vested with the administration of the practice and hospital, shall be in possession of and in control of the joint practice of both partners and shall administer, direct, charge, audit and collect fees therefor.

Fourth: All income for the joint practice shall be banked by the Senior Partner, and after all expenses of practice are paid, the net profits shall be shared as follows: First fiscal year, Senior Partner 75%, Junior Partner 25%; second fiscal year, Senior Partner 70% , Junior Partner 30%; third fiscal year, Senior Partner 65%, Junior Partner 35%; fourth fiscal year, Senior Partner 60%, Junior Partner 40%. Thereafter the proportionate share of the net proceeds from the joint practice shall be Senior Partner 55%, and Junior Partner 45% until the dissolution of the co-partnership or upon the death of one partner.

Fifth: The Senior Partner shall deduct and place in a savings first fund in the name of the joint co-partnership ten percent (10%) of the Junior Partner's proportionate share of the net proceeds at the current rate of interest.

Sixth: This monthly deduction recited in the fifth article shall continue each fiscal year until the dissolution of the co-partnership or the death of one of the partners, and shall be banked in the prescribed manner.

Seventh: Upon the death of either party, these accumulated funds shall become the property of the surviving partner. Upon retirement or death of the Senior Partner, or upon dissolution of this co-partnership at the time stated above, these accumulated funds shall become the property of the Junior Partner. Upon the termination of this contract before the time stated above, these accumulated funds shall become the property of the Junior Partner. Upon the termination of this contract before the time stated above, upon written petition of either or both parties, these accumulated funds shall become the property of the Senior Partner.

Eighth: Each partner is to devote his entire time and attention to the joint practice and to engage in no other business enterprise without the written consent of the other.

Ninth: It is expressly stipulated that the Junior Partner will help in all cases when needed, and will perform those duties assigned to him at the discretion of the Senior Partner.

Tenth: Either party shall assume the entire joint practice in the absence of the other partner on account of sickness, vacation or other reason.

Eleventh: The Senior Partner shall have one month's vacation a year and the Junior Partner two weeks' vacation each year, both in addition to attendance at medical meetings. These vacations shall be at the discretion of the Senior Partner.

Twelfth: Neither partner is to become surety or bondsman for anyone without the written consent of the other.

Thirteenth: In case of the death of either party, a list of outstanding accounts shall be submitted to the deceased partner's family, and the surviving partner shall be honor-bound and legally obligated to attempt to collect and return to the deceased's family the proportionate share of such outstanding accounts as determined by the fiscal year and month in which the death of the deceased partner occurred.

Fourteenth: In case of the death of either party, the proportionate share of the hospital property and equipment shall become the purchasable property of the surviving partner, and the deceased's family shall be paid the full amount of the deceased's share thereof from the accumulated trust fund as recited in Article Five herein.

Fifteenth: It is expressly stipulated that each partner will be liable only for the acts, indebtedness and liabilities of the other partner as occur in the actual pursuance of the joint practice of veterinary medicine, and that to his proportionate share in the partnership that exists at the time of the commission thereof.

Sixteenth: An AVMA insurance policy against malpractice, issued in the name of the co-partnership, shall be maintained and paid from the funds accruing from the joint practice, and this expense shall be considered general office expense of the practice.

In witness whereof, the parties aforesaid have hereunto set their hands and affixed their seals on the day and year above written.

_____
Senior Partner
_____
Junior Partner

All of the provisions in this suggested agreement might not apply in a particular case. For example, partners might wish to work out a scheme or division of income which would differ from that suggested in paragraphs four, five and six of the above form.

151. Partnership Accounting and Dissolution. The Uniform Act provides that "the partnership books shall be kept, subject to any agreement between the partners, at the principal place of business of the partnership, and every partner shall at all times have access to and may inspect and copy any of them,"[373] that "partners shall render on demand true and full information of all things affecting the partnership to any partner or the legal representative of any deceased partner or partner under legal disability."[374] The Act further provides that every partner must account to the partnership for any profit derived by him without the consent of the other partners, from any transaction connected with the partnership. Besides the responsibility to account, the law provides that any partner may demand a formal accounting when:

1. He is wrongfully excluded from the business by his co-partners.
2. A right exists under the articles of agreement.
3. Circumstances render it just and reasonable.

The affairs of a partnership may be terminated voluntarily by the partners, or by a change in relation due to one partner no longer being associated with the business. In either case, the Partnership Act provides certain machinery for determining the rights of partners or the heirs and assigns of partners. Dissolution may be decreed by a court on application by or on behalf of a partner. Also, the partnership agreement itself may contain specific provisos on the death of a partner and how his interest is to be handled. Except for obligations already incurred, dissolution terminates the existence of the partnership together with the rights and liabilities incident to it.

CHAPTER 20

TAXES AND INSURANCE

152. **Property Taxes.** Assessment against property is a common device for raising revenue. These assessments fall into two categories, those against personal property and those against real estate. Some states do not use a personal property tax. In a state where a personal property tax is used, an owner's automobile, equipment, furnishings and supplies would be appraised annually, and the tax rate for his unit of government applied to determine his tax. If a partnership is involved, all personal property belonging to the partnership would be assessed and the tax would be an obligation of the partnership. Exemptions of various kinds have been written into many state laws. Some of a veterinarian's property, therefore, may be exempt in particular states—his professional instruments and equipment, for example.

Evaluations of real estate for assessment purposes are generally made for periods longer than one year. Four years is the usual period. A veterinarian's office and the land on which it is situated, or an animal hospital and the land on which it is situated would be evaluated by the assessor and the tax liability then determined by applying the combined rates for schools, roads and other purposes to this valuation. A reviewing authority is provided in each county, and if an owner is not satisfied with the valuation placed on his property, he may be heard. Real estate located in a municipality, drainage district, or other public corporation with the authority to raise revenue, is subject to special assessments levied by those entities. Generally, however, all such assessments against property are collected at one time with the general property tax, and are included on the same tax bill. Property taxes may be paid in installments, as provided by law. Failure to pay such a tax subjects the property to forfeiture, and it may be sold at public sale to satisfy the obligation.

153. **Sales and Service Occupation Taxes.** Many states have a "service occupation tax," imposed on certain sales to the veteri-

narian. Medicines or other items purchased for use as incident to his professional treatment of animals are taxable when sold to the veterinarian but are **not** taxable when transferred to his clients. Medicines or other items sold not as incident to the treatment of an animal are taxable when sold by the veterinarian, and he must make an accounting for the tax on all such sales.

Obviously there is a puzzling strip of gray between clear cases on each end of this example, and rules from the revenue department must further clarify the meaning of "incident to his service." It should be noted that taxation of sales by the veterinarian are not imposed by the "service occupation tax," but by provisions of the current sales tax (retailers occupational tax) and by the "service use tax." However, these tax laws are so worded as to prevent double taxation. If the veterinarian pays a tax on a sale by him, then he should not have paid a service occupation tax to the company which sold to him. It is presumed that anything purchased to be used as incident to the treatment of animals is taxed when sold to the veterinarian, and not thereafter.

If the veterinarian does not know exactly how a stock of supplies will be disposed of, he must then give his supplier a certificate reporting his Department of Revenue registration number, and make an accounting. He will then pay service tax, sales tax, or no tax as his various methods of disposal indicate. Obviously the veterinarian who uses all materials purchased as incident to his practice will have fewer accounting headaches, because his suppliers will have to collect and remit the tax.

Both the service tax and the sales tax have provisions making the purchasing veterinarian liable for payment of the tax when the seller is not a resident of the state and does not qualify as a collector of the tax. Veterinarians should familiarize themselves with the laws of their state on these taxes.

154. **Income Taxes.** Federal income tax is based on one's net income, as determined under federal laws and regulations. One man may gross $25,000 and another $35,000, while their income tax liability may be about the same. Business expenses, depreciation, and other legitimate deductions account for the difference. Many professional men are entitled to deductions which many times are not claimed—or which could be claimed if adequate records were maintained. This suggests the importance of

a good accounting system and the maintenance of good business records. Competent assistance with income tax problems should be employed. Frequently, personnel in a collector's office can clarify specific problems for the taxpayer, but a veterinarian needs someone to help him plan his whole system of records and business procedures with the tax angle—as well as other angles— in mind. Without any pretense at being exhaustive, here are some examples of deductions which a veterinarian may make.

Building. Heating, lighting, insurance, maintenance, repair, depreciation, and other expenses necessary to keep his office going—even moving expenses—may be included. If a building is rented, the rent plus any additional expense borne by the lessee may be deducted.

Travel. All automobile expenses including depreciation may be deducted. If the vehicle is used partly for family purposes, then a percentage figure should be used to determine the proportion of all costs chargeable to the business. Travel by public carrier may be deducted when it is in connection with the business —even trips to meetings and conventions.

Equipment, services and supplies. Equipment other than that on which depreciation may be taken, supplies of all kinds for the business, laundry and other services for the business, tax and accounting fees, telephone, books and subscriptions and dues may all be deducted.

Bad debts and interest on money borrowed may also be deducted.

Partnerships are required to make an income tax return, though the partnership itself pays no tax. Each partner includes in his return his distributive share as disclosed by the partnership return.

155. **Sales Tax.** Sales taxes or retailer's occupation taxes are state taxes, and apply to the sale of goods at retail. These laws all provide for some exemptions. Ordinarily exempted are "occasional sales," or sales not normally a part of one's business. A veterinarian using drugs, medicines and other products in the course of his practice would probably not have to make a tax return on such products in most states. However, if he engages in the business of dispensing drugs, and makes substantial sales

from his place of business, which sales are not associated with his treatment of animals, he might very well be required to make a return. The revenue laws and regulations of the particular state should be checked on these points.

156. Insurance Against Property and Business Losses. Certain hazards are a part of every business. The veterinary profession is no exception. A veterinarian's property may be damaged or destroyed by fire or wind, his premises may be burglarized, his car may be wrecked, or he may lose profits and be unable to pay his creditors because of illness and inability to carry on his practice. Insurance is available to cover these and other hazards. Fire and windstorm, burglary and theft, collision, mortgage, and health and accident insurance are among the policies which may be procured. The best procedure for a veterinarian is to talk over his needs with a reliable insurance agent and get the coverage he feels he needs.

For the livestock owner, fire and windstorm insurance is available, but policies covering death of animals by disease or accident are costly, and are generally justified only on valuable animals. Insurance against loss in transportation is available at reasonable premiums.

157. Liability Insurance. The veterinarian is concerned about the liability which may result from four sources—his negligence toward clients in carrying on his professional work or operating an animal hospital; his negligence toward third parties (another motorist, for example); his negligence toward his employees; and his employees' negligence toward clients and others. Liability insurance is available to cover all these risks.

Professional liability insurance, covering liability to clients, is available through the American Veterinary Medical Association. This is in a sense "malpractice" insurance.

Insurance covering **liability to persons and property** in the use of an automobile is widely available. This may be made to cover both owned and rented cars, and to cover either the owner or any other authorized person using his car.

Comprehensive liability insurance covers injuries to third parties by the veterinarian or his employees and agents which might not be covered in an automobile liability policy—escape of animals and dog bites, for example.

Employer's liability insurance, either as required by the state workmen's compensation law, when such a law applies to the veterinarian, or as sold by private insurance companies, covers liability to one's employees where they are injured in the course of the business.

In purchasing any insurance, it pays to read the policy. In a Missouri case, for example, an accident policy was held not to cover the death of a veterinarian from blood poisoning resulting from a cut on his finger accidentally received while inoculating a hog, upon the ground that a veterinarian is not a "surgeon," within the meaning of clause in the policy making the insurer liable "in the event that a legally qualified physician, surgeon, or dentist, while holding an autopsy or performing a surgical operation, . . . actually cuts or wounds himself, and by reason of such cutting or wounding and simultaneously therewith be inoculated with poison."[375]

CHAPTER 21

REAL ESTATE, LEASES AND WILLS

158. Property Ownership. The chief distinction between real property (real estate) and personal property is that real property is relatively immovable. The land and the improvements permanently attached to it are regarded as real property. Ownership of real property is usually called holding the title to it. "Holding title" usually means that the ownership is evidenced by an instrument that the law recognizes as a proper means of transfer, ordinarily a deed or will.

The legal interest an owner has in real estate may be one of several kinds. He may hold the land in fee simple (the highest kind of ownership). He may have a life interest in it, or he may stand to take it on the death of the life tenant. He may also have one of several other kinds of legal interest, some of which, especially those dependent on future events, may be highly contingent. Also, if one is purchasing property under a contract, or mortgages the property to another, he does not have the "legal" title any longer, but has what is spoken of as an "equitable" interest.

Much land is held by persons entitled only to a life interest. Technically, such a person is known as a life tenant. Actually, he is not a tenant in the same sense that a farm tenant is, but resembles an owner. During his lifetime he may rent the land to others, farm it himself, and take all the income or make nearly any use of it he sees fit. He cannot sell or mortgage the land, however, because he is entitled only to the use of the property and not to the fee or title interest. This interest belongs either to some person who has been designated to take the land at the death of the life tenant or, in case no one has been designated, to the one who created the life estate, or to his heirs. The former are known as remaindermen, the latter as reversioners.

Life estates may be created by will or deed, or may come about by operation of law. The dower interest which may be elected by a surviving spouse is an example of the latter. Life estates are usually created by persons who want to make sure that some particular individual is given a means of income during life, but who wish also to designate what shall happen to the land at the termination of the life tenancy. For example, farm owners frequently deed the farm to their children, reserving a life estate in themselves; or a husband may make a will giving the land to his children, subject to a life estate in his wife.

Although life tenants cannot willfully destroy buildings, timber or other parts of the real estate, the remainderman cannot compel them to use sound farming practices.

One who rents from a life tenant must yield possession at the time the life tenant dies, regardless of the length of time for which he may have rented the premises. If possible, it is good practice to secure the signatures of the remaindermen when renting from a life tenant.

When two or more persons have "undivided" interests in the same piece of land, they are known as "tenants in common." Suppose, for example, that two children inherit a 200-acre farm from their mother. Each of them will own 100 acres, but it will not be any particular 100 acres; rather, it will be an undivided ½ of 200 acres. Suppose there were five children. Then each would own an undivided 1/5 of the 200 acres, or an undivided 40 acres.

These tenancies in common may be created by deed or will, but generally they arise when property is not disposed of by will and passes to the heirs by the laws of descent. The undivided interests need not be equal. Also, these undivided interests may be sold, the purchaser then becoming a tenant in common with the other owners.

Frequently, the term "estate" is used to describe undivided ownership by several heirs, a reference to the "Jones estate" meaning the undivided holding by Jones' heirs following his death. Sometimes "estates" are so held, without partition or division, for many years.

There is a particular kind of undivided ownership known as a "joint tenancy." By joint tenancy is meant an undivided ownership of property by two or more persons, each having the right to take immediately all the property or his increased interest in it on the death of the other joint tenants. When a husband and wife are joint tenants, should one or the other die, title and ownership of the property immediately pass to the other spouse. It would not be a part of the decedent's estate and would not be subject to administration. However, federal estate and state inheritance taxes may be payable, depending on the size of the interest passing from one joint tenant to the other. There are circumstances in which the creation of a joint tenancy may increase the tax liability of an estate. This is a point—along with others—which should be checked carefully by a competent lawyer, and discussed with him, before deciding that a joint tenancy is desirable.

A tenancy in common differs from a joint tenancy in that it does not carry the all-important right of survivorship, so that when a tenant-in-common dies, his share must be set aside, administered and divided among heirs. Joint tenancies may be created by will as well as by deed.

Husbands and wives like joint tenancy because it is a certain way of passing the whole legal interest in the property immediately to the survivor. However, there are some objections to it, apart from the fact that it does not always represent a tax saving. The heirs are assured of nothing, because the surviving spouse has complete freedom to sell or otherwise dispose of the property. Also, if a surviving spouse remarries, the second husband or wife automatically qualifies for dower rights in the property; and if children are born to the second marriage, they are in position to inherit a portion of the property. Also, during the existence of the joint tenancy relation, either joint tenant may sell his or her undivided interest. This destroys the joint tenancy and the right of survivorship, and makes the purchaser and the remaining joint tenant owners in common without any right of survivorship.

159. **Titles.** Prospective buyers of real estate need to know at least two important things: the true value of the property and the state of the title. Information about the title can be gained only through a summary of the essential facts contained in all conveyances or encumbrances that in any way affect the land. An abstract is such a summary. Generally, abstracts are prepared by private companies which make a charge for their services.

In the preparation of an abstract, a search must be made through records in the offices of the county recorder, county clerk, circuit clerk, or other local office maintaining records affecting property. Each instrument or record, whether a deed, mortgage, release, divorce decree or other document, is carefully abstracted for essential facts, numbered and placed chronologically with other summaries. When all such records have been summarized and arranged, they are stapled together. The document is called an abstract.

Contrary to the belief of many people, an abstract is not a guarantee of good title. It is simply a record of what has legally affected the property. An abstract may disclose that the title is very insecure. One of the benefits of such a document is that weaknesses are disclosed and the purchaser is given an opportunity to have defects removed before taking title.

Abstracts should be examined by a person competent to pass judgment on the facts that have been abstracted and capable of discerning the absence of necessary facts. Such persons are generally lawyers who have had a great deal of experience in preparing and examining real estate documents.

Regardless of how sound a buyer may consider the title to be, it is good business for him to procure an up-to-date abstract from a reliable company and have it examined by an experienced person. He may give himself still further protection by purchasing a title guaranty policy. In this latter case, his title will be registered in the private registration system used by the guaranty company, and future transfers are then greatly simplified.

The buyer is further protected through the use of a warranty deed. This does not mean that the title is perfect. It means only that if imperfections come to light, the seller will "make the buyer whole."

160. Procedure Involved in Buying Property. Assuming that an adequate appraisal of a prospective purchase has been made and that a site satisfactory to the veterinarian can be purchased for what it is worth, what steps need to be taken to effect a satisfactory change of ownership? This is a question which every buyer should ask himself. A list of some of the appropriate answers follows.

1. Find a credit agency that will finance the purchase under suitable terms. A financing plan should provide for an amortized method of payment over a fairly long term of years at not more than the going interest rate. Twenty years may be considered as a reasonable period for a loan. However, many sound loans are made for shorter periods.

2. A contract should be drawn up with the seller and signed by seller and buyer. Among other things, this contract should:

a. Specify the amount of the purchase price and how and when it is to be paid.

b. Specify that insurance policies in force on the property shall be transferred to the buyer and that any payments for losses occurring following the date of the contract shall be payable as the interests of the parties appear.

c. Designate by whom current taxes, assessments, and insurance premiums shall be paid. These may be apportioned between the buyer and seller, depending upon the amount of the current term for each item that has elapsed at the time of the sale date or of taking possession or title. Sometimes the buyer simply agrees to pay installments that become due after the date of purchase.

d. Provide that the seller shall pay all past assessments, taxes, or obligations of any kind against the land, prior to final settlement.

e. Require the seller to provide an abstract containing all entries up to the present transaction and showing a clear and merchantable title.

f. Provide for the delivery of a warranty deed free of exceptions or conditions, at the time final settlement is made with the seller.

g. Provide for any special things which the seller agrees to do before delivery of possession, such as repairing a building.

3. Reach an agreement with the lending agency specifying:

a. The amount borrowed.

b. The interest rate.

c. The period for repayment.

d. The number, amount, and date of annual installments.

e. Repayment privileges, particularly with respect to the amount of principal that can be repaid in any one year.

f. Appraisal fees or other loan service charges.

g. Any special provisions in case of default in repayment of the loan.

4. The warranty deed should:

a. Be executed by the seller and, if a long term purchase contract is involved, placed in the hands of an escrow agent. The bank where installments are paid frequently acts as escrow agent.

b. Specify in whom the title is to vest: for example, "John Jones" or "John Jones and Nellie Jones, his wife, as joint tenants and not as tenants in common."

c. Be signed and sealed by the seller and his or her spouse, contain a properly executed waiver of dower and homestead rights, and be acknowledged before an authorized person.

5. The abstract should be examined by a competent attorney.

6. Any defects in the title should be cleared by the seller before making final settlement.

7. When the deed has been received, it must be recorded.

8. When the deed is recorded, a mortgage is issued to the lending agency to secure the notes given for the amount advanced to pay for the property. The mortgage and notes should be in accord with the original agreement relative to the terms of the loan. Frequently, a trust deed is used in place of a mortgage.

9. Other points to consider:

a. Who is now occupying the premises you are buying? If a tenant, what are his rights? Does he have a written lease? When and how can his term be terminated and you take possession? What are his rights in improvements now on the land?

b. If you buy through a real estate firm and the firm offers to find a loan for you, or get your title examined, or draw up your contract with the seller, or place your insurance for you, be sure you are getting competent service in all these things; that you are dealing with companies or individuals as reliable as you could pick for yourself; and that costs are not out of line with those you could get from companies or individuals selected by you to perform these services.

c. Be certain there are no valid liens, judgments, or other obligations not appearing in the abstract; that any mineral leases or deeds which may have been executed have been released, that there are no transcripts of records of proceedings in a federal court affecting the property, which have not been examined.

d. Find out if anyone has an easement to the use of the land as a driveway or for other purposes and if there are any existing controversies over such easements.

10. When final payment has been made on the loan, a release of the mortgage or trust deed must be executed and recorded.

161. Leasing Space for a Veterinary Practice. When one leases space to establish and carry on a profession, certain considerations become very important: How long can tenure be provided? How much latitude will the tenant have in remodeling and changing? Can the premises be sub-leased?

Though a short term lease with an option to renew may be desirable at the outset, the veterinarian may eventually desire a long term lease, with the right to sub-lease or assign. A lease with an "automatic continuation" clause, keeping it in effect year after year unless one of the parties gives notice as prescribed, is a good type of lease. The lease should state the purpose for which the property is to be used, but should go as far as the owner and possible zoning regulations or other restrictions will permit in allowing the lessee to change the use.

Among the specific items for which the lease should spell out responsibility are heat, light, water, repairs, paint and improvements. Also, the lease should permit the veterinarian to remove improvements made by him in case the lease is terminated. The right to make such improvements as are necessary to carry on his profession should be stated in the lease. The property leased should be accurately described. If the property for any reason becomes untenantable—the tenant should be excused from continuing under the lease. If the owner reserves the right to terminate the lease in case of sale, or for some other reason, the lease should provide for an adequate period of notice to the lessee.

It is a good idea to secure the services of an attorney in working out a lease agreement.

162. The Will. When one dies without leaving a will, his property, both real and personal, is distributed among his next of kin according to the rules of descent adopted by the legislature of the particular state. In most cases, some improvement could be made in this distribution, and some tax saving made, by leaving a will.

Generally speaking, good wills are not as difficult to make as most people believe. Bad wills are nearly always a result of wanting to provide for too many contingencies, hasty preparation, poor wording, or failure to regard the fairly simple requirements of the law. Since the courts have had to construe the meaning of particular phrases in wills, they have oftentimes found it necessary to give these phrases meanings which may not correspond with the particular maker's intent. Hence, the maker should always consult a competent lawyer, not only for aid in planning the distribution of his estate, but also about the wording and execution of the instrument. Though the laws of each state prescribe how wills may be made, there are a few principles which apply generally. Any person of sound mind and memory, and of the age prescribed by law may make a will. With a few limited exceptions, wills must be in writing and signed in the presence of the maker by two or more credible witnesses who will swear before the probate court that they saw the deceased sign the will, or that he acknowledged it to be his act. When witnesses are dead or otherwise unavailable, their signatures may be proved.

Dates and addresses, though not necessary, should be inserted—particularly the date showing when the will was made. The language should be simple and direct so that it will not be misinterpreted, and it must show that the instrument is to be effective only in the event of death.

Wills may be used to dispose of all kinds of property, both real and personal, to create trusts or to give many different kinds of interests to desired parties.

When a will is left, it must be presented for probate by the person having it in his possession. Letters testamentary are then issued to the executor named in the will, or to another in accordance with provisions of the law. When there is no will, the person appointed by the court is known as an administrator. When both testate (included in a will) and intestate property are involved, the court may issue letters to an administrator with the will annexed. In all cases, an executor and administrator are charged by law with the preservation and management of the estate during administration, the collection and payment of debts, and with making a final accounting and settlement. There are many other specific duties prescribed by law, but these are the principal ones.

The procedures are so involved that most executors and administrators need legal assistance. When estates are not settled quickly, the honesty, interest and managerial ability of the executor become highly important.

Sometimes when people die, they leave more than one will. By law, any will that has not been revoked must be admitted to probate. When two or more wills are "construed together," as the courts say, confusion often results. This situation may be avoided in one of two ways: 1. by retaining the original will and adding to it a "codicil" containing desired changes or alterations, or 2. by revoking all earlier wills and substituting a new one. Much litigation has arisen out of the question of revocation. Was the will revoked, or wasn't it? To help clarify this problem, legislatures have specified the ways in which a person may revoke his will. Burning, cancelling, tearing or obliterating, making another will declaring the previous will revoked, inconsistent provisions of a later will—but only as to matters not consistent—or a separate instrument executed like a will, declaring the will revoked, are all ways of revoking a will.

Marriage generally revokes a will made prior to the date of the marriage. Divorce does not revoke a will.

TABLE OF CASES

1. Hendershot v. Western Union Telegraph Company, 106 Ia. 529, 76 N.W. 828.
2. Erickson v. Webber, 58 S.D. 446, 237 N.W. 558 (1931).
3. Pearson v. Zehr, 138 Ill. 48, 29 N.E. 854 (1891).
4. Rouse v. Youard, 1 Kan. App. 270, 41 P. 426.
5. Grayson v. Lynch, 163 U.S. 468, 16 S.Ct. 1064 (1896).
6. Bekkemo v. Erickson, 186 Minn. 108, 242 N.W. 617 (1932).
7. Miller v. Horton, 152 Mass. 540 (1891).
8. Saunders v. Commonwealth, 117 Ky. 1, 77 S.W. 352 (1903).
9. Seigle v. Bromley, 22 Colo. App. 189, 124 P. 191.
10. Miller v. Buach, 32 Texas 208.
11. Peet Stock Remedy Co. v. McMullen, 32 F. 2d 669 (1929); Barnes v. State, 83 Neb. 443, 119 N.W. 662 (1909); Pistole v. State, 68 Ca. R 127, 150 S.W. 618 (1912).
12. Barnes v. State, 83 Neb. 443, 119 N.W. 662 (1909).
13. Folsom v. State Vet. Bd., 158 Mich. 277 (1909).
14. Pistole v. State, 68 Ca. R. 127, 150 S.W. 618 (1912).
15. Royal College of Veterinary Surgeons v. Robinson, 12 B. 557, 66 L.T. 263 (1892).
16. Royal College of Veterinary Surgeons v. Groves, 57 J.P. 505 (1894).
17. Attorney-General v. Churchill's Veterinary Sanitorium, Ltd., 2 Ch. 401, 103 L.T. 368 (1910).
18. 44 and 45 Vict. C. 62.
19. Royal College of Veterinary Surgeons v. Collinson, 2 K.B. 248, 99 L.T. 122 (1908).
20. 1 K.B. 92, 109 L.T. 866 (1914).
21. Commonwealth v. Palmer, 71 Pa. Super. 188 (1919).
22. Commonwealth v. Pearce, 23 Dist. 1048, 42 C.C. 409 (1914).
23. Commonwealth v. Heller, 277 Pa. 539, 121 A. 558 (1923).
24. Ex parte Oliver, 134 S.E. 657 (1925); Gregory v. McInnis, 140 S.C. 48, 134 S.E. 527 (1926).
25. See note 11.
26. Rader v. Elliott, 181 Ia. 156, 163 N.W. 406 (1917).
27. Kerbs v. State Veterinary Board, 154 Mich. 500 (1908).
28. Jennings v. State Veterinary Board, 156 Mich. 417 (1909).
29. 157 Mich. 246 (1909).
30. See note 22.
31. Staniforth v. State, 34 O.A. 241, 170 N.E. 578 (1929).
32. Reid v. Robertson, 304 Ky. 509, 200 S.W. 2d 900 (1947).
33. Dollar v. Reid, 308 Ky. 348, 214 S.W. 2d 584 (1948).
34. Cooper v. State Board, 114 N.J.L. 10, 175 A. 207 (1934); affirmed 115 N.J.L. 115, 178 A. 748 (1935).
35. 305 Ky. 528, 204 S.W. 2d 954 (1947).

36. 138 Mich. 428 (1904).
37. See note 26.
38. Drummond v. Rowe, 155 Va. 725, 156 S.E. 442 (1931).
39. See note 26.
40. Conkey v. Carpenter, 106 Mich. 1 (1895).
41. Barfield v. State, 71 Okla. Cr. 195, 110 P. 2d 316 (1941).
42. State v. Ramsey, 31 N.D. 626, 154 N.W. 731 (1915).
43. Missouri Veterinary Medical Assoc. v. Glison, 230 S.W. 2d 169 (1950).
44. Rhoden v. Oregon State Veterinary Medicine Examining Board, 223 P. 2d 804 (1950).
45. Commonwealth v. Weber, 32 Lanc. 341 (1915).
46. Buttersworth v. Sevint, 186 S.E. 770 (1936).
47. D. Harcourt Kitchin, *Legal Problems in Medical Practice*, p. 13 (1936) —England.
48. Hurley v. Eddingfield, 156 Ind. 416, 59 N.E. 1058 (1901).
49. Tomer v. Aiken, 126 Ia. 114, 101 N.W. 769 (1904).
50. Limbaugh v. Watson, 37 Ohio L. Rep. 6 (1932).
51. Childers v. Faye, 201 N.C. 42, 158 S.E. 744 (1931).
52. Boom v. Reed, 69 Hun. 426, 23 N.Y.S. 421 (1893).
53. William v. Gilman, 71 Me. 21 (1880).
54. 30 CYC 1573.
55. Dashiell v. Griffith, 84 Md. 363, 35 Atl. 1094.
56. Brent v. Kimball, 60 Ill. 211, 14 Am. Rep. 35 (1871).
57. Durand v. Dyson, 271 Ill. 382, 111 N.E. 143 (1916); Thompson v. State, 4 Ill. Ct. Cl. 26; People v. Anderson, 355 Ill. 289, 189 N.E. 338 (1934).
58. Miller v. Horton, 152 Mass. 540 (1891).
59. See note 3.
60. Polar Wave Ice and Fuel Co. v. Alton Branch of Illinois Humane Society, 153 Ill. App. 310 (1910).
61. Becker v. Janinski, 15 N.Y.S. 675, 27 Abb. N.C. 45.
62. Conner v. Winton, 8 Ind. 315, 65 Am. Dec. 761 (1856).
63. Morrison v. Altig, 157 Ia. 265, 138 N.W. 510 (1912).
64. Carroll v. Bell, 15 West. Law. Rep. 327 (Canada, 1910).
65. Citpion v. Fields, 30 Cal. App. 2d 51, 85 P. 2d 534 (1939).
66. Wheaton v. Johnson, 55 Ill. App. 53 (1893).
67. Baird v. Smith, 21 Cal. App. 2d 221, 68 P. 2d 979 (1937).
68. Yeates v. Boyd, 50 Ga. App. 331, 177 S.E. 921 (1935).
69. Moyer v. Piechocinska, 31 N.Y.S. 2d 308 (1942).
70. Smith v. Quayle, 14 N.Y.S. 2d 741, 258 App. Div. 769 (1939).
71. Scanlon v. Anderson, 49 R.I. 470, 144 A. 146 (1929).
72. Henderson and Campbell v. Hall and Hughes, 87 Ark. 1, 112 S.W. 171.
73. Orr v. Meek, 111 Ind. 40, 11 N.E. 787 (1887); Adams Adm. v. Stewart, 5 Har. 144 (Mich.); Prevosty v. Nichols, 11 Mart. O.S. 21 (La.).
74. McKleroy v. Sewell, 73 Ga. 657.
75. 21 Ruling Case Law 387.
76. Leighton v. Sargent, 27 N.H. 460 (1853).
77. Wood v. Clapp, 4 Sneed 65, 36 Tenn. 65 (1856).
78. United States v. Russell and Tucker, 95 F. 2d 684 (1938).

120. 21 U.S.C. 101-105.
121. 21 U.S.C. 71-96 and 141-149.
122. 46 U.S.C. 466a,b.
123. Estes v. United States, CCA 8, 227 Fed. 818 (1915).
124. 30 O.A.G. 325.
125. 21 U.S.C. 71-96.
126. 21 U.S.C. 96.
127. 21 U.S.C. 111-133.
128. 49 U.S.C. 177.
129. 7 U.S.C. 426.
130. United States v. Hoover, 133 F. 950 (1904).
131. 21 U.S.C. 123.
132. United States v. Pennsylvania, 235 F. 961 (1916).
133. Missouri K. and T. Ry. Co. v. Haber, 169 U.S. 613, 18 S.Ct. 488 (1898).
134. 21 U.S.C. 121.
135. Robinson v. Atlantic Coast Line Ry. Co., 28 Ga. App. 484, 112 S.E. 389 (1922).
136. Chicago B & O Ry. Co. v. Faye-Bauhn Co., CCA 8, 184 F. 15 (1910).
137. U.S. v. Slater, DC-Nev. 123 Fed. 115 (1903).
138. Carter v. U.S., CCA 5, 138 F. 2d 227 (1930).
139. Ill. Central Railroad v. Edwards, 203 U.S. 531, 27 S.Ct. 159 (1906); Illinois Central Railroad v. McKendree, 203 U.S. 514, 27 S.Ct. 153 (1906).
140. Asbell v. Kansas, 209 U.S. 251, 28 S.Ct. 485 (1907).
141. Must Hatch Incubator Co. v. Patterson, DC-Ore., 27 F. 2d 447 (1928).
142. U.S. v. Starkey, DC-Ill., 52 F. Supp. 1 (1943).
143. Payne v. Cotner, 148 Ark. 401, 230 S.W. 275 (1921).
144. Mintz v. Baldwin, DC-NY, 2 F. Supp. 700 (1933), Aff'd. 289 U.S. 346, 53 S.Ct. 611 (1933).
145. Atlantic Coast Line Ry. v. Bahnsen, DC-Ga., 300 F. 233 (1924).
146. San Antonio U. & G. R. Co. v. Johnson and Weathersbee, 1 S.W. 2d 350 (1927).
147. Grimes v. Eddy, 27 S.W. 479 (1894).
148. 45 U.S.C. 71-74.
149. Kroplin v. Truax, 119 Ohio St. 610, 165 N.E. 498 (1929); Loftus v. Dept. of Agriculture of Iowa, 211 Ia. 566, 232 N.W. 412 (1930).
150. Campoamor v. State Livestock Sanitary Board, 136 Fla. 451, 182 So. 277 (1938); People v. Anderson, 355 Ill. 289, 189 N.E. 338 (1934).
151. Gomes v. Merced County, 30 Cal. App. 2d 650, 86 P. 2d 1060 (1939).
152. Thome v. Merced County, 32 Cal. App. 2d 521, 90 P. 2d 364 (1939).
153. Aguiar & Bello v. Brock, 24 F. Supp. 692 (1938); Durand v. Dyson, 271 Ill. 382 (1915).
154. Abbott v. State, 63 So. 667 (1913).
155. Dederick v. Smith, 88 N.H. 63, 184 A. 595 (1936).
156. Yoder v. Givens, 179 Va. 229, 18 S.E. 2d 380 (1942).
157. Neer v. State Livestock Sanitary Board, 40 N.D. 340, 168 N.W. 601 (1918).
158. People v. Teuscher, 248 N.Y. 454, 162 N.E. 484 (1928).
159. Atlantic Coast Line Ry. Co. v. Bransen, 300 F. 233 (1924).

196. Barnum v. Vandusen, 16 Conn. 200 (1844).
197. See note 185.
198. Fultz v. Wyloff, 25 Ind. 321 (1865).
199. Jeffrey v. Bigelow and Tracy, 13 Wend. 518 (1835).
200. Missouri Pac. Ry. Co. v. Finley, 38 Kan. 550, 16 P. 951 (1888).
201. Selvege v. St. Louis and S. F. Ry. Co., 135 Mo. 163, 36 S.W. 652 (1896).
202. Wilson v. Missouri K. & T. Ry. Co., 129 Mo. App. 658, 108 S.W. 590 (1908).
203. Grimes v. Eddy, 126 Mo. 168, 28 S.W. 756 (1894).
204. Reynolds v. Galveston H. & S. A. Ry. Co., 101 Texas 2, 102 S.W. 724 (1907).
205. San Antonio V. and G. R. Co. v. Johnson and Weatherbee, 1 S.W. 2d 350 (1928).
206. San Antonio V. and G. R. Co. v. Schmidt, 18, S.W. 2d 237 (1929).
207. 21 U.S.C. 301-392.
208. 21 U.S.C. 72, 87, 91.
209. 21 U.S.C. 71.
210. 21 U.S.C. 73.
211. 7 U.S.C. 1622 h.
212. 21 U.S.C. 76.
213. 21 U.S.C. 80.
214. 21 U.S.C. 115, 116.
215. 21 U.S.C. 111.
216. 21 U.S.C. 83.
217. 21 U.S.C. 85.
218. 21 U.S.C. 82.
219. 21 U.S.C. 18.
220. 21 U.S.C. 61.
221. 21 U.S.C. 62.
222. U.S. v. Carolene Products Co., 304 U.S. 144, 58 S. Ct. 778 (1937).
223. 21 U.S.C. 25.
224. 21 U.S.C. 94a.
225. 21 U.S.C. 142.
226. Ill. Rev. St., Ch. 38, Sec. 10, 14.
227. Hauls v. Berg (Civ. App.) 105 S.W. 1176 (1907).
228. 182 Ill. App. 117 (1914).
229. 108 F. 2d 974 (1940).
230. 264 Ill. App. 504 (1932).
231. Sloan v. F. W. Woolworth Co., 193 Ill. App. 620 (1916).
232. Rosenbusel v. Ambrosia Mills Co., 168 N.Y.S. 505, 181 App. Div. 97 (1917).
233. Price v. People of the State of Illinois, 238 U.S. 446, 35 S. Ct. 892 (1914); People v. Quality Provision Co., 367 Ill. 610, 12 N.E. 2d 615 (1938).
234. Of greatest substantive significance is 26 U.S.C. 4701-4776.
235. Dow Drug Co. v. Nieman, 13 N.E. 2d 130, 57 Ohio App. 190 (1938).
236. 19 C. J., *Druggists*, Sec. 38 (citing numerous cases).
237. 21 U.S.C. 153.

238. 42 U.S.C. 262.

239. 21 U.S.C. 154.

240. 21 U.S.C. 155.

241. 21 U.S.C. 156.

242. 7 U.S.C. 851, 852.

243. See Jnl. AVMA, Vol. 106, page 179 (1945).

244. Law 1915, Ch. 170, Sec. 2.

245. Hall v. State, 100 Neb. 84, 158 N.W. 362 (1916).

246. Ferald v. Board of Supervisors of Webster County, 202 Ia. 1019, 210
      N.W. 139 (1926).

247. Fisher v. Board of Regents of University of Nebraska, 108 Neb. 760,
      189 N.W. 161 (1922).

248. Pechoes v. Johnson, 106 Wash. 163, 179 P. 78 (1919).

249. 18 U.S.C. 1716.

250. See Vet. Rec. Vol. 55, page 146 (1943).

251. Elwyn L. Cady, "Interstate Trade Barriers Affecting the Sale of
      Livestock Remedies," *University of Kansas City Law Review*, Vol.
      15, P. 25, at P. 30. (1937).

252. H. E. Maslsey, V.M.D., "Veterinary Medicinal Preparation Under the
      Federal Food, Drug and Cosmetic Act," *Food Drug Cosmetic Law
      Quarterly*, Vol. 3, p. 398 (1948).

253. People v. Fisher, 83 Ill. App. 114 (1898).

254. Smith v. Hays, 23 Ill. App. 244 (1887).

255. Ankenbrandt v. Joachim, 173 Ill. App. 158 (1913).

256. Lee v. Burk, 15 Ill. App. 651 (1884).

257. Buckley v. Clark, 21 Misc. 138, 47 N.Y.S. 42 (1897); Commissioner v.
      Barrett, 13 Ky. L. Ref. 451, 17 S.W. 336 (1891).

258. Lincoln v. Ramsey, 75 Ill. 246 (1874).

259. Wichita County Water Improvement District v. Curlee, 120 Texas
      103, 35 S.W. 2d 671 (1931).

260. Hughes v. William, 1 KB 574 (1943); Heath's Garage, Ltd. v. Hodges,
      2 KB 370 (1916); Fitzsimmons v. Snyder, 181 Ill. App. 70 (1913);
      Ensley Mercantile Co. v. Otwell, 12 Ala. 515, 38 So. 839 (1904);
      Haynes v. Kay, 111 S.L. 107, 96 S.E. 623 (1918).

261. Ill. Rev. Stat., Ch. 44, §5 (1957).

262. Atchison, T. and S. F. Ry. Co. v. Elder, 149 Ill. 173, 36 N.E. 565
      (1894); Indianapolis and C. Ry. Co. v. McKinney, 24 Ind. 283 (1865).

263. Sinram v. Pittsburgh, Ft. W. and C. Ry. Co., 28 Ind. 244 (1867);
      Baltimore and Ohio Ry. Co. v. Wood, 47 Ohio St. 431, 24 N.E. 1077
      (1890); Knight v. New York L. E. and W. Ry. Co., 99 N.Y. 25, 1
      N.E. 108 (1885).

264. Estey v. Susquehanna Pipeline Co., 98 N.Y.S. 2d 560 (1950).

265. Hill v. Southern Ry. Co., 6 Ala. App. 488, 60 So. 450 (1912).

266. Lancaster v. Futrell, 218 S.W. 805 (Texas Civ. App. 1920).

267. Liming v. Ill. Cent. Ry. Co., 81 Ia. 246, 47 N.W. 66 (1890).

268. Cook v. Johnson, 58 Mich. 437, 25 N.W. 388 (1885).

269. Warren v. DeLong, 57 Nev. 131, 59 P. 2d 1165 (1936).

270. State v. Akers, 106 Mont. 43, 74 P. 2d 1138 (1938).

271. Heckethorn v. State, 48 Ariz. 151, 59 P. 2d 331 (1936); Cahill v. People, 111 Colo. 29, 137 P. 2d 673 (1943); Ontario Nat. Bank v. Rouse, 152 Ore. 71, 52 P. 2d 176 (1936).

272. Bohart v. Songer, 110 Mont. 405, 101 P. 2d 64 (1940).

273. Lewis & Johnson v. Stracner, 165 So. 334 (1936).

274. State v. Marton, 158 Kan. 503, 148 P. 2d 760 (1944).

275. Holder v. State, 136 Fla. 880, 187 So. 781 (1939).

276. Sawyer v. Gerrish, 70 Me. 254, 35 Am. Ref. 323.

277. Scarfe v. Morgan, 4M. and W. 270.

278. Harley v. Wills, 52 S.C. 156, 29 S.E. 563.

279. State v. Withrow, 228 Wis. 404, 280 N.W. 364.

280. Gone v. Watson, 61 N.H. 136; Collins v. Bennett, 46 N.Y. 490; Johnson v. Weedman, 5 Ill. 495 (1843).

281. Norlin v. Nolan, 195 Ia. 1208, 193 N.W. 544; Coleman v. Carstens Packing Co., 147 P. 893, 85 Wash. 179.

282. George Adams & Frederick Co. v. South Omaha National Bank, 123 Fed. 641, 60 CCA 579 (1903).

283. Citizens Rapid Transit Co. v. Dew, 100 Tenn. 317, 45 S.W. 790.

284. Dickerman v. Consolidated R. Co., 79 Conn. 427, 65 A. 289; Woolf v. Chalker, 31 Conn. 121, 81 Am. Dec. 175; Jemison v. Southwestern R. Co., 75 Ga. 444, 58 Am. Dec. 476; Graham v. Smith, 100 Ga. 434, 28 S.E. 225; State v. Topeka, 36 Kan. 76, 12 P. 310; State v. McDuffie, 34 N.H. 523, 69 Am. Dec. 516; Fox v. Mohawk & H. R. Humane Soc., 165 N.Y. 517, 59 N.E. 353; State v. Lymns, 26 Ohio St. 400, 20 Am. Rep. 772; McCallister v. Sappingfield, 72 Ore. 422, 144 P. 432.

285. Duff v. Louisville and N. Ry. Co., 219 Ky. 238, 292 S. W. 814; Hodges v. Causey, 77 Miss. 353, 26 So. 945.

286. Wilcox v. State, 101 Ga. 563, 28 S.E. 981; Dodson v. Mock, 20 N.C. 282, 32 Am. Dec. 677.

287. Hamby v. Sampson, 105 Ia. 112, 74 N.W. 918; Harrington v. Miles, 11 Kan. 480, 15 Am. Ref. 355.

288. Hurley v. State, 30 Texas App. 333, 17 S.W. 455.

289. Jenkins v. Ballantyne, 8 Utah 245, 30 P. 760.

290. Vantreese v. McGee, 26 Ind. App. 525, 60 N.E. 318 (1901).

291. McDonald v. Castle, 116 Okla. 46, 243 P. 215.

292. Chunot v. Larson, 43 Wis. 536, 28 Am. Ref. 567.

293. Andrews v. Jordan Marsh Co., 283 Mass. 158, 186 N.E. 71 (1933).

294. Clinkenbeard v. Reinert, 284 Mo. 569, 225 S.W. 667.

295. Kittredge v. Elliott, 16 N.H. 77, 41 Am. Dec. 717; Rider v. Clarkson, 77 N.J. Eq. 469, 78 A. 676.

296. Holmer v. Murray, 207 Mo. 413, 105 S.W. 1085; Adams v. Hall, 2 Vt. 9, 19 Am. Dec. 690.

297. McClain v. Lewiston Interstate Fair and Racing Assoc., 17 Idaho 63, 104 P. 1015; Melicker v. Sedlacek, 189 Ia. 946, 179 N.W. 197; Serio v. American Brewing Co., 141 La. 290, 74 So. 998; Quilty v. Battie, 135 N.Y. 201, 32 N.E. 47; Wood v. Campbell, 28 S.D. 197, 132 N.W. 785; Plummer v. Ricker, 71 Vt. 114, 41 A. 1045; see also Strouse v. Leipf, 101 Ala. 433, 14 So. 667; Marsh v. Jones, 21 Vt. 378, 52 Am. Dec. 67.

298. Schultz v. Griffith, 103 Ia. 150, 72 N.W. 445.
299. Buck v. Brady, 110 Md. 568, 73 A. 277; Brice v. Bauer, 108 N.Y. 428, 15 N.E. 695 (1888).
300. Twigg v. Ryland, 62 Md. 380, 50 Am. Ref. 226.
301. Conway v. Grant, 80 Ga. 40, 13 S.E. 803; Schmid v. Humphrey, 48 Ia. 652, 30 Am. Ref. 414.
302. Montgomery v. Kaester, 35 La. Am. 1091, 48 Am. Ref. 253; Loamis v. Terry, 17 Wend. 496, 31 Am. Dec. 306; M'Caskill v. Elliott, 36 S.C.L. 196, 53 Am. Dec. 706.
303. Ryan v. Marren, 216 Mass. 556, 104 N.E. 353 (1914).
304. Holton v. Moore, 165 N.C. 549, 81 S.E. 779; Muller v. McKesson, 73 N.Y. 195, 29 Am. Ref. 123.
305. Brune v. DeBendetty, 261 S.W. 930 (Mo. App.).
306. Robinson v. Marino, 3 Wash. 434, 28 P. 752.
307. Meibus v. Dodge, 38 Wis. 300, 20 Am. Ref. 6.
308. Nelson v. Nugent, 106 Wis. 477, 82 N.W. 287.
309. Nabre v. Wright, 98 Minn. 477, 108 N.W. 865; Van Steenbury v. Tabias, 17 Wend. 562, 31 Am. Dec. 310; Stine v. McShane, 55 N.D. 745, 214 N.W. 906.
310. Blair v. Foreband, 100 Mass. 136, 97 Am. Dec. 82.
311. Sentell v. New Orleans & C. Ry. Co., 166 U.S. 698, 17 S. Ct. 693 (1897).
312. Longyear v. Buck, 83 Mich. 236, 47 N.W. 234; McGlove v. Womack, 129 Ky. 274, 111 S.W. 688.
313. Clinkenbeard v. Reinert, 284 Mo. 569, 225 S.W. 667.
314. Woolf v. Challser, 31 Conn. 121, 81 Am. Dec. 175.
315. Perry v. Phipps, 32 N.C. 259, 51 Am. Dec. 387.
316. Chapman v. Decraw, 93 Me. 378, 45 A. 295; Brown v. Carpenter, 26 Vt. 638, 62 Am. Dec. 603.
317. Ex parte Minor, 203 Ala. 481, 83 So. 475; McChesney v. Wilson, 132 Mich. 252, 93 N.W. 627.
318. Melicker v. Sedlacek, 189 Ia. 946, 179 N.W. 197.
319. Knowles v. Mulder, 74 Mich. 202, 41 N.W. 896, 16 Am. St. Ref. 627; Schmid v. Humphrey, 48 Ia. 652; 30 Am. Ref. 414.
320. Forsythe v. Kluckholm, 150 Ia. 126, 129 N.W. 739.
321. Sprague v. Foster, 48 Ill. App. 140 (1891).
322. Leggat v. Sands' Ale Brewing Co., 60 Ill. 158 (1871).
323. Adams v. Johnson, 15 Ill. 345 (1854).
324. Roberts v. Appelgate, 153 Ill. 210, 38 N.E. 676 (1894).
325. Kermer v. Harding, 85 Ill. 264, 28 Am. Ref. 615 (1877).
326. Crabtree v. Kile, 21 Ill. 180 (1859).
327. Tanell v. Gatewood, 3 Ill. 22, 33 Am. Dec. 437 (1830).
328. Dewor v. Loy, 248 Ill. App. 396 (1937).
329. Kemett v. Knerlet, 221 Ill. App. 601.
330. See note 327.
331. Green v. Ryan, 242 Ill. App. 466.
332. Trowsdale v. Burkhardt, 207 Ia. 1133, 224 N.W. 93 (1929).
333. See note 329.

334. Redwood Bros. v. Wyoming Cattle Investment Co., 126 Ia. 410, 102 N.W. 144 (1905).
335. Snowden v. Waterman, 105 Ga. 384, 31 S.E. 110 (1898).
336. Hoffman v. Oates, 77 Ga. 701 (1886).
337. Roddan v. Brain, 201 Ala. 109, 77 So. 403 (1917).
338. Beston v. Alexander, 185 Mo. App. 16, 171 S.W. 582 (1914).
339. Doose v. Watkins, 151 Fed. 340 (1907).
340. Renfrow v. Citizens State Bank, 87 Ind. App. 318, 158 N.E. 919 (1927).
341. Klinge v. Farris, 128 Ore. 142, 268 P. 748 (1928).
342. Watson v. Smith, 15 Ga. App. 62, 82 S.E. 633 (1914).
343. Fawcett v. Osborn, 32 Ill. 411, 83 Am. Dec. 278 (1863).
344. Linton v. Porter, 31 Ill. 107 (1863).
345. *California.* Merguire v. O'Donnell, 103 Cal. 50, 36 P. 1033 (1894).
    Georgia. Lewis v. Bracken, 97 Ga. 337, 20 S.E. 943 (1895); Snowden v. Waterman, 105 Ga. 384, 31 S.E. 110 (1898).
    Illinois. Crabtree v. Kile, 21 Ill. 180 (1859).
    Kansas. Broquet v. Tripps, 36 Kan. 700, 14 P. 227 (1887).
    Kentucky. Sapp v. Bradfield, 137 Ky. 308, 125 S.W. 721 (1910).
    Maryland. Horn v. Buck, 48 Md. 358 (1878).
    Michigan. Murphy v. McGraw, 74 Mich. 318, 41 N.W. 917 (1889).
    Missouri. Galbreath v. Carnes, 91 Mo. App. 512 (1902).
    North Dakota. Larson v. Calder, 16 N.D. 248, 113 N.W. 103 (1907); Needhorn v. H. S. Halverson and Company, 22 N.D. 594, 134 N.W. 203 (1912).
    Vermont. Pinney v. Andrus, 41 Vt. 631 (1869).
346. Merrick v. Wiltse, 37 Minn. 41, 33 N.W. 3 (1887).
347. Sapp v. Bradfield, 137 Ky. 308, 125 S.W. 721 (1910).
348. Cummins v. Ennis, 4 Pa. 424, 56 A. 377 (1903).
349. McGuire v. Thompson, 152 Neb. 28, 40 N.W. 2d 257 (1949).
350. Forbes v. Hunter, 223 Ill. App. 400 (1921).
351. Chamberlain v. Bain, 27 Ill. App. 634 (1887).
352. Barker v. Kean, 67 Ill. App. 433 (1896).
353. Myers v. Sirville, 155 Ill. App. 96 (1910).
354. Dayton v. Kidder, 105 Ill. App. 107 (1902).
355. Bartholomew v. Case, 219 Ill. App. 133 (1920).
356. Wade v. Moffett, 21 Ill. 110, 74 Am. Dec. 79 (1859).
357. Flanigan v. Crull, 53 Ill. 352 (1870).
358. Palfrey v. Killian, 224 Mo. App. 325, 27 S.W. 2d 462 (1930).
359. Benton S. Oppenheimer, *A Treatise on Medical Jurisprudence*, Sec. 60, p. 219.
360. Birmingham Baptist Hospital v. Crews, 229 Ala. 398, 157 So. 224 (1934); Children v. Frye, 201 N.C. 42, 158 S.E. 744 (1931).
361. Shields v. Dodge, 14 Lea (Tenn.) 356.
362. Marlin v. Nolan, 193 N.W. 544, 195 Ia. 1208; Coleman v. Carstens Packing Co., 147 P. 893, 85 Wash. 179.
363. Gould v. Hill, 251 P. 167, 43 Idaho 93; Othoudt v. Addison Fur Corporation, 247 N.W. 723, 262 Mich. 481; El Paso Cattle Loan Co. v. Hunt, 228 P. 888, 30 N.M. 157; Nemi v. Todd, 96 A. 14, 15, 89 Vt. 502;

INDEX